Hebrews

THE CROSSWAY CLASSIC COMMENTARIES

Hebrews

by
John Owen

Series Editors
Alister McGrath and J. I. Packer

CROSSWAY BOOKS
A DIVISION OF GOOD NEWS PUBLISHERS
WHEATON, ILLINOIS • NOTTINGHAM, ENGLAND

First printing, 1998

Printed in the United States of America

Library of Congress Cataloging-in-Publication Data
Owen, John, 1616-1683.
  Hebrews / by John Owen.
     p.   cm. — (Crossway classic commentaries)
    ISBN 1-58134-026-5 (TPB : alk. paper)
    1. Bible. N.T. Hebrews—Commentaries. I. Title. II. Series.
BS2775.083 1998
227'.87077—dc20   98-33632
                                          CIP

15	14	13	12	11	10	09	08	07	06	05	04	03	02	01	00	99	98
15	14	13	12	11	10	.9	8	7	6	5	4	3	2	1			

First British edition 1998

Production and Printing in the United States of America for
CROSSWAY BOOKS
Norton Street, Nottingham, England NG7 3HR

ISBN 1-85684-184-7

Contents

Series Preface

The purpose of the Crossway Classic Commentaries is to make some of the most valuable commentaries on the books of the Bible, by some of the greatest Bible teachers and theologians in the last 500 years, available to a new generation. These books will help today's readers learn truth, wisdom, and devotion from such authors as J. C. Ryle, Martin Luther, John Calvin, J. B. Lightfoot, John Owen, Charles Spurgeon, Charles Hodge, and Matthew Henry.

We do not apologize for the age of some of the items chosen. In the realm of practical exposition promoting godliness, the old is often better than the new. Spiritual vision and authority, based on an accurate handling of the biblical text, are the qualities that have been primarily sought in deciding what to include.

So far as is possible, everything is tailored to the needs and enrichment of thoughtful readers—lay Christians, students, and those in the ministry. The originals, some of which were written at a high technical level, have been abridged as needed, simplified stylistically, and unburdened of foreign words. However, the intention of this series is never to change any thoughts of the original authors, but to faithfully convey them in an understandable fashion.

The publishers are grateful to Dr. Alister McGrath of Wycliffe Hall, Oxford, Dr. J. I. Packer of Regent College, Vancouver, and Watermark of Norfolk, England, for the work of selecting and editing that now brings this project to fruition.

THE PUBLISHERS
Crossway Books
Wheaton, Illinois

Introduction

John Owen (1616-1683), sometime chaplain to Oliver Cromwell and vice-chancellor of Oxford University, was by common consent the greatest of the Puritan theologians. He was a prolific and masterful writer, as his treatises on trinitarian faith and life, the person and work of Christ and of the Holy Spirit, justification by faith, the Christian's communion with God, the eternal security of the saints, and the nature, life, and order of the church abundantly show. Built on mainstream Reformed covenant theology and buttressed by polemics against Arminianism, Roman Catholicism, and Socinian unitarianism, these works have classic status, and it is for them that Owen is chiefly remembered by the minority (it is, alas, a quite small minority) who know his name today.

But Owen the theologian was first and foremost a Bible-man. All his theology, like Calvin's (which it closely resembles), rests on biblical texts exegeted in their context. And in Owen's own estimate, his main legacy to the ongoing church was not any of the books referred to above but his massive two-million-word exposition of Hebrews, which fills seven of the twenty-three volumes of the standard edition of his works and is boiled down for our convenience in the following pages.

John Owen wrote on Hebrews with several purposes in mind. In the first place, the glory of Jesus Christ as the divine Savior and Lord of Christians and churches was always his supreme theological, devotional, and doxological concern, and he wanted to expound Hebrews because of all the New Testament epistles it seemed to him to display that glory most fully and directly. We do not have to follow him in supposing that Paul wrote it to concur with him in his estimate of it. Then, too, he wanted to bring out the vast quantity of instruction on living by faith in Christ that he found in its pages; and on top of that he wished to vindicate the true meaning of the letter as a sermon on sovereign grace against the mishandlings of Socinian commentators who, to his mind, dishonored Christ directly by their Arian account of who and what he was and their

Pelagian denial of original sin and God's renewing work in the human heart. To get through this agenda he first spent half a million words on introductory topical essays ("exercitations" as he called them) and then dug into the text itself in minutest detail and on the grandest scale. Nothing to match Owen's achievement was done before him, nor has been done since his day.

"After all my searching and reading, prayer and assiduous meditation have been my only resort, and by far the most useful means of light and assistance. . . . I always went nakedly to the Word itself, to learn humbly the mind of God in it, and to express it as he should enable me." So wrote Owen in his preface to the work. Of his achievement Andrew Thomason declared: "It is like some vast minster [medieval cathedral] filled with solemn light, on whose minuter details it might be easy to suggest improvement; but whose stable walls and noble columns astonish you at the skill and strength of the builder the longer you gaze." "This greatest work of John Owen," Thomas Chalmers told his students, ". . . is a work of gigantic strength as well as gigantic size; and he who has mastered it is very little short . . . of being an erudite and accomplished theologian."

Today's evolutionary mind-set makes us expect Puritan Bible-work to be cruder and shallower than ours, but this classic work joins hands with Matthew Henry's great exposition of the entire Bible to prove us wrong, even when downscaled as drastically as it is in this abridged version. To present it in this way, in a form more palatable to a modern readership, is for me a privilege indeed.

J. I. PACKER

Hebrews
Chapter 1

This first chapter encourages the Hebrews to persevere in the teaching of the Gospel. The Messiah, the Son of God, is described in two ways. First, his person and offices and what he has done for the church are declared. Second, he is compared with others who have revealed the mind and will of God, and his preeminence above angels is especially emphasized.

Verses 1-2

In the past God spoke to our forefathers through the prophets at many times and in various ways, but in these last days he has spoken to us by his Son, whom he appointed heir of all things, and through whom he made the universe.

The apostle compares the Mosaic law and the Gospel. First, he compares their *revelation and institution,* through which the obligation to observe them arose; and, second, their *whole nature, use, and efficacy.*

They agree about the principal cause of their revelation, or the prime author from whom they originated. This is God. He was the author of the law and the Gospel. He spoke of old **through the prophets**, he spoke in these last days **by his Son**. Neither of them was from men; both have the same divine origin (see 2 Timothy 3:16; 2 Peter 1:20-21).

Their difference in this respect, namely, in their revelation, he refers to under four headings.

First, in the *manner* of their revelation. This is shown in two ways. 1. The revelation of God's will under the law was given **at many times**; but under the Gospel in one dispensation of grace and truth. 2. As for **in various ways**, there was only one way under the Gospel, and that was through the Spirit dwelling in the Lord Christ in his fullness, and through him, communicated to his apostles.

Second, *the times and seasons of their revelation.* The law was revealed **in the past,** but the Gospel was revealed **in these last days.**

Third, *the people to whom the revelation was made.* The law was to *our forefathers* and the Gospel is to *us.*

Fourth, and principally, *the people through whom these revelations were made.* The law was through **the prophets,** the Gospel was through **his Son.** God spoke then through the prophets; now he has spoken through the Son.

The law and Gospel both agree that God was the author of them both. The apostle moves on to the differences between the law and the Gospel, concerning their revelation from God.

In the past. First, the revelation of the will of God under the old testament was **in the past,** or "formerly," or "of old." This word comprises the whole time from the giving of the first promise up to the end of all public revelation under the old testament. The correct extent of **in the past** is from the giving of the law of Moses to the close of public prophecy in the days of Malachi.

Our forefathers. God spoke through the prophets **in the past.** Another comparison between the law and the Gospel is that he spoke to **our forefathers.** They were all the faithful of the Jewish church, from the giving of the law until the end of prophecy in the days of Malachi.

In these last days. Most expositors take this expression as a circumlocution for the times of the Gospel. But they are never called this, nor were they ever known by that name among the Jews. Some seasons, indeed, under the Gospel are called *the last days* (2 Timothy 3:1); but the whole time of the Gospel is nowhere referred to in this way. It is the last days of the Jewish church and state, which were then drawing to their close, that are here and elsewhere called the **last days,** or "the latter days" or "the last times" (2 Peter 3:3; 1 John 2:18; Jude 18). The end of their church and state was foretold to be a perpetual desolation (Daniel 9:27), and the last days were now upon them, so that they might understand what they were soon to expect.

To us. That is, to the members of the Jewish church who lived in the days of the personal ministry of Christ and later under the preaching of the Gospel (2:3).

These are two examples of the comparison between the *times* and the *people.* The next difference is the manner of these several revelations of God's will. Under the law, the revelation was made **at many times.**

At many times. The gradual discovery of the mind and will of God, by the addition of one thing after another, at different times, as the church could bear the light, and as it served the purpose of reserving all the preeminence to the Messiah, is what this expression intends to convey. The expression denotes the whole progress of divine revelation from the beginning of the world and consists of four principal parts.

The first was the promise given to Adam of a descendant, which was the principle of faith and obedience to the fathers before the flood.

The second was to Noah after the flood, in the renewal of the covenant and the establishment of the church in his family (Genesis 8:21-22; 9:9-10).

The third part is the revelations made to Abraham, restricting the promise to his descendant and the further explanations about its nature (Genesis 12:1-3; 15:17-20; 17:1-2).

The fourth is the revelation to Moses, in the giving of the law and the building of the Jewish church in the wilderness. This had three subsidiary revelations that were given to David (1 Chronicles 23:25-32; 28:11-19), to the prophets after the division of the kingdom, and to Ezra.

In contrast to this *gradual revelation* of the mind of God under the old testament, the apostle intimates that now through Jesus, the Messiah, the Lord has at once begun and finished the whole revelation of his will, according to their own hopes and expectation. So the faith was "once for all entrusted to the saints" (Jude 3) not in one day, not in one sermon, or by one person, but at one time, or under one dispensation, consisting of all the time from the start of the Lord Christ's ministry to the closing of the canon of Scripture, which period was now present.

In various ways. This refers either to the various ways God revealed himself to the prophets, through dreams, visions, voices, and angels; or, through the prophecies and sermons of the prophets. The latter is principally intended, although the former is not excluded.

Through the prophets. This is the last comparison between the law and the Gospel. In the past God spoke **through the prophets**, but now **by his Son.** These prophets, through whom God spoke in the past, were all those who were divinely inspired and sent to reveal his will and mind concerning the duty of the church, which they declared through their inspired words, both spoken and written.

In contrast to God speaking through the prophets, it is asserted that the revelation of the Gospel came through God speaking **by his Son.** This is the main hinge on which all the arguments of the apostle in the whole letter turns. To support this argument, the following arguments must be remembered.

First, I take it for granted that the Son of God appeared to the prophets under the old testament. Whether he ever spoke to them directly, or only through angels, is not so clear. That the Son of God did appear to the fathers in the old testament is seen from Zechariah 2:8-11. He was also called "an angel" in Exodus 23:20-21.

Second, there is a difference between the Son of God revealing God's will in his *divine person* to the prophets, and the Son of God as *incarnate*, revealing God's will directly to the church. This difference is insisted upon by the apostle. So, **in these last days,** the Lord did with his own hands the work that from the foundation of the world he had used angels and men to do.

We must now establish that the revelation of God's mind was in and through the Son.

This happened, first, by virtue of the Lord Jesus Christ, from the womb, being filled with the light and knowledge of God and his will.

Second, this was accomplished through the commission, mission, and equipping of the Son, as incarnate and mediator, with the ability to declare God's mind and will for the church. This was given to the Son by the Father, who had sent him (John 7:16). It was from the Father that he heard the word and learned the teaching that he declared to the church. This is asserted wherever it is said that the Father sent, sealed, anointed, commanded, or taught the Son; and wherever the Son did the Father's will, spoke his words, sought his glory, and obeyed his commands (see John 8:26, 28, 40; 14:10; 15:15; Revelation 1:1).

Third, the Son received the revelation of God's will since his own nature was divine, and because he was the eternal Word and Wisdom of the Father.

Fourth, the Lord Christ carried out his office of revealing the Father's will through his human nature, in which he dwelt among us (John 1:14).

Fifth, Christ's human nature was, from the moment of its union with the person of the Son of God, a "holy thing."

Sixth, Christ had a special endowment of the Spirit that is beyond our understanding (John 1:33; Luke 4:1).

Seventh, Christ's prophecies were superior to those of Moses and all other prophets. This arose because the person of Christ is infinitely superior to them. This is also demonstrated by the nature of the revelation Christ received (John 1:17; 3:34). The giving of the law through Moses, which instructed the church through its typology and imagery, stands in marked contrast with the grace and truth that came through Jesus Christ (John 1:17-18; see also Ephesians 3:8-11; Colossians 1:26-27; 2 Timothy 1:9-10; Titus 2:11).

Eighth, the Jews had an expectation of a new and final revelation of the will of God, to be made by the Messiah in the last days; that is, of their church-state, and not, as they now fondly imagine, of the world. The general expectation of the church for the full revelation of God's will was upon the Messiah (John 4:25).

From all these observations we note the force of the apostle's argument. The apostle has opened the spring from which all his successive arguments flow. He focused on him who brought life and immortality to light through the Gospel, and from that moved on to the doctrinal part of the letter, describing the person of Christ, the Son of God, in his excellency, in whom God spoke to them, so that they might consider whom they were dealing with.

Having declared the Son to be the immediate revealer of the Gospel, the apostle now declares the Son's glory. The apostle assigns two things to him in verse 2: that he was appointed heir of all things, and, that through him the universe was made.

Whom. That is, the Son, in whom the Father spoke to us; and as such, the revealer of the Gospel. The Son, as God, has a *natural dominion* over everyone. To this he can be no more appointed than he can be to be God. Nothing, indeed, can be added to him as *God,* but there may be to him *who is God,* about the humble way he carried out his work in an assumed nature. He who is God and exalted so high as to be the eternal Son of the Father, who was made man, may, in respect of the office that he performed in the nature of man, by his Father be made **heir of all things.**

Heir. Three things are signified by this word. First, *title, dominion, lordship.* The heir is the lord of that which he is heir of. The heir is lord of all (see Galatians 4:1). Second, *possession.* Christ is made actual possessor of what he has title to. Chrysostom and Theophylact affirm that this word denotes "the propriety of his sonship, and the immutability of his lordship." Third, this title and its possession was *granted* to Christ by the Father.

Of all things. This is the object of Christ's heirship, his inheritance. Elsewhere it is stated that all things were subject to him (see Romans 9:5; 1 Corinthians 15:27). That God is over all suits the apostle's argument. For the author of the Gospel is heir and lord of all things. Since he is heir of all things it is easy to conclude that any participation of anything good in heaven or on earth must be through him. The next words **through whom he made the universe** support this. He made everything, and it was fitting that he should be Lord of everything. Chrysostom has well said that it is as if he had said, "he appointed one head to them all," angels and human beings. The object and extent of Christ's inheritance is expressed in **of all things.**

Appointed. He "placed," "set," "made," "appointed." The way Christ the Son came to his inheritance is expressed by this word. God "appointed" or "placed" him there. This word may denote either those special acts by which he came into the full possession of his inheritance, or it may be extended to other preparatory acts that preceded them. In the former sense, the glorious investiture of the Lord Christ in the full actual possession of his kingdom after his resurrection, with the manifestation of it in his ascension, and token of its stability in his sitting at the right hand of God, is meant.

It may also refer to certain preparatory things that preceded this, such as the following five matters. First, the *eternal purpose of God,* ordaining him before the foundation of the world to his work and inheritance (1 Peter 1:20). Second, the *covenant* that was of old between the Father and the Son for carrying out the great work of redemption, which included this inheritance (Isaiah 53:10-11). Third, the *promises* made to him in his types, such as Abraham, David, and Solomon (Genesis 15; Psalms 72). Fourth, the *promises recorded in the Old Testament* for his assurance of success (Psalm 2; Isaiah 49). Fifth, the *solemn proclamation* of him to be the great heir and lord of all, at his first coming into the world (Luke 2:11, 30-32). But it is the consummation of all these, whatever was intended or declared in these previous acts of the will and wisdom of God, that is principally intended in this expression.

Through whom he made the universe. These words give added weight to the apostle's argument, and he further considers the person of the Messiah. He also reveals the foundation of the preeminence ascribed to him in these words, so that they were "his own" (John 1:11), and it was fitting that he should be Lord of them all. Moreover, if all things were made by him, all disobedience to him is certainly most unreasonable, and will be met with inevitable ruin. The apostle sets out to convince the Hebrews of this truth.

God, in his infinite wisdom, ordered all things in the first creation, so that the whole of that work might be subservient to the glory of his grace in the new creation of all by Jesus Christ. Through the Son he made the universe in the beginning of time, that in the fullness of time he might be the just heir and lord of all. The Jews have a saying that "the world was made for the Messiah"; which is thus far true, that both it and all things in it were made, disposed of, and ordered in their creation, so that God might be everlastingly glorified in the work which Christ was designed for, and which through him he had to accomplish.

Verse 3

The apostle, pursuing his argument, proceeds with the description of Christ. He does this, partly, to give a further account of what he had previously affirmed concerning his divine power in making the universe, and, partly, to teach the Hebrews, from their own typical institutions, that it was the Messiah who was figured and represented previously to them in those signs and pledges of God's glorious presence that they enjoyed. In this way he confirmed the proposition he had in hand concerning the excellency and eminence of him through whom the Gospel was revealed, that their faith in him and obedience to him might not be shaken or hindered.

The Son is the radiance of God's glory and the exact representation of his being, sustaining all things by his powerful word. After he had provided purification for sins, he sat down at the right hand of the Majesty in heaven. This description of the person in whom God spoke in the revelation of the Gospel has three parts: first, declaring *what he is*; second, *what he does,* or did; and, third, the *consequence* of the first two. Of the first part of this description of the Messiah there are two branches: for he affirms about him, first, that he is the "brightest beam," or "splendor of the glory"; and, second, "the exact representation," or "character of his Father's person."

In the second also two things are assigned to him—the former relating to his power, as he is the radiance of God's glory, **sustaining** or ruling **all things by his powerful word**; the latter relating to his love and work of mediation—**he,** in his own person, has **provided purification for sins.**

His present and perpetual enjoyment, as a consequence of what he was and did, or does, is expressed in the last words: **he sat down at the right hand of the Majesty in heaven.**

The radiance of God's glory. Why does the apostle express the divine glory of Jesus Christ in these words? "Who is the radiance, light, luster, or majesty of God's glory." The apostle here alludes to something the people were familiar with as a type under the old testament, in the great mystery of the manifestation of the glory of God to them in and through the Son. The ark, which was the most signal representation of the presence of God among them, was called "his glory." So the wife of Phinehas, when the ark was taken away, affirmed that the glory had departed from Israel, for the ark of God had been taken (1 Samuel 4:22). The Psalmist, mentioning the same thing, calls it "his glory," "the ark" (Psalm 78:61).

The apostle reminds the Jews that God had promised to live among them by his glorious presence, from which Jerusalem derives its name, "THE LORD IS THERE" (Ezekiel 48:35). So he who had revealed the will of God to them was none other than he who had dwelt among them from the beginning, representing in all things the person of the Father, being typically revealed to them as **the radiance of God's glory.**

The apostle adds that the Son is **the exact representation of his being,** that is, of the person of God the Father.

The **exact representation** of the Father is the Father himself. As is the Father, so is the Son. And this agreement and likeness between the Father and the Son is essential. What the Father is, does, has, that the Son is, does, has; or else the Father, as the Father, could not be represented by him.

The Son in himself is "in very nature God" (Philippians 2:6). To us he is "the image of the invisible God," representing him to us (Colossians 1:15).

This expression is taken from the ordinary engraving of rings, or seals, or stones. It may also be that the apostle had in mind the representation of the glory of God by engraving among the institutions of Moses. There was hardly anything that more gloriously represented God than the engraving of his name on the gold plate that was worn on the front of the high priest's miter. At its sight the great conqueror of the east fell down before him. It is mentioned in Exodus 28:36: "Make a plate of pure gold and engrave on it as on a seal: HOLY TO THE LORD." Here was that name of God that denotes his essence and glory to his people.

Sustaining all things by his powerful word. After the description of the person, the apostle returns to an assertion of the power of Christ, the Son of God, and so makes his transition from the kingly and prophetic to his sacrificial work, which he intends to enlarge on later.

The apostle had previously shown that by Christ, the universe was made. As further evidence of his glorious power, and of his continuing to act in the same way, the apostle adds that Christ also lives to uphold, or rule and dispose of all things that were made by him. To understand these words two questions must be asked: first, How, or in what sense, is Christ said to **sustain all things**? Second, how does he do this **by his powerful word**?

Sustaining. Some translate this as "upholding, supporting, bearing, carrying." These commentators maintain that it refers to the divine power that is exerted in the conservation of creation that keeps it from sinking into its original confusion and nothingness. About this our Savior says, "My Father works hitherto and I work." This refers to the providential sustaining of all things made from the beginning. "And this," says Chrysostom in his commentary, "is a greater work than that of the creation." By the former all things were brought forth from nothing; by the latter they are preserved from returning to nothing, which is their own nature.

Some take the word to mean his *ruling,* governing, and disposing of all things made by him and sustained by him. So it may denote the power over all things given to the Son as mediator, or else that providential rule over everything that he has with his Father.

Our next inquiry concerns the way the Son upholds all things. He does it **by his powerful word.** In the New Testament the word *word* can mean a word of blessing (Matthew 4:4), any word spoken (Matthew 26:75), a word of promise (Luke 1:38), a blasphemous word (Acts 6:11), the word of God (Luke 3:2), or an authoritative command (Luke 5:5). In this letter it is used in different ways.

In this verse the efficacy of divine Providence is called the *word of God* to indicate that as rulers accomplish their will by a word of command in and about things subject to their pleasure (Matthew 8:9), so God accom-

18

plishes his whole will in all things by his power. Therefore, **by his powerful word** is added here to distinguish which word it is that the apostle means. It is a word that is *effectual and operative*—namely, exerting his divine power with authority to accomplish his purpose in and through all things.

In Ezekiel's vision this is the communication of a spirit of life to the cherubs and wheels, to act and move them as seems good to him by whom they are guided. It is probable that the apostle used these words, **by his powerful word,** which show the divine power of the Son in ruling creation, to remind the Hebrews that the Lord Christ, the Son, is seen by Ezekiel in the form of a man, ruling all things. The Son, ruling from a throne over the cherubim and wheels, governs the whole creation with his power.

This, then, is what the apostle assigns to the Son, as he sets out the dignity of his person, so that the Hebrews may think carefully before they reject his teaching. He partakes of God's nature, **being the radiance of God's glory and the exact representation of his being,** who manifests his divine power both in the creation of all things, and also as he rules over them, since they were made by him. From this it follows that, just as he had power and authority to change the Mosaic institutions, so he also possesses truth and faithfulness in the revelation of God's will, and that it is their duty to embrace and adhere to this.

We move on with our apostle now in his description of the person and work of the Messiah.

He began by declaring him to be the great prophet of the new testament, and, then, the lord, and ruler of all things. He now ends his general proposition with a brief account of his priestly office. He explains what he did in this office and what resulted from this, in the rest of this verse.

Before he could speak about the work of purification of our sins, which, as a priest, is assigned to Christ, the apostle had to show Christ's divine nature. For this is a work of him who is God and man. For as God takes it to be his property to blot out our sins, so he could not have done it had he not been man also. This is asserted in the words that follow.

After he had provided purification for sins. The apostle says two things here about the Messiah; one, which is the foundation of both, he takes for granted. First, he says *what* he did: **he provided purification for sins;** second, he says *how* he did this: he did it **after he . . .** The basis for these things he assumes we know: that Christ was the great high priest of the church. The apostle's readers knew well enough that this matter of purging sins belonged only to the priest.

Here, then, the apostle makes a tacit comparison between Christ and Aaron, the high priest. Christ is superior to Aaron in both of the things that are attributed to him here as high priest. First, in that **he had pro-**

vided purification for sins—that is, really and effectually before God and in the conscience of the sinner, and that for all time. In contrast, the purification of sins that Aaron brought was but external and representative of what was true and real. Second, Christ did it himself, as the offering was himself, whereas what Aaron did he did through the offering of bulls and goats.

Purification. Let us see what is ascribed to our Lord Christ. It is **purification for sins.** "To purify" most often denotes *real actual purification,* either of outward defilements, by healing and cleansing, as in Mark 1:40; 7:19; or from spiritual defilements of sin, by sanctifying grace, as in Acts 15:9 and 2 Corinthians 7:1. But this word is also often used in the sense of "to purge by atonement," as in Hebrews 11:22-23. This is how the word **purification** is used in this verse. This is how the word is used in Exodus 29:36 where the "day of atonement" occurs.

This **purification for sins,** then, which the apostle says happened before the ascension of Christ, is not the actual sanctification of believers by the Spirit, but the atonement made by Christ in his sacrifice, that our sins should not be imputed to us. Therefore it says **he provided purification for sins,** not that he purged us from our sins. And wherever sins, not sinners, are made the object of any mediatory act of Christ, that act refers to God and not the sinner, and removes sin, so that it should not be imputed (see 2:17).

After he. The apostle shows how **purification for sins** was made. It was by the sacrifice and offering of himself (Ephesians 5:2; Hebrews 9:12, 14). The high priest of old made atonement, and typically purged the sins of the people, by sacrificing the beasts according to the instructions of the law (Leviticus 16); this high priest did it through the sacrifice of himself (Isaiah 53:10; Hebrews 9:12).

He sat down at the right hand of the Majesty in heaven. The apostle, having thus asserted in general the priestly office of Christ and the sacrifice that he offered, with its consequence, as it could not be accomplished without the greatest humiliation and abasement of the Son ever conceivable, he now adds the blessed event and result of his great work: **He sat down at the right hand of the Majesty in heaven.** We now look at the scope of these words and how they were expressed.

The apostle means two things by these words. First, that the Lord Christ, providing purification for sins, did so perfectly through the one offering of himself, and so discharged the whole work of his priesthood as he made atonement for sinners. This is seen in the immediate result of his work. He entered into the glorious condition mentioned in this verse. This is evidence that his work was complete and that God was totally satisfied with what he had done. Second, the glorious condition of the Lord Jesus after his humiliation is seen in these words. His Spirit did of old signify both his "sufferings" and the "glories that would follow" (1 Peter 1:11).

We now turn to the way the apostle describes the glory of the Son of God after he had provided purification for sins. First, we note the *security* of Christ from all his enemies and from all future sufferings. The Jews knew what he suffered from God and man. Now he lets them know the reason for this. It was for the purging of our sins; and, moreover, he declares now that he is everlastingly secured from all opposition, for where he is, his enemies cannot come (see John 7:34). He is above their reach, secure in the throne and presence of God. Thus the fruit of the church, being secure from the rage and persecution of Satan, is said to be "snatched up to God and to his throne" (Revelation 12:5). So, although people continue to show malice and anger against the Lord to the end of the world as though they wanted to crucify him afresh, yet he dies no more, being secure out of their reach at the right hand of God.

Second, we note Christ's *majesty and glory.* This cannot be expressed. It includes all that can be given by God in heaven. God on his throne is God in the full manifestation of his own majesty and glory; on his right hand sits the Mediator, yes, so he can be in the middle of the throne (Revelation 5:6). How little our weak minds can comprehend this majesty (see Matthew 20:21; Romans 8:34; Ephesians 1:20; Philippians 2:9; Colossians 3:1).

Verse 4

So he became as much superior to the angels as the name he has inherited is superior to theirs.

There are five things to be noted about this verse.

As much superior. First, the apostle's general assertion, namely, that the Son, as the great priest and prophet of the church, was *preferred above,* and made more glorious and powerful than the angels. How this was done is also mentioned. Christ is made "more excellent" than the angels. So, to say that Christ is **as much superior** is to say that he is "exalted" and actually given more power, glory, and dignity than the angels. The Lord Jesus Christ, the revealer of God's will in the Gospel, is exalted above, preferred before, made more excellent and glorious than the angels themselves, all or any of them, who ministered to the Lord in the giving of the law on Mount Sinai.

Second, this verse tells us *when* Christ was exalted above the angels. While some say that this happened at the time of his incarnation or his baptism, it must be the time of his resurrection, ascension, and exaltation at God's right hand.

Third, we see the *extent* of Christ's exaltation. It was **much superior to the angels.** "Look," says the apostle, "how much the name given to the Messiah exceeds the name given to the angels. It is as much as he himself exceeds them in glory, authority, and power. God gives names to signify their state and condition."

Fourth, the *proof* of this assertion is seen from Christ's name. His name was not given to him by man, or assumed by himself, but ascribed to him by God himself. So here the name of Christ or the name of angels is not intended in the sense of their individual meaning. Rather, the apostle is emphasizing that the titles were given to them by God, and this tells you about their relative importance.

Inherited. Fifthly, the last important thing to note is *how* the Lord Christ *came by this name,* or obtained it. He **inherited** it as his particular possession forever. As he was made heir of everything, so he inherited a more excellent name than the angels. Now he was made heir of everything in that all things were made by him; so the Father committed to him, as mediator, a special power over all things.

Verse 5

For to which of the angels did God ever say, "You are my Son; today I have become your Father"?

The apostle continues to strengthen his proposition about the superiority of the Lord Christ over the angels with testimonies from the Old Testament.

We note the *method* the apostle uses to produce the testimony that he intends to use—**For to which of the angels did God ever say;** and then we look at the *evidence* itself—**"You are my Son; today I have become your Father."**

The apostle insists that testimonies in matters of faith must be from the Scripture. He confidently sends the Hebrews to the acknowledged rule of their faith and worship, whose authority he knew they would not dismiss (Isaiah 8:20). The apostle also argues negatively from the authority of Scripture in matters relating to faith and the worship of God. "It is *nowhere said in the Scripture to angels;* therefore they do not have the name ascribed to the Messiah." So an argument taken negatively from the authority of the Scripture in matters of faith is valid and is here consecrated forever by the apostle to be used by the church. Then the apostle mentions that there is a distinction of degrees among the angels themselves. To confirm his general assertion of Christ's preeminence over all the angels, he challenges them to mention any angel that either in fact or in their minds was superior to other angels, to whom such words were ever spoken: **For to which of the angels did God ever say.**

We now move on to the evidence itself. First, the words *especially* to the one they are applied to; that is, it is the Messiah who is prophesied about in Psalm 2:7. All Christians agree about this as such quotations are applied to Christ in several other places, such as Acts 4:25-27; 13:33; Hebrews 5:5. It is also certain that the Jews always applied this psalm to the Messiah, which they do to this day.

Second, the testimony should give a *special name* to the Messiah, a name that was his forever, which neither men nor angels could share. It needed to be a name that would distinguish him from everyone else. Many were called beloved of the Lord, but only Solomon was especially called "Jedidiah," and that name distinguished him from others. In the same way the Messiah had his name given to him. God decreed from eternity that he should be called by that name: **"You are my Son; today I have become your Father."**

Third, this name must show the Messiah's preeminence above the angels. Now, the name is *the Son of God*: **You are my Son.** While angels may be called the sons of God in a general way, it was never said to any angel personally, "You are my Son." God never said to any of them, "Today I have become your Father." So it is not the general name of a son, or sons of God, that the apostle refers to here; he is emphasizing that this name is specially assigned to the Lord Jesus, with the extra words, **"today I have become your Father."**

Or again, "I will be his Father, and he will be my Son"? This is the second piece of evidence the apostle produces to prove the preeminence of the Lord Christ above the angels, from the excellency of the name given to him. For this evidence to be valid it must be seen that these words *originally* referred to Christ, and, that there is a *name* in it assigned to him that is superior to any given to angels.

For the first of these, we must not ignore the difficulties that commentators have mentioned. The words quoted in this verse come from 2 Samuel 7:14. They are part of the answer given by God through Nathan to David, concerning his resolve to build a house for God. (The whole answer comes in 2 Samuel 7:11-16; also 1 Chronicles 17:12ff.) We say that both Solomon and the Lord Christ are intended in this whole oracle; Solomon *literally*, and also as the *type*; the Lord Christ *principally* and mystically, as he who was *represented* by him. So, these words first applied to Solomon, denoting that fatherly love, care, and protection that God would give him in his kingdom, inasmuch as Christ was represented by him in this. This means that these words need not apply exclusively to

Solomon. Principally, therefore, they refer to Christ himself, expressing that eternal, unchanging love that the Father bore him, based on the father-son relationship.

These words support the apostle's argument, for to which angel had God ever said, **"I will be his Father, and he will be my Son"**? They contain a great privilege, referring to the Messiah, and nothing like them was ever spoken to any angel. The name of the Son of God was never given to any of them in such a way. This demonstrates the preeminence of Christ above everything that the angels can attain to.

Verse 6

And again, when God brings his firstborn into the world, he says, "Let all God's angels worship him."

This is the second argument the apostle uses to confirm his assertion about the preference of the Son above angels, and it is supported by God's command to the angels to worship Christ. It is quite clear that the person worshiped is greater than the person whose duty it is to worship. We consider the apostle's preface and the evidence he brings forward.

His preface, or the way he produces this second testimony is this: **And again, when God brings . . . he says.** Christ's second coming is not intended here. So we ask what **when God brings his firstborn into the world** means. This does not refer to any one special act, or any one particular day. Rather, it means God's whole work in bringing the Messiah, through his conception, birth, anointing with the Spirit, resurrection, sending of the Holy Spirit, and preaching of the Gospel. These words **when God brings his firstborn into the world** describe this happening. So, after he had kept his church, under the administration of the law given by angels through the hand of Moses the mediator, in the expectation of the coming of the Messiah, when he brings him forth and enables him to carry out all his work, he says, **"Let all God's angels worship him."** This supports the apostle's argument that as Christ accomplished his work of revealing God's will, he was worthy of worship and honor from the angels themselves.

Firstborn. In what sense is Christ called **firstborn** here? The Lord Christ is never called **firstborn** with respect either to his eternal generation or to the conception and nativity of his human nature. About the former he is called "the Son," and "the only begotten Son of God," but nowhere "the firstborn." About the latter, he is called the "firstborn son" of the virgin, because she had no children before him, but not absolutely "the firstborn," which title is here and elsewhere in the Scripture ascribed to him. It is not, therefore, the thing itself of being the firstborn, but the dignity and privilege that came with it which are meant in this name. So, in Colossians 1:15, he is said to be "the firstborn over all creation," which means no more than that he has power and authority over all of God's creatures.

He says. That is, "God himself says." The words that follow are his words. Whatever the Scripture says in his name, God says, and continues to speak to this day. He speaks in the Scripture to the end of time. This is the foundation of our faith.

The apostle's words may be summarized as follows: "Again, in another place, where the Holy Spirit foretells the bringing forth into the world among men him who is the Lord and Heir of all, to undertake his work, and to enter into his kingdom and glory, the Lord speaks to this end, Let all God's angels worship him."

Verse 7

In speaking of the angels he says, "He makes his angels winds, his servants flames of fire."

The apostle now brings his third argument to demonstrate the preeminence of the Lord Christ above the angels.

The providence of God in disposing and using angels in his service is meant here. God employs his angels and heavenly ministers in producing those winds, fire, thunder and lightning, through which he executes many judgments in the world. The sense here is completed by seeing this as a simile, which is stated in the Targum (an Aramaic translation) on Psalm 104: "He makes (or sends) his angels like the winds, or like a flaming fire," making them fast, spiritual, agile, powerful and effective to accomplish the work they are appointed to do.

God uses his angels in carrying out the works of his providence here below. "This," says the apostle, "is the testimony that the Holy Spirit gives about them, their nature, duty, and work, as they serve the providence of God. But now," he says, "consider what the Scripture says concerning the Son, how it calls him God, how it ascribes a *throne* and a *kingdom* to him" (shown in the next verses), "and you will clearly see his preeminence above them."

Verses 8-9

But about the Son he says, "Your throne, O God, will last forever and ever, and righteousness will be the scepter of your kingdom. You

have loved righteousness and hated wickedness; therefore God, your God, has set you above your companions by anointing you with the oil of joy."

Having given an account of what the Scripture teaches and testifies about angels, in these next verses the apostle shows how many other things, far more glorious, are spoken to and of the Son, through whom God revealed his will in the Gospel.

It is the Christ, the Son, that is spoken to and denoted by the name, "Elohim," **"O God,"** as being the true God by nature. But what is affirmed about him here is not about him being God, but being king of his church and people; as elsewhere God is said to redeem his church with his own blood.

We now consider what is assigned to him, which is his kingdom. The first royal ensign mentioned is his **throne.** This **throne** denotes the kingdom itself. A throne is the seat of a king in his kingdom and is frequently used metonymically for the kingdom itself (see 1 Kings 8:20; Daniel 7:9).

The throne does not simply denote the kingdom of Christ, or his supreme rule and dominion, but the glory also of his kingdom. Being on his throne, he is in the height of his glory. And thus, because God manifests his glory in heaven, he calls that his throne, as the earth is his footstool (Isaiah 66:1). So Christ's throne is his glorious kingdom, which is also referred to in the words "he sat down at the right hand of the Majesty in heaven" (verse 3).

Forever and ever. To this throne *eternity* is attributed. So Christ's throne is contrasted with the frail, mutable kingdoms of the earth (see Psalm 72:7, 17; 145:13; Isaiah 9:7; Daniel 7:14; Micah 4:7). It will not decay or fall into any enemy hands, for he must reign until all his enemies become his footstool (1 Corinthians 15:24-27).

The second royal ensign is his **scepter.** Here the scepter denotes the actual administration of rule, as the word **righteousness** indicates. So the scepter stands for the laws of the kingdom and the efficacy of the government itself. What we call a righteous government is here the meaning of, **righteousness will be the scepter.**

The scepter of Christ's kingdom is one of **righteousness** because the laws of Christ's Gospel are righteous, holy, just, and full of truth (Titus 2:11-12). And all his administration is full of grace, mercy, justice, rewards and punishments, pardon, sanctification, trials, discipline, and preservation of his elect.

You have loved righteousness and hated wickedness. This shows the complete righteousness of God's kingdom. The laws of his rule are righteous, and his administrations are righteous. They all proceed from a constant love of righteousness and hatred of iniquity.

The result of this righteous rule in Christ is his **anointing you with the oil of joy and gladness.** God is the giver of this privilege.

Anointing you with the oil of joy. The privilege itself is being anointed with the oil of joy. Oil and anointing were normally used to make the face look cheerful at feasts and public solemnities (Psalm 104:15; Luke 7:37). On special occasions priests, kings, and prophets were anointed with oil (Exodus 30). That the ceremony was typical is evident from Isaiah 61:1-3. It denoted the giving of the Holy Spirit to enable the anointed person to carry out a special service. While it is true that Christ was anointed by the Spirit at his conception, baptism, and ascension, the apostle, with the psalmist, is here, most probably, referring to the glorious exaltation of Jesus Christ when he was solemnly instated in his kingdom. This was called making him both Lord and Christ (see Acts 2:36), when God raised him from the dead and gave him glory (see 1 Peter 1:21).

Verse 10-12

He also says, "In the beginning, O Lord, you laid the foundations of the earth, and the heavens are the work of your hands. They will perish, but you remain; they will all wear out like a garment. You will roll them up like a robe; like a garment they will be changed. But you remain the same, and your years will never end."

10. O Lord. The person spoken of and spoken to in these words is **O Lord.** Concerning this person, or the **Lord,** the author affirms two attributes. 1. The *creation of heaven and earth.* 2. The *abolition or change of them.*

In the beginning. The time or season of the creation is intimated to be **in the beginning,** or, as the word says here, "of old," before they were or existed. **You laid the foundations of the earth, and the heavens are the work of your hands.**

11. They will perish. This fading nature of the fabric of heaven and earth, along with everything contained in them, he sets out, first, by their future end, **they will perish,** and, second, their tendency to that end, **they will all wear out like a garment.** The gradual decay of the heavens and earth is seen in the words, **they will all wear out like a garment.** These words also indicate the close proximity of the ending.

12. You remain the same. In contrast to the fading earth and heavens Christ remains the same and **will never end.** One thing is meant by both these expressions—Christ's eternal and absolute immutable existence. It is not wrong to call eternity *nunc stans*, present existence, where nothing is past or future, and where everything is wholly present in and of itself. To emphasize God's eternal nature in contrast with the world's frailty and all of its creation, it is said that his **years will never end.** The world comes to an end but there is no end to Christ's existence.

Verse 13

This verse contains the last testimony produced by the apostle for the confirmation of the preeminence of the Lord Christ above angels. **To which of the angels did God ever say, "Sit at my right hand until I make your enemies a footstool for your feet"?** The usefulness of this testimony as confirmation of the Messiah's majesty and authority is seen from the frequent quotations about this in the New Testament (see Matthew 22:44; Acts 2:34-35; 1 Corinthians 15:25).

The introduction to this evidence starts with a question: **To which of the angels did God ever say?** From this we note that the question contains a definite negative. He never said these words or anything like them. The emphasis of the question is on the denial. Included in these words is a tacit application of this testimony to the Son, or the Messiah: "To the angels he did not say these words, but to the Son he said, 'Sit at my right hand.'"

The testimony itself centers on Christ's sitting at God's right hand. **Sit at my right hand.** This is Christ's exaltation to the glorious administration of the kingdom which was given to him with honor, security, and power; or as our apostle calls it, his reigning (1 Corinthians 15:25).

These words explain the purpose of this sitting down at God's right hand. It is to make his enemies the footstool for his feet. We inquire: Who are these enemies? How do they become his footstool? Who makes them his footstool?

We have shown that Christ's glorious exaltation in his kingdom is spoken about here. So the enemies must be the enemies of his kingdom. Christ's kingdom can be viewed in two ways: first, its inner, spiritual power and efficacy in the hearts of his subjects; and, second, in outward administration in the world. Both of these aspects of Christ's kingdom have many enemies that must be made his footstool.

The kingdom, rule, or reign of Christ, in the first sense, is the authority and power that converts, sanctifies, and brings salvation to his elect. As he is their king, he brings them to life by his Spirit, sanctifies them by his grace, preserves them through his faithfulness, raises them from the dead on the last day by his power, and gloriously rewards them for all eternity in his righteousness. In this work the Lord Christ has many enemies; such as the law, sin, Satan, the world, death, the grave, and hell. All these are enemies of the Christ's work and kingdom, and consequently to his person, who has undertaken this work.

Footstool. This word is used in a metaphorical sense. The allusion in general is taken from Joshua's actions against his enemies (Joshua 10:24). To demonstrate the loss of their power and his absolute supremacy over them, he told his people to put their feet on the necks of these enemies (see 2 Samuel 22:39; Psalm 8:6). To have his enemies put under his feet is to have complete victory over them. Their being made his footstool implies the constant nature of their condition under the weight of whatever burden he chose to put on them.

The second meaning of Christ's kingdom, his administration of it visibly in this world, is included in these words. God the Father, in Jesus Christ's exaltation, has given him all nations for his inheritance and the ends of the earth for his possession (Psalm 2:8). This means that Christ has a right to build his church in any part of the world and authority to order all nations for the benefit of his kingdom.

Until. The word **until** in this verse does not intimate any limit to the kingdom's duration. It only emphasizes Christ's secure and glorious reign while his work is carried out, which includes the subduing of his enemies (see Isaiah 9:7; Daniel 2:44; Hebrews 7:27).

Verse 14

Are not all angels ministering spirits sent to serve those who will inherit salvation?

The apostle has demonstrated the preeminence of the Son, as mediator of the new covenant, above all the angels, from those attributes of honor and glory that are given him in the Scriptures and that are not given to the angels. So that he may not appear to be arguing merely in a negative way, from what is not said about the angels, he adds in this verse a description of their nature and use, to show once more that nothing he affirms about them can be said about the Son.

Spirits. Their nature is that they are **spirits,** spiritual subsistences and not natural faculties, as the Sadducees imagined. They are created spirits and cannot be compared with Christ who made all things.

Ministering. Their works are seen from their description of being **ministering spirits.** They minister to the Lord. **Ministering spirits** wait on God concerning his holy services for the good of the church. Hence angels and the church are in the same family (Ephesians 3:15). They are all fellow servants in the same family who keep the testimony of Jesus (Revelation 19:10).

To serve those who will inherit salvation. These words indicate the limit of their ministry. It is **to serve those who will inherit salvation.** It is for their good, on their behalf, and for their sake.

Who will inherit salvation. This indicates that at present the saved are heirs and will inherit later, that is, obtain salvation by virtue of being heirs. This refers to elect believers. However, the apostle does not refer to them as elect, nor, directly, as believers, but as heirs. They receive their inheritance from their adoption. They are adopted children, heirs, and co-heirs with Christ (Romans 8:16-17). This is one of the many privileges we have as adopted members of God's family. These blessed angels specially minister to this family and have us under their constant care.

Hebrews
Chapter 2

In this second chapter the apostle explains the purpose of his letter and how it affects his readers. It was not just their instruction that he had in mind, although that was important and did serve the overall purpose of his letter. They had, by their instability and buckling under trials, made the apostle write to them in this way. In addition to this, the apostle foresaw that they would have great difficulties and temptations to contend with, and he was concerned that they would become like some other believers (2 Corinthians 11:2-3). The apostle's main aim, therefore, in this whole letter was to encourage the Hebrews to be steadfast in the faith of the Gospel and diligent about all the ways and means by which they might be established in their faith.

The apostle uses the incomparable excellency of the Author of the Gospel as the basis of his argument. He reminds them, and us, in general, that in handling the doctrines of the Gospel about the person and work of Jesus Christ, we should not be satisfied with mere intellectual assent but should endeavor to have our hearts set on fire by them through faith, love, obedience, and perseverance. The apostle emphasizes that the previously declared excellencies of Christ and the glory of his kingdom should prevent his hearers from becoming barren and unfruitful. The apostle had overwhelmed the Hebrews in the first chapter with a flood of divine testimonies about the person of the Messiah. He now gives them time to reflect where this divine discourse will lead them and how it particularly applies to them.

The apostle interposes his exhortation with arguments about another aspect of Christ's nature. He tells them to consider the priestly office of Christ and the effects this has. The apostle's exhortations are always based on the doctrines he has just expounded. We see this in the exhortations he gives at the beginning of this chapter, before he moves on to the priestly work of Christ in verses 5-9. The first verses, then, of this chapter are purely hortatory, spiced with some reasons for making the exhortations weighty.

Verse 1

We must pay more careful attention, therefore, to what we have heard, so that we do not drift away.

The first verse contains the exhortation itself. **Therefore,** for this cause, refers to the previous discourse, and the whole verse is an exhortation, which is taken as a conclusion to the previous teaching. From the proposition he made about the glory and excellency of the Author of the Gospel he draws the inference, "Therefore we ought . . ." The exhortation refers to a specific duty, **we must pay more careful attention.** A reason for doing this is added, **so that we do not drift away.**

We must pay more careful attention. This must be given with reverence, assent, and readiness to obey. It should be like the heart of Lydia, which "the Lord opened" to respond to Paul's message (see Acts 16:14). Lydia did not just listen, she responded immediately with humility and resolved to obey the Word. The apostle does not want his hearers to squander the benefits that are to be derived from what they **have heard.**

Verses 2-4

For if the message spoken by angels was binding, and every violation and disobedience received its just punishment, how shall we escape if we ignore such a great salvation? This salvation, which was first announced by the Lord, was confirmed to us by those who heard him. God also testified to it by signs, wonders and various miracles, and gifts of the Holy Spirit distributed according to his will.

The apostle's purpose in these three verses is to confirm his exhortation in verse 1.

Message. This verse opens with a description of the law that the apostle does by using a periphrasis, **the message spoken by the angels.** The word **message** has the word **spoken** added to it, meaning that the **message** was published, preached, or declared. The **message** is the teaching of the law. That is, the law itself is spoken, declared, and promulgated. This is done **by angels,** that is, by the ministry of angels. The law was given from God, but it was given by angels.

For if. The apostle's argument springs from these words. "For if the law that was proclaimed to our fathers by angels was so vindicated against the disobedient, how much more will the neglect of the Gospel be avenged?"

Binding. The apostle affirms that the proclaimed Word was **binding,** or "firm," or "steadfast"; that is, it became an assured covenant between God and the people. The law proclaimed by angels became a steadfast covenant

between God and the people (Joshua 24:21, 22, 24). As it was firm and rat-
ified in this way, obedience to it became necessary and reasonable.

The apostle refers to disobedience to the law in the words **every violation and disobedience received its just punishment. Just punishment** is
a fair recompense, proportional to the crime according to God's judgment.
It is stated that God's judgment is on those "who do such things," who
"deserve death" (Romans 1:32).

3-4. The subject of these verses is **such a great salvation.** The originator of this salvation is **the Lord** who **announced** it. It is distributed
through **signs, wonders and various miracles, and gifts of the Holy
Spirit. If we ignore** this **salvation,** a punishment is indicated by the words
how shall we escape?.

3. Such a great salvation. This refers to the Gospel, as is clear from
verse 1. What was referred to as "what we have heard" is here spoken of as
great salvation. The Gospel is called **salvation** by metonymy, for it is the
grace of God that brings salvation (Titus 2:11); this is the Word that is able
to save us; the doctrine and basis of salvation (Romans 1:16).

First announced by the Lord. The apostle here describes the principal
author or revealer of the Gospel. It began to be spoken of by the Lord.
This asserts that the first preacher of the Gospel, before he used apostles
and disciples for this work, was the Lord himself. As the angels declared
the law, so the Lord himself proclaimed the Gospel.

Was confirmed to us by those who heard him. The apostle describes
how the Gospel came to us. It was **confirmed to us by those who heard
him.** Most of the Hebrews were not personally acquainted with the Lord's
ministry. They had never heard the words he spoke. But, although they
may not have heard the Lord, the same Word that this apostle now
preaches to them was not only declared but **confirmed to us by those
who heard him.**

He does not just say that the Word was preached to us by them but was
confirmed, made firm and steadfast, as it was delivered infallibly to us
through the ministry of the apostles. There was a divine "firmness," certainty, and infallibility in the apostolic declaration of the Gospel, just as
there was in the writings of the prophets.

4. God also testified to it. The nature of this testimony follows: it was
through **signs, wonders and various miracles, and gifts of the Holy Spirit.**

First come **signs,** that is, miraculous deeds, performed to signify God's
presence in the powerful actions.

Second came **wonders,** deeds beyond the power of nature. They were
performed to fill people with wonder and awe, pointing people to what
was signified by them.

Third come **various miracles,** "mighty works," where God's mighty
power is clearly discernible.

Fourth are **gifts of the Holy Spirit,** which are enumerated in 1 Corinthians 12 and Ephesians 4:8. These **gifts** are "free gifts," freely bestowed and **distributed** for the reason explained in 1 Corinthians 12:7-11.

3. Ignore. A neglect of the Gospel is mentioned here. It means, "if we do not take due care about it." This word intimates an omission of all the duties that are necessary if we are to retain the Word that has been preached to us.

Escape. There is a punishment intimated on this sinful neglect of the Gospel: **how shall we escape?** or, "how shall we flee from, or avoid" this punishment? The apostle does not mention what this punishment is. But from the preceding words it is clear that it is a "just retribution," that is, it is a **just punishment** (verse 2). A punishment is given to such a great crime. To see what this punishment is, see Matthew 16:26; 25:46; 2 Thessalonians 1:9.

How shall we escape? This denies any way of deliverance. No one can rescue us (see 1 Peter 4:17-18). The punishment is certain, and this event of being punished will definitely take place. It is an unavoidable evil. So, **how shall we escape?** We will not, there is no way out, and we do not have the ability to bear what we are liable to (Matthew 23:33; 1 Peter 4:18).

Verses 5-9

It is not to angels that he has subjected the world to come, about which we are speaking. But there is a place where someone has testified: "What is man that you are mindful of him, the son of man that you care for him? You made him a little lower than the angels; you crowned him with glory and honor and put everything under his feet." In putting everything under him, God left nothing that is not subject to him. Yet at present we do not see everything subject to him. But we see Jesus, who was made a little lower than the angels, now crowned with glory and honor because he suffered death, so that by the grace of God he might taste death for everyone.

5. The whole verse contains a negative assertion about the apostle's argument. This is the thrust of it: "The world to come is not made subject to angels; but it was made subject to Jesus: and therefore he is exalted above the angels."

The world to come. The subject of the apostle's proposition is **the world to come,** the new heavens and new earth, which God promised to create (Isaiah 65:17; 66:22). This **world to come** is the state and worship of the church under the Messiah. Concerning this world the apostle first declares, negatively, that it is not made subject to angels. The church was not put in subjection to angels when it was founded. The church is not subjected to angels in its work. The role of angels in this world is a ministry (1:14), not one of ruling or reigning. Angels have no rule in or over the church. They join the church in giving testimony to Jesus (Revelation 19:10; 22:9). The angels are, like us, subject to him, in whom they and we are gathered into one head (Ephesians 1:10). As for the power to judge and reward on the last day, it is clear that God has not put the world to come in subjection to angels, but only to Jesus.

6. The apostle has shown that the world to come, which the Jewish church looked for, was not made subject to angels, as no mention of any such thing comes in the Scriptures. The apostle, as he pursues his objective of demonstrating the preeminence of the Lord Jesus above the angels, maintains that the world to come is put in subjection under him. He does not state this using his own words, but from a testimony in the Scriptures that he quotes for this purpose.

There is a place where someone . . . The way the apostle cites this quotation is unusual. Neither the person nor the place in the Scriptures are specified. The reason for this is obvious. Both person and place were sufficiently well known to the people the apostle wrote to. The Hebrews were not ignorant about who spoke the words in the quotation. The **someone** mentioned there is David, and the **place** is Psalm 8:4-6.

The testimony itself comes in verses 6-7, **What is man . . . ?** It is made up of a contemplation of the infinite love and condescension of God toward mankind. It is expressed by the words **What is man?**, which the apostle cries out in near astonishment. The apostle does not mention the context for these words, as the psalmist does in Psalm 8:3, "When I consider your heavens, the work of your fingers, the moon and the stars, which you have set in place. . . ." David contemplates the greatness, power, wisdom, and glory of God, manifesting itself in his mighty works, especially in the beauty, order, majesty, and usefulness of the heavens. From this David moves on to say that this infinitely wise God, through whose Word all this came into being, condescended to care about mankind.

So **what is man that you are mindful of him, the son of man that you care for him?** That is, why do you remember him, or set your heart on him for good? This expresses the heart and mind of God toward human nature in the person of Jesus Christ. The whole counsel and purpose of God about the salvation of mankind, in and through the humiliation, exaltation, and whole mediation of "the man Christ Jesus," is contained here.

7. You made him a little lower than the angels. This was part of God's visitation. Christ was **made lower than the angels** through an act of God. The extent of Christ's humiliation is seen in that he was made **lower than the angels.**

35

Another result of God visiting mankind is Christ's exaltation. He is given rule and dominion. He **crowned him with glory and honor.** This is the royal badge and token of supreme kingly power. To be crowned is to be invested with sovereign power, or with the right and title of a sovereign. To be crowned with glory and honor is to have a glorious and honorable crown, or rule and sovereignty. **Glory** denotes the weight of the crown. It is a weight of glory (see 2 Corinthians 4:16). **Honor** is its beauty and glory.

8. To expand on the objective extent of this rule and dominion, he adds, **In putting everything under him, God left nothing that is not subject to him.** To apply this testimony to the correct person, he declares negatively who it does not relate to: **Yet at the present we do not see everything subject to him.** These words refer to mankind. He asserts this by appealing to a common experience: **we . . . see.** "This is a matter that everyone can judge." "We do not need testimony or argument to instruct us on this point; our own condition, and what we see in other people, are sufficient to instruct us."

The word **yet** puts a limit on this experience. **Yet at present we do not see.** "It has been a long time since this testimony was given, much longer than the creation of any and all other things, and yet all this time we see that all things are far from being placed under his feet." So, by our own observation, we can easily discern that this word does not principally apply either to the first man or to his posterity.

9. The apostle now shows who these words apply to and in whom these words had their complete fulfillment. **But,** he writes, **we see Jesus.** The apostle positively applies this testimony to Jesus. Two things are stated here. First, that he was made **a little lower than the angels.** Second, that he had all things put in subjection to him. "Both these," says the apostle, "we see accomplished in Jesus." That is what the words **we see Jesus** mean: that is, these things are fulfilled in him. As the apostle had just appealed to their experience in his negative statement, that all things are not made subject to man in general, he is here affirmative and says, **we see Jesus.** Now they saw it, partly through what he had previously demonstrated about him, partly through the signs and wonders he had just spoken about, and partly through his calling and gathering of his church, giving laws, rules, and worship to it, by virtue of his authority in and over this new world.

Who was made a little lower than the angels, or was brought into a condition that exposed him in a way angels never experienced. These words from the psalm do not apply to the condition of mankind, as if he were saying, "He is so excellent that he is only a little beneath angels." For the apostle ascribes to Christ a dignity far above all angels, in that as all things are put under his feet, so he clearly states that these words refer to the abasement of Jesus, as he was so humbled that he might die. The apostle also takes the opportunity to expound another aspect of Christ's mediation, since it is prophesied here. For although he was abased, this was not for his own benefit but that **by the grace of God he might taste death for everyone.**

The other part of the testimony states, **we see Jesus . . . now crowned with glory and honor,** and consequently that all things are put under his feet. The state of the church is meant by this statement, so that Christ's teachings should be carefully observed by everyone who wishes to benefit from all his promises.

Numerous things are contained in this verse. There is the humiliation of Christ, so that he might suffer **death**; and his exaltation and authority over all things, in particular in the world to come: **crowned with glory and honor.** Christ's death is explained: its cause is **the grace of God**; its nature was that **he might taste death**; it purpose was for others; and its extent was for all: **so that by the grace of God he might taste death for everyone.**

He suffered death. Christ was so humbled that he might suffer death. To complete the application of the testimony produced, his exaltation after his suffering, he was **crowned . . . with glory and honor.** This exaltation contained absolute dominion over everything, except for God, and so over the world to come, which was not put in subjection to angels. With these words the apostle ends his argument for the excellency of Christ above the angels from the subjection of all things to him.

The apostle now moves on to expand on the result of Christ's humiliation. He mentions four things.

First, he mentions the reason behind Christ's humiliation: **so that by the grace of God.** Sometimes it is called his "goodness," "kindness," or his "love of mankind," or his "love" (see John 3:16; Romans 5:8; 1 John 3:16); or his "pleasure," "the riches of God's grace" (see Ephesians 1:5, 7); or "called according to his purpose" (Romans 8:28). For thus it is seen that **grace,** God's grace, was the impulse behind Christ's death. It was the gracious, free, sovereign purpose of God's will, suited to and arising from his natural grace, love, goodness, pity, mercy, and compassion, working together. It was not of any anger or displeasure on God's part against Christ that caused Christ's death. It was out of love and kindness toward others, who would not otherwise have been brought to glory, that Christ was thus appointed to die.

Second, the kind of death Christ died is described as: **he might taste death for everyone.** To die in this way is to experience the sorrows, bitterness, and penalties of death. To **taste death** is, first, really to die. No pretense about dying is described here. It is indicated here that his death involved *bitterness.* Christ himself compares it with a cup of suffering that he had to drink (see Matthew 26:39). Christ's tasting death also implies his *conquest over death.* For the phrase **taste death,** as applied to Christ, indicates that he only had a thorough taste of it and that he neither was nor could be detained by its power (see Acts 2:24). So through God's grace Christ tasted death.

Third, the result of Christ tasting death is mentioned: **for everyone.** Christ died for others. He died **for** them. He died on behalf of others. David wished that he could have died in Absalom's place (see 2 Samuel 19:1). David longed to die for Absalom, so that Absalom could live. So the most common way of interpreting these words is to "die for another," meaning that the death is in his place. The Jews understood this about their sacrifices, where the life of the animal was accepted in the place of the life of the sinner. In this way Christ tasted death **for** everyone. Christ was, through God's grace and wisdom, substituted as a mediator, a surety, in their place, to go through the death that they should have undergone, so that they might go free.

Fourth, this dying of Christ is said to be **for everyone.** This refers to all those many children whom God intended by his death to bring to glory (verse 10); those sanctified by him, whom he calls "brothers" (verses 11-12), and "the children God has given him" (verse 13); whom through death he delivers from the fear of death (verses 14-15); even "Abraham's descendants" (verse 16).

Verse 10

In the previous verses the apostle mentioned the thing that most Jews found most offensive, and which is most important to believe, namely, the sufferings of the Messiah. This, Christ's own disciples were slow to believe (see Matthew 16:21-22; 17:22-23; Luke 24:25-26), and the Jews generally stumbled over. They thought that it was strange that the Messiah, God's Son, the Savior of his people, the Captain of their salvation, concerning whom so great and glorious things have been foretold, should be brought into such a low and despised condition, and there to suffer and die. The Jews expected an outward, glorious, and regal deliverance to come with the mighty weapons of an army. What could they expect from a Messiah who had suffered and died?

So the apostle, having asserted the sufferings of Christ, found it necessary to emphasize this point and to expand on it. He taught them about the priestly office of the Messiah and how he accomplished redemption. As for the salvation itself he declares that it was not to be of the same kind they had previously experienced when they escaped from Egypt, but a spiritual and heavenly deliverance from sin, Satan, death, and hell. The apostle tells them that this will be performed through the sufferings and death of the Messiah and that it could not be accomplished in any other way. He mentions the first reason for this in verse 10.

In bringing many sons to glory, it was fitting that God, for whom and through whom everything exists, should make the author of their salvation perfect through suffering.

The reason for Christ tasting death (verse 9) is given here: **it was fitting that God . . .** This verse explains why Christ tasted death. It was to **bring many sons to glory.** The apostle here declares the nature of the salvation that was to be performed by the Messiah. His purpose was not to carry them into a new Canaan and bring them into a wealthy country, into an earthly country. Rather, he wanted his children, in and through the Messiah, to come into eternal glory with himself in heaven. So it was little wonder that the way to achieve this was totally different from an earthly deliverance but rather through the death and sufferings of the Messiah himself.

In bringing many sons to glory, all the sovereign acts of power, wisdom, love, and grace are especially assigned to the Father, as all the ministerial actions are assigned to the Son as mediator. So there is every reason why he might be called the one who was **bringing** or leading the sons to glory.

Make . . . perfect. These words express the special way through which God fitted the Lord Christ for his office, of being the **author of their salvation.** To understand this correctly we observe that the apostle does not refer to the redemption of the elect absolutely, but of bringing them to glory, when they were made sons in a particular fashion. So he does not treat absolutely the designation, consecration, or fitting of the Lord Christ to his office of mediator in general, but just that part of it which affected the bringing of the sons to glory. This sheds light on the phrase, **make . . . perfect through suffering. Perfect** here signifies to consecrate, dedicate and sanctify for an office, for some special part of an office. Hence the old commentators called baptism "perfection," or consecration to Christ's sacred service. The word in the next verse refers to this as making men **holy.** This word is used by Christ himself when he says, "For them I sanctify myself" (John 17:19), that is, "dedicate, consecrate, separate" myself to be a sacrifice. It is also said in Hebrews that "the blood of the covenant . . . sanctified him" (Hebrews 10:29)—this word is not used in any other sense in this letter when applied to Christ (see 5:9; 7:28).

So it was appropriate that God should dedicate and consecrate the Lord Christ for this part of his work through his own sufferings. He formerly consecrated Aaron to be priest, but through the hands of Moses, and he was set apart for his work through the sacrifice of other things. But the Lord Christ must be consecrated by his own sufferings and the sacrifice of himself. Through all the sufferings, then, of the Lord Christ in his life and death, which brought about the salvation of the elect, God consecrated him to be a prince, leader, and author of the salvation of his people. Peter declares this to be so in Acts 2:36 and 5:30-31. So the whole work of saving the sons of God, from first to last, is committed to the Lord Jesus (see Isaiah 55:4).

When the people came out of Egypt with Moses, they all died in the wilderness. But they were delivered again through Joshua, the type of Christ, and none of them failed to enter Canaan. Christ is the **author of their salvation.** This is seen in his care and watchfulness. "He who watches over Israel will neither slumber nor sleep" (Psalm 121:4). There is no time or season when the sons committed to his care will ever be neglected. They are never out of his heart or mind. They are engraved on the palms of his hands. Christ shows how he is the **author of their salvation** through his tenderness and love. "He tends his flock like a shepherd: He gathers the lambs in his arms and carries them close to his heart; he gently leads those that have young" (Isaiah 40:11). Christ also leads them with power, authority, and majesty. "He will stand and shepherd his flock in the strength of the LORD, in the majesty of the name of the LORD his God" (Micah 5:4). The "name of the LORD his God" is in him and is accompanied by his power and majesty as he rules and feeds his people.

Verses 11-13

The reason for the necessity of Christ's sufferings has been declared. It was fitting that God should make the author of salvation perfect through suffering. It is not yet apparent how this suffering could be beneficial to the sons who were to be brought to glory. The law denounced the sinner himself with the judgment of death. While the Lord Jesus undertook to be the author of salvation for the sons of God and might be willing to suffer for them, how could one's person's punishment be accepted for the sin of another? In these verses the apostle discovers reasons for this. He assumes that there was an agreement between the Father and the Son in this matter, and he gives details about this in chapter 10. He also assumes that in his sovereign authority, God had relaxed the law about the person suffering, but not about the penalty that had to be suffered. God had abundantly declared this to the church of the Jews in all their sacrifices. The apostle then goes on to state the grounds for Christ's substitution in the place of the sons and how they benefit from his suffering.

Both the one who makes men holy and those who are made holy are of the same family. So Jesus is not ashamed to call them brothers. He says, "I will declare your name to my brothers; in the presence of the

congregation I will sing your praises." And again, "I will put my trust in him." And again he says, "Here am I, and the children God has given me."

These verses contain, first, a further description of the author of salvation and the sons to be brought to glory by him, taken from his office and work toward them concerning their sanctification. Second comes the assertion that they will be **of the same family.** Third comes a consequence from this that **Jesus is not ashamed to call them brothers.** Fourth, there is a triple confirmation about this from the Old Testament.

First, the apostle describes the author of salvation and the sons to be brought to glory by their mutual relation to one another in terms of sanctification. Christ sanctifies, and they are the ones he makes **holy.** Christ, the author of salvation, is the sanctifier. As Christ sanctifies, so the children are sanctified. Christ's action here is what he did for the sons, when he suffered for them, in line with God's will (see verse 10). Now the sanctifier separates and dedicates them for sacred use, or he purifies them and makes them holy. The latter sense is principally intended here.

Second, the apostle affirms that they are of **the same family,** "one." This made it fitting for Christ to suffer and for them to partake of his sufferings. One common nature is intended here. Christ and they have the same nature. In this way it was fitting that he should suffer for them, and they were now in a position to benefit from his sufferings. An offering made to the Lord of firstfruits, or meat or grain, had the same nature as the rest of the fruits it was taken from, and all the fruits were sanctified (see Leviticus 2). In the same way, the Lord Jesus Christ was taken as the firstfruits of the nature of the children and offered to God so that the whole lump, or the whole nature of man in the children, that is, all the elect, are or separated to God and effectually sanctified in their season.

This is the basis of all the testimonies that the apostle now draws on from the Old Testament. As he was of one nature with them, he **is not ashamed to call them brothers,** as he demonstrates from Psalm 22. Also, Christ's participation of their nature made it necessary for him to trust God, which the apostle demonstrates by quoting, **"I will put my trust in him."** This could in no sense be said of Christ had he not shared that nature, which is exposed to all kinds of needs and troubles, which the angels never experience. As his nature was thus one with ours, that made him our brother and made it necessary for him to trust in God for deliverance. As the principal head and firstfruit of our nature and the author of our salvation, he is a father to us and we are his children. This, the apostle demonstrates with his third quotation from the Old Testament, **"Here am I, and the children the LORD has given me"** (Isaiah 8:18). The apostle says the same thing in verse 14, where he shows in what sense Christ and the children were one, namely, since they both participated in "flesh and blood."

41

This interpretation reflects the apostle's arguments accurately. But if anyone wishes to show further links between Christ and his members, I will not object. There may be references here to their being *one God* and *one mystical body, one church,* with Christ as the head, and the sons the members.

We now turn to the double duty that the Lord Christ places upon himself in these verses. First, he will declare God's name to his brothers; and, second, he will praise God in the congregation. In the former we must ask what is meant by the **name** of God, and in the latter how it is or was **declared** by Jesus Christ.

Your name. God's name is unknown to men by nature. So is the way he communicates his goodness and grace to them. And this is the name of God meant here, which the Lord Jesus "revealed . . . to those whom you gave me out of the world" (John 17:6). This is the same as his declaration about the Father: "no one has ever seen God" (John 1:18).

The second part of this testimony goes on to state what Christ will do: he **"will sing your praises"**; and where he will do this: **"in the presence of the congregation."** Both these expressions come from the temple. Singing hymns of praise to God in the great congregation was then a main part of worship. He would praise God by declaring his name. There is no way to celebrate the praise of God like declaring his grace, goodness, and love toward mankind. In this way they may believe in him and so give him glory. He would do this **"in the presence of the congregation,"** that is, in the great assembly of people in the temple. This was a type of the whole church of the elect under the new testament. The Lord Christ, in his own person, by his Spirit in the apostles, by his Word, and by all his messengers to the end of time, set forth the love, grace, goodness, and mercy of God in him the mediator. This sets forth the praise of God in the middle of the congregation.

The apostle then quotes from Psalm 18:4 [NIV footnote has Isaiah 8:17, **"I will put my trust in him."**—*Ed.*] The whole of Psalm 18 is literally about David's trials and deliverances, but not absolutely, as he was a type of Christ. In all the difficulties and troubles he had to contend with, he put his trust in God (see Psalm 22:19; Isaiah 50:7-9). Christ could not have done this if he had been *only God.* But the apostle is now demonstrating that he *was also man,* like us in all things, except for sin. So his duty was, in all times of trouble, to exercise faith in God's care and protection.

The last testimony is, **"Here am I, and the children the LORD has given me."** It is taken from Isaiah 8:18. It is a prophecy about Christ. The apostle quotes it to reinforce his argument about the united nature of the author of salvation and the sons to be brought to glory. He can now call them **brothers,** as they share the same condition of facing troubles. Also, by God's appointment, they are his children. As he has the same nature as them, it is fitting for him to be their parent. God, through an act of sovereign grace, gives them to him to be his children. This is the purpose of the apostle using this testimony here.

Through this triple testimony the apostle confirms the relation between the children to be brought to glory and the author of their salvation. So it became righteous that Christ should suffer for them and fitting that they should enjoy the benefit of his sufferings.

Verses 14-15

The apostle has outlined the unity of Christ and the children as they are related to a common root and take part of the same nature. He now declares the result, use, and necessity of that union, in respect of the work that God has appointed Christ to, and the ends which he had to accomplish thereby. They are two in number: the destruction of the devil, and the freeing of those who have been in slavery because of death. Neither of these things could have happened except through the author of salvation, which Christ could not have performed unless he had the same nature as the children, which is clear from the opening words of verse 14.

Since the children have flesh and blood, he too shared in their humanity so that by his death he might destroy him who holds the power of death—that is, the devil—and free those who all their lives were held in slavery by their fear of death.

The apostle examines in detail the common nature Christ and his children have, how they are all one, and the special reasons why the Lord Christ was made to take part of the nature. Chrysostom gives these verses this sense: "Having shown the brotherhood" (between Christ and the children) "he lays down the causes of that dispensation."

There are a number of things that the apostle takes for granted will be known by the Hebrews: first, that the devil had the power over death; second, that because of this, people were full of fear of death and so lived a life of anxiety because of their fear of death; third, that the Messiah could deliver people from this state; and, fourth, that the Messiah would accomplish this through his suffering.

The apostle proceeds to explain the state of the children to be brought to glory. Their *natural* state is that they were all partakers of flesh and blood—**the children have flesh and blood.** Their *moral* state meant that they deserved death, the penalty for sin, and were enslaved in their fear of death. So verse 15 states that Christ might **free those who all their lives were held in slavery by their fear of death.**

There is a double affirmation about Christ, the author of salvation: first, he took part in their natural condition—**he too shared their humanity;** second, he freed them from their moral condition—**and free those . . .**

The apostle states how this was done, emphasizing the necessity of Christ's participation in the children's nature, so that he might relieve them from their trouble. He did it by death: **by his death.**

Then the apostle shows the immediate effect of Christ's death, resulting in the children's freedom, the destruction of the devil's power over death. The result of Christ's death was that **he might destroy him who holds the power of death.**

14. Flesh and blood. The apostle explains the natural condition of the children, that is, the children whom God planned to bring to glory, those who were given to Christ. These children **have flesh and blood.**

Flesh and blood usually stands for the whole human nature; not as if by "blood" the soul was meant, because the life is said to be in it. But in this expression, as used in this verse, because human nature is not absolutely considered, it is rather human mortality that is under consideration. So it is as if he said, "the children were people subject to death." For the apostle explains why the Lord Christ was made a man subject to death—so he and the children should be of one nature. So, just as this was the condition of the children, that they were all partakers of human nature, liable to suffering, sorrow, and death, he was also like them in this. This is expressed to demonstrate the love and condescension of Jesus Christ.

Now the apostle explains the moral condition of the children. They were subject to death and lived in fear and slavery of their condition that continued throughout their lives.

It is implied that they are subject to death as a penalty due to their sin. On this supposition lies the whole weight of Christ's mediation. The children who were to be brought to glory were under God's curse, which Christ came to deliver them from.

The first effect of this death was that they lived in **fear of death.** This fear of death came about because their minds were troubled about their expectation of death on account of their sins. This apprehension is common to all people since it stems from a general presumption that death is penal. Death is God's judgment on those who commit sin (see Romans 1:32; 2:15). The sentence of the law is well known, "The soul that sinneth shall die."

Their fear of death brought slavery with it—**all their lives were held in slavery by their fear of death.** This slavery is involuntary. No one is in slavery because he wants to be. This slavery generates a strong desire to seek freedom by any possible means. This slavery clouds and tires the mind. Where slavery is total it generates greater future evils. Such is the slavery of condemned criminals; such is the slavery of Satan, who is kept in chains of darkness for the judgment of the great day. All these things concur with the slavery mentioned here. This is the state of sinners who are outside of Christ.

All their lives. They are said to continue in this state **all their lives.** They had no way to deliver themselves from it. This was the state of the children whose rescue was undertaken by the Lord Christ, the author of salvation.

Two things are stated about the Lord Christ, linked to the premise that the children have flesh and blood, and are in slavery by their fear of death. First, Christ took part in their natural condition himself; second, he delivered them from their moral condition. In order to achieve the second, he had to take part in the first.

He too shared in their humanity. Christ really took part in human nature.

These verses explain the effects of Christ's death, **that he might destroy him who holds the power of death.** We note *who* holds the power of death; *what* that power consisted of; *how* he was destroyed; and how this happened *through Christ's death.*

The person who had the power of death is described by name, **the devil.**

Destroy him who holds the power of death—that is, the devil. He is the great enemy of salvation and the great accuser.

His power lay in his power in and over death, for he **holds the power of death.** He was the means of bringing death into the world. He was able to introduce sin and so he had power to bring in death also. Romans 5:12 states, "just as sin entered the world through one man, and death through sin, and in this way death came to all men, because all sinned." Satan is called the "prince of this world" (John 12:31), and the "god" of this world (2 Corinthians 4:4) in that all in the world are under the guilt of that sin and death that he brought to them. God passed the death sentence against sin, and then Satan's power frightened men's consciences and so brought them into slavery.

He might destroy him. Satan is destroyed. This does not apply to the devil's nature and being but to his power in and over death, as is stated elsewhere: "Now is the time for judgment on this world; now the prince of this world will be driven out" (John 12:31). What here, in Hebrews, is called the destroying of the devil is there, in John, called the driving out of the prince of this world. It is the driving him out of his power, from his princedom and rule, as in Colossians 2:15, "having disarmed the powers and authorities, he made a public spectacle of them, triumphing over them by the cross." Conquerors did this when they had not slain their enemies but had deprived them of their rule and led them captive. The destruction, then, is meant here of him **who holds the power of death;** it is the removing of that power that he had in and over death, with all the effects and consequences of it.

The *means* by which Satan was thus destroyed is also described. It was **by his death**, that is, by Christ's own death. Of all possible ways this seemed to be the most unlikely, but it was not only the best, but the only way by which this might be accomplished. How this happened must be declared and vindicated. All of Satan's power over death was founded on sin. The obligation of the sinner to death gave Satan his power. If this obligation was removed, Satan's power would also be taken away. Now this, with reference to the children for whom he died, was done in the death of Christ—*virtually* in the death itself, *actually* in its application to them. When the sinner ceased to be a slave of death, Satan's power was broken. This happens to everyone who has an interest in Christ's death: for "therefore, there is now no condemnation for those who are in Christ Jesus" (Romans 8:1). This is because of Christ's death. He died for their sins and took on himself the death that they deserved. Once death was conquered and their obligation to death was taken away, Satan's power dissolved.

The first branch of Satan's power consisted in the bringing of sin into the world. This is dissolved by Christ "who takes away the sin of the world" (John 1:29), which he did as "the Lamb of God," by the sacrifice of himself in his death, typified by the paschal lamb and all the other sacrifices under the old covenant. Again, Satan's power consisted in his rule in the world, which was under the shadow of sin and death. From this, Satan was driven out in the death of Christ (see John 12:31). When contending with Christ for the continuance of his sovereignty, he was conquered. The ground on which he took his stand was taken away from him as the guilt of sin was taken away from under him and his title defeated. And, actually, believers are translated from his rule, from the power of darkness, into the kingdom of light and the Son of God. Satan can no longer make any use of death as penal in order to terrify people. Since people are justified by faith, in the death of Christ, they "have peace with God" (Romans 5:1). When Christ makes peace between God and us by the blood of his cross (see 2 Corinthians 5:19-21; Ephesians 2:14-15), the weapons of this part of Satan's power are taken out of his hand, since death has no power to terrify consciences. The people whom Christ died for will never have the death sentence passed on them. So Christ's death stops Satan from ever pronouncing death over anyone. So Satan, as far as his power over death is concerned, is completely destroyed by Christ's death. And all this depended on God appointing the satisfactory sufferings of Christ and accepting them instead of the sufferings of the children themselves.

Verse 16

For surely it is not angels he helps, but Abraham's descendants.

What the apostle denies in these words is taught nowhere in the Scriptures (see 1:5, "For to which of the angels did God ever say"). So we might say these words mean, "Nowhere in Scripture does Christ help angels." But his help of **Abraham's descendants** is referred to in the Scriptures. There it is promised, there it is spoken about, and there it is done by him.

What the apostle asserts has the ring of an axiom about it. The same thing is denied and affirmed of the different things mentioned, "He took not angels, but he took the seed of Abraham." How did Christ help the descendants of Abraham in the Scriptures? It is clear that this refers to Abraham's "seed," and it is said in Galatians 3:16a, "the promises were spoken to Abraham and to his seed." This was the great principle, the great expectation of the Hebrews, that the Messiah should be the seed of Abraham. "The Scripture does not say 'and to seeds,' meaning many people, but 'and to your seed,' meaning one person, who is Christ" (Galatians 3:16b). This was declared to them in the promise; and this accordingly was accomplished. Here Christ is said to be the seed of Abraham, because in the Scripture it is so plainly, so often affirmed that he should be so, when not one word is anywhere spoken that he should be an angel or take their nature on him. This gives the true meaning to this verse. In this verse the apostle affirms what he had previously affirmed about his being a partaker of flesh and blood together with the children. This, the apostle says, the Scripture declares, where it is promised that he would be the seed of Abraham, which he there takes on himself, and which was already accomplished in his being made partaker of flesh and blood (see John 1:14; Romans 9:5; Galatians 3:16; 4:4).

This, then, the apostle teaches us, that the Lord Christ, the Son of God, according to the promise, took to himself the nature of mankind, coming from the seed of Abraham—that is, into personal union with himself; but he did not take the nature of angels, and there is no such thing said of him anywhere in the Scripture.

Verses 17-18

For this reason he had to be made like his brothers in every way, in order that he might become a merciful and faithful high priest in service to God, and that he might make atonement for the sins of the peo-

ple. Because he himself suffered when he was tempted, he is able to help those who are being tempted.

In these two verses the apostle illustrates what he had taught before and confirms what he had asserted concerning the Son's participation of flesh and blood in the same way as the children. He does this in one particular way. He emphasizes that Christ is a high priest. The Hebrews knew that the Messiah was a high priest, and the apostle would enlarge on this later on. Christ was a high priest in a way that suited his office and benefited those he ministered to. This the wisdom of God and the nature of the thing itself require. Now, as these people were prone to being tempted and suffered all sorts of things, Christ must be able to help, relieve, and save such people. All this the apostle declares in these verses.

17. For this reason. This is an important illative expression. Chrysostom understood the connection between these verses and the previous ones in this way, "Therefore he was made man, that he might be a sacrifice able to purge our sins."

He had to be made. The *necessity* of the matter of the apostle's assertion is expressed by "he ought," "it must be so," **he had to be made.** On the supposition that he was to be a high priest, it could not be otherwise. God having designed him to that office and work, it was indispensably necessary for him to be made like his brothers in all things.

Made like his brothers in every way. The apostle's assertion concerns Christ's being; he had to be **made like his brothers in every way.**

In every way can have numerous limitations placed on it. For, whereas the brothers are sinners, Christ was not made like them in sin. This exception the apostle mentions in 4:15. Christ was made like them in the essence of human nature, a rational spiritual soul, and a mortal body. It was necessary that he should have a human nature, as truly and really as the brothers, and be like them, in order that he might be an offering priest and have of his own to offer to God.

It was also necessary that in and with his human nature he should take on him all the properties and affections of it, so that he might be made like his brethren. He had human affections like love, joy, fear, sorrow, shame, and the like. His body was not free from hunger, thirst, cold, pain, and death itself.

The main purpose of his conformity to the brothers is that he **might become a merciful and faithful high priest.** Two things are mentioned here. The *office* Christ was appointed to—he was to be **high priest**; and, his *qualifications* for that office—he was to be **merciful and faithful.**

His conformity to his brothers consisted of his *participation* in their nature and his *partnership* with them in their condition of suffering and temptation. The first of these was necessary for his *office;* the latter for his *qualifications.* He was made man that he might be a high priest; he suffered being tempted that he might be merciful and faithful. Nothing more was required for him to be a high priest but that he should take our nature. But in order that he might be merciful and faithful with that kind of mercy and faithfulness that the brothers needed, it was necessary that he should suffer and be tempted.

In order for Christ to be a high priest, it was necessary that he should take the nature of those he was going to minister the things of God to. So the apostle informs us, "Every high priest is selected from among men" (5:1).

His nature had to be *perfectly holy* so he could exactly discharge according to God's will all that was required of him in his role of high priest. But this was not all that the condition of the brothers required. Their sorrows, weakness, miseries are such that their comfort in this life required Christ's compassion. Therefore, Christ was made like them in the infirmities of their nature, their temptations and sufferings, from where all their sorrows arise. So Christ's sufferings and temptations equipped him with all the necessary qualifications for his office.

Merciful. Christ was **merciful,** "tenderly compassionate," as the Syriac version translates the word. He was *misericors,* one who lays all the miseries of his people to heart, so caring for them, to relieve them.

Faithful. The other qualification mentioned is that Christ should be **faithful.** Christ was **faithful** in his exact, constant, careful consideration of the concerns of his brothers, as they were tempted and as they suffered. This he knew about through his own experience in serving God in such conditions as are described in Isaiah 40:11. The faithfulness mentioned in this verse is not Christ's faithfulness in general, in which he carried out his whole work, mentioned in John 17:4, but, rather, his care and compassion for the needs and sorrows of his brothers as they suffer and are tempted. That is what is intended here.

The apostle, having asserted Christ's priesthood, now describes its office. In general terms it is in **service to God**; and specifically, **that he might make atonement for the sins of the people.**

In service to God. Christ was a high priest in God's service. This is either in things done for God with men (see 2 Corinthians 5:20), or in things that were done with God for men. For there were two general parts of the office of high priest; one was to preside in the house over the worship of God, to do the things of God with men. This was assigned by the prophet Zechariah to Joshua the high priest, a special type of Christ: "This is what the Lord Almighty says: 'If you will walk in my ways and keep my requirements, then you will govern my house and have charge of my courts'" (Zechariah 3:7). It is also assigned to Christ himself, "It is he who will build the temple of the LORD, and he will be clothed with majesty and will sit and rule on his throne. And he will be a priest on his throne" (Zechariah 6:13). This is "the high priest whom we confess" (Hebrews

3:1). He was set authoritatively over God's house, to take care that the whole worship was performed according to his appointment and to declare his statutes and ordinances to the people. In this sense the Lord Christ is also the high priest of his church, feeding and ruling them in the name and authority of God (see Micah 5:4).

However, this is not the part of his office that is referred to here by the apostle. The other part of the high priest's office was to perform the things to God that had to be performed on behalf of the people. So Jethro advised Moses, "You must be the people's representative before God" (Exodus 18:19). This was the principal part of the office and the duty of the high priest. The apostle shows that this was also Christ's office when he writes, **that he might make atonement for the sins of the people.**

The people. These are Abraham's descendants. As there was a special people under the old covenant for whom God made atonement, so Christ has a people, his elect.

Might make atonement for the sins. Make atonement is usually translated "appease," "atone," "propitiate," or "reconcile." But here it is linked with **sins,** and how can anyone be said to please, atone, or reconcile sin? The answer is that to make atonement reconciliation for sin appeases the wrath of God against sin. This is clearly taught in the Old Testament. Moses told the people, "You have committed a great sin. But now I will go up to the LORD; perhaps I can make atonement for your sin" (Exodus 32:30). It is God who is the object of the act of appeasing or atoning, "to make atonement with God for your sin." So when this word **atonement** is used there is always understood an offense, crime, guilt, or debt to be taken away; there is an offended person to be pacified, atoned, reconciled; the offending person needs to be pardoned, accepted; and a sacrifice or other means is needed to make atonement.

The Jews knew that the principal work of the high priest was to make atonement with God for sin so that their freedom would be gained. They understood this act, as it was the normal way in which the apostle applied it to them. They knew that the great work of their high priest was to make atonement for them, for their sins and transgressions, that they might not die, that the punishment threatened in the law might not come on them (see Leviticus 16:10, 21).

There is a further double enforcement of the necessity of what was previously affirmed, concerning Christ being **made like his brothers,** with reference to his priesthood. The first is taken from what he did or suffered in that condition, the other from the benefits that flowed from this. The first comes in the following words, **Because he himself suffered when he was tempted.**

18. He himself suffered when he was tempted. Here it is affirmed that Christ suffered when he was tempted, not that "Christ just happened to be

tempted." It is not the suffering of Christ in general that is intended, nor
is the end mentioned that of his suffering in general, which would make
reconciliation. Rather, it was the succoring of those who were tempted,
which links to the sufferings that came on him during his temptations.

While Christ was in the world countless particular temptations came to
him, and he suffered under them all. There were temptations from his relatives, as he was disbelieved, which deeply affected his compassionate
heart with sorrow; there were temptations from his followers, who for-
sook him when he preached the mysteries of the Gospel to them; there
were the temptations from his chosen disciples, all of whom deserted him,
one denied him, and one betrayed him; there was the anguish of his
mother, when "a sword pierced through her soul" in his sufferings; and
there were numerous temptations from his enemies.

The result of this is expressed in these words, **he is able to help those
who are being tempted.**

Those who are being tempted. Those for whom Christ went through
this condition are those whom he reconciled to God by his sacrifice as a
high priest, but they are described here by a special reference to their obedience, which, producing all their sorrow and trouble, makes them always
in need of his assistance. They are "the tempted ones," **those who are
being tempted.** Even though they have been reconciled to God by
Christ's death, they still have to follow the path of obedience. As they
travel along this path they meet many difficulties, dangers, and sorrows,
which all stem from temptations. Hence they are described as those who
are tempted and suffer greatly on that account. Other people are little concerned about temptations. Outwardly they may have many or few troubles, but what troubles they do have are not temptations. As far as inward
troubles are concerned, like yielding to sin, they are not tempted because
they put up no resistance to temptation. It is reconciled people who are
definitely the tempted ones, especially as temptations are seen as the reason for sufferings.

He is able. The ability arises from that special mercy that Christ is disposed to as a result of that experience that he had of suffering under temptation. This is a moral power, not a natural power. It is not the power of
the hand, but the power of the heart and will, an ability of having a prepared mind, which is here assigned to Christ.

Christ had particular experience about weakness, sorrows, and the miseries of human nature as he was attacked by temptations. He felt this and
will never forget it. His heart is therefore inclined to compassion and
knows what brings relief. This compassion moves him to bring succor.
This is the effect of mercy and compassion.

The benefit the brothers derive from this lies in the comfort they are
given. This in general consists in speedy relief when they cry out for help.

There are three things that tempted believers are in special need of. First, they need strength to withstand their temptations so that they are not overcome by them; second, they need consolation to strengthen their spirits; and, third, they need deliverance from the temptations. Our high priest is suitably endowed to provide all the help that the tempted need. This comfort is administered in various ways. It is given by his Word or promises. It is given by his Spirit who supplies them with grace or spiritual strength and who also rebukes their tempters and temptations.

Hebrews
Chapter 3

The teachings throughout this letter are constantly used as the basis for exhortations. This is a method employed in all branches of learning, especially in the Scriptures, where the wisdom and knowledge of the living God are found. In the previous chapters our apostle has demonstrated the excellency of Christ, both in his person and his work, comparing him with the angels. At the beginning of this chapter the apostle tells the Hebrews his reason for insisting on these things. They should reflect on them so that they may persevere in the faith and worship of God. This is the purpose of this chapter. But, as he does throughout the letter, he has no sooner intimated his intentions in verse 1 than he gives an additional reason for his exhortation, which continues to verse 6. From there he returns to his general exhortation with a supply of new reasons, arguments, and inferences.

There are three parts of this chapter.

1. An exhortation to perseverance. Observe:

a) The *means* of accomplishing the duty commanded (verses 1, 8, 9, 12, 13).

b) Its *nature* (verses 6, 14).

c) The things that are *contrary* to it (verses 12, 15).

d) Its *benefits* (verse 14).

e) The *danger* of neglecting it (verses 8-11, 15-19).

2. A new enforcement of the exhortation, taken from the faithfulness of Christ in carrying out the office committed to him (verses 2-6). Observe:

a) The faithfulness of Christ asserted.

b) The way this is put: by comparing him with and preferring him above Moses.

3. The special reasons relating to his general argument, taken from scriptural testimonies (verses 7-11).

This whole chapter is thus an exhortation, reinforced with many cogent reasons, to persevere in the faith and obedience of the Gospel.

Verses 1-2

Therefore, holy brothers, who share in the heavenly calling, fix your thoughts on Jesus, the apostle and high priest whom we confess. He was faithful to the one who appointed him, just as Moses was faithful in all God's house.

In these two verses the apostle starts to apply the teaching that he had declared in the previous two chapters.

1. Therefore. The first word refers to what had gone before—**therefore,** or, "seeing things are as I showed you, namely, that the person about whom I speak is so excellent and so highly exalted above all, and that although he was humbled for a season, it was for the unimaginable benefit of the church—it cannot but be your duty to consider him; that is, both what he is in himself and what he is to us." The apostle's purpose is to confront them with his general exhortation to persevere in their profession of the Gospel.

As the apostle presses home these exhortations, he calls them **holy brothers,** and he describes one of their privileges, that they **share in the heavenly calling.**

Holy brothers. The apostle calls them "brethren," **brothers,** adding that they are **holy** brothers. Although the apostle was related in a human way to the Hebrews, he calls them here **brothers** because he is related to them in a spiritual way, as they are in the same family of God with him.

Holy. This is the usual epithet, along with "saints," with which our apostle adorns believers (see Romans 1:7; 1 Corinthians 1:2; 2 Corinthians 1:1; Philippians 1:1). What he means by **holy** is illustrated when he calls the same people "sanctified" (see John 17:19; 1 Corinthians 1:2; 6:11; Ephesians 5:26; 1 Thessalonians 5:23). He regarded them as **holy,** not because of an external separation, but because of an internal, real sanctification and purity.

Who share in the heavenly calling. The apostle describes them as those who **share in the heavenly calling.** This is usual with our apostle, who uses similar phrases such as "called to be saints," and "sanctified in Christ Jesus." He describes the quality of this calling or vocation. It is a **heavenly calling,** or "super-celestial"; or, as elsewhere, "the calling that is from above." It is a **heavenly** calling because of where it comes from: that is, from God, the Father, who is in heaven. As it is with our election, so our calling is ascribed to the Father in a special way (see Romans 8:28-30;

1 Corinthians 1:9; Galatians 5:8; Philippians 3:14; 1 Thessalonians 2:12; 1 Peter 1:15; 2:9; 5:10). For no one can come to the Son unless the Father draws him. Believers are rightly termed "those who are called to belong to Jesus Christ" (Romans 1:6).

Who share. Here the apostle shows that the Hebrews participate in this calling. They **share** in the heavenly calling. They have an interest in it.

Fix your thoughts on Jesus, the apostle and high priest whom we confess. The words may be read either, "Consider Christ Jesus, the apostle and high priest whom we confess," and so the person of Christ is placed as the immediate object of the required consideration, and the other words are added only as a description of him through his offices. Or, the words may be read, "Consider the apostle and high priest whom we confess, Christ Jesus," and then the apostle and high priest whom we confess are the proper objects of this consideration.

This is the immediate duty that the apostle presses on them, namely, the consideration of that apostle and high priest whom we confess, whose greatness, glory, excellency, and preeminence in all things he had declared.

Fix your thoughts. This is the diligent use of the mind in its considerations, thoughts, meditations, and conceptions about Jesus Christ, so that they may understand and perceive correctly who and what he is, and what follows as a consequence of this. This rational consideration is of singular use to the proposed end. Later, the apostle blames them for being backward in learning the teaching of the Gospel (5:11-14). Here, he appears to intimate that they had not sufficiently weighed and pondered the nature and quality of the person of Christ and his offices, and so remained entangled in Judaism.

The object of this consideration is **Jesus,** who is **the apostle and high priest whom we confess.** In addition to the name **Jesus,** we have the description of him as he is to be considered, by his offices, an **apostle** and a **high priest.**

The apostle. He is said, and he is here only said, to be the **apostle.** An apostle is someone who is sent, a legate, ambassador, or public messenger. This is one of the characteristic features of the Messiah. He is one sent from God on his great mission to the children of men. He is God's apostle. Speaking of himself by the Spirit, he says, "And now the Sovereign LORD has sent me, with his Spirit" (Isaiah 48:16). Again, he says, "He has sent me to bind up the brokenhearted" (Isaiah 61:1). So, according to God's promise he was sent to the church as a savior: "he will send them a savior and defender, and he will rescue them" (Isaiah 19:20).

In the Gospels Christ refers to himself as being sent by God, or of being his apostle, more frequently than anything else. "The one whom God has sent" is his description of himself (John 3:34); and Christ refers to God as "the one who sent me" or made him an apostle (Matthew 10:40).

John speaks about this most frequently (see John 3:17, 34; 4:34; 5:23, 24, 30, 36-38; 6:29, 38-40, 44, 57; 7:16, 28, 29; 8:16, 18, 29, 42; 9:4; 10:36; 11:42; 12:44, 45, 49; 13:20; 14:24: 15:21; 16:5; 17:3, 18, 21, 23, 25; 20:21).

High priest. The Hebrews are to look on Christ as **high priest.** This is the kingdom and priesthood promised in Zechariah 6:13.

To demonstrate to the Hebrews how the Lord Christ has the preeminence in all things, the apostle instructs them that both the offices, that of an apostle, which was executed by Moses, and that of the high priest, which was committed to Aaron, were invested in Christ alone.

Whom we confess. Our profession is the faith and worship of God. This we **confess** with worship and obedience as required. The Lord Christ was and is the apostle of this confession, as he also is the high priest of our confession.

Verse 2

He was faithful to the one who appointed him, just as Moses was faithful in all God's house.

Here is a comparison of the Lord Christ with Moses, as he was the apostle of God or one sent by him to reveal his will.

He was faithful. The chief qualification of an apostle or ambassador is that he is **faithful.** God's apostle is the chief steward or dispenser of his mysteries, and it is principally "required that those who have been given a trust must prove faithful" (1 Corinthians 4:2).

To the one who appointed him. Christ's appointment, being made an apostle of God, was foreordained before the foundation of the world (see 1 Peter 1:20). He was in particular designated by God to be his apostle for the instruction of his church (Proverbs 8:22-31; Isaiah 48:16; Zechariah 6:13). Hence the eternal life that he was to manifest (1 John 1:2) and to bring to light through the Gospel (2 Timothy 1:10) is said to be "promised before the beginning of time" (Titus 1:2). Herein lies the foundation of the appointment of Christ to his office.

As Moses was faithful in all God's house. This further asserts Christ's faithfulness when compared with Moses, who **was faithful in all God's house.**

Moses was commended for being faithful. "Moses did everything just as the LORD commanded him" (Exodus 40:16).

The extent of Moses' faithfulness was **in all God's house.** That is, says Chrysostom, "in the whole people." **In God's house** means in his household, his family. Also notice how "house" and "household" are used in

Acts 16:15; 1 Corinthians 1:16; 2 Timothy 1:16. Thus, **God's house** is his household, his family, the church.

God's house also means his church because God lives in his church, through his special presence, as a man lives in his own house (Revelation 21:3). Both are springs of care, love, and delight. In this house Moses is **faithful.** And this commendation of Moses is celebrated by the Jews in their hymns in the ritual on the Sabbath: "You called him your faithful servant, and put a glorious crown on his head, when he stood in front of you on Mount Sinai" (*Machzor*, part i, fol. 49).

The apostle moves on to demonstrate Christ's preeminence over Moses. He says that both were prophets, both God's apostles, sent by God to declare the divine mind and will. He says they were both faithful in carrying out their work. The difference between them comes in the next verse.

Verses 3-6

Jesus has been found worthy of greater honor than Moses, just as the builder of a house has greater honor than the house itself. For every house is built by someone, but God is the builder of everything. Moses was faithful as a servant in all God's house, testifying to what would be said in the future. But Christ is faithful as a son over God's house. And we are his house, if we hold on to our courage and the hope of which we boast.

The apostle shows here Christ's superiority over Moses, as he had done previously with reference to angels and all other revealers of God's will to his church. He has just told the Hebrews that they should fix their thoughts on Jesus, on his person, and on his offices.

To understand verses 3-6 correctly two things must be borne in mind. First, that the apostle is now telling the Hebrews about the greatest example of the excellency of the Gospel. Here he puts Christ above Moses. Nothing can match the authority and honor of Jesus Christ. Second, the apostle uses this argument to urge the Hebrews to persevere.

3. For (KJV). The causal conjunction **for** links this verse to verse 1. The apostle indicates why the Hebrews should fix their thoughts on Jesus. It is because Christ's glory, honor, and dignity are superior to Moses'. The apostle illustrates this in verses 3-6, before he returns to his exhortation in verse 7.

The proposition of verses 3-6 is clear, but the illustration he uses and the inferences he draws from his illustration are involved. The proposition is this, that **Jesus was found worthy of greater honor than Moses.** This is supported by the words, **just as the builder of a house has greater**

honor than the house itself. It is further illustrated in verse 4, **For every house is built by someone, but God is the builder of everything.**

The apostle argues that in the comparison between Christ and Moses, he agrees that Moses was faithful, as is demonstrated by God's testimony that "Moses was faithful in all God's house" (verse 2). The church or people of God are meant by "the house of God." The apostle uses the same metaphor to show Christ's dignity in his relation to the church, using the words "over God's house" (verse 6). In Scripture the things stated are important, but so are the ways that they are expressed. The apostle ascribes a double relationship between Christ and this house, which are the main attributes of any house. The first is the builder, from whom he draws his first argument in verses 3 and 4; the second is the owner, the possessor of the house, from whom he draws his second argument in verses 5 and 6. Without a builder a house does not exist, and without an occupant a house has no use.

In the apostle's first argument, verse 3, only the proposition is set out, as the assumption is included, and the conclusion is left to an obvious inference. The proposition is, "He who builds the house has more honor than the house." The assumption included is, "Christ built the house, and Moses was only a part of the house. Therefore Christ had more glory than Moses."

Jesus has been found worthy of greater honor than Moses. This proposition contains two things: first, a supposition—that Moses is worthy of honor; and, second, an assertion—that the Lord Christ was worthy of much more glory.

The apostle supposes that Moses was "counted worthy of honor" because of the work he did. He was the sole mediator between God and the people (see Galatians 3:19); as he said himself, "At that time I stood between the LORD and you to declare to you the word of the LORD " (Deuteronomy 5:5).

4. For every house is built by someone, but God is the builder of everything.

In this verse the apostle confirms and illustrates what he had just asserted. Up to this point two things were necessary. First he had to show that his argument had a proper basis in the illustration he was drawing on. This he does in the words, **every house is built by someone.** Every single house has its builder. The builder is more honorable than the house. The apostle uses this fact in his argument.

Second, if that building of the house, which alone would make good the apostle's inference (namely, that Christ was more honorable than Moses, because he built the house and Moses was only part of the house), was such as we have described, who could possibly build the church throughout the ages? Who could do such a task? Why, replies the apostle, **God is the builder of everything.**

Everything. This word is nowhere used in Scripture to express the creation of everything, nor does it mean to create, but rather to prepare or to build. It is often used in the preparing of the church or for preparing for the worship of God (see Matthew 11:10; Luke 1:17; 7:27; Hebrews 9:2, 6).

God. Who is here meant by the name **God?** If God the Father was intended, then **the builder of everything** would mean the creation of the world, but this is not the case, as we have just shown. The apostle is showing here why the house was or could be built by Christ, because Christ is God, and so Christ could do this.

Verses 5-6

Moses was faithful as a servant in all God's house, testifying to what would be said in the future. But Christ is faithful as a son over God's house. And we are his house, if we hold on to our courage and the hope of which we boast.

The apostle uses another argument here to make the same point. It is a comparison between Christ and Moses in relationship to the building of the house of God. In the building they were both faithful, Christ as the chief *builder*, and Moses as a principal *part of the house*. Once the house was built, they were both faithful to it in their different ways. Moses was a servant in God's house; Christ was a son over his own house, the house he had built.

As for Moses, these words show his relation to the house of God, where he was **a servant,** and, the purpose of his ministry, **testifying to what would be said in the future.**

As for the Lord Christ, these verses reveal his relation to the house, where he was **a son,** or lord **over God's house.**

The argument of the apostle here is clear: "The son, faithful over his own house, is more glorious and honorable than a servant who is faithful in the house of his lord and master; but Christ was thus a son over the house, Moses only a servant in it."

5. Moses was faithful as a servant in all God's house. The office ascribed to him is that of a **servant,** a servant of God and of the people: a servant, minister, or officer in the things belonging to religious worship. This was his place, office, dignity, and honor.

Testifying to what would be said in the future. These words express the purpose of the service and ministry of Moses. In his ministry he was a testimony, and by what he did in the service of the house he gave testimony. What did he testify about? To the things that were later spoken about, namely, in the fullness of time, by the Messiah. Moses testified about the things concerning the Gospel. This was the proper end of all that Moses did or ordered in the house of God.

Moses was faithful. Moses was faithful in testifying about the Gospel. And here the apostle takes his leave of Moses. He does not mention him again, and so he gives him an honorable burial here. He puts this glorious epitaph on his grave, **Moses was faithful as a servant in all God's house.**

6. But Christ is faithful as a son over God's house. The word **faithful** is repeated here. Moses was faithful. Christ is faithful. Nearly every word demonstrates the asserted preeminence of Christ over Moses. Christ is a *son*, Moses is a *servant;* Christ is *over* the house, Moses is *in* the house; Christ is over his *own* house, Moses is in the house of *another*.

Christ has absolute and supreme authority over everyone and everything. Everyone who belongs to God's house is at his disposal, and the institution of its whole worship is in his power alone.

We are his house. The apostle explains his metaphor. "I have," he said, "spoken about these things as a house and a house being built; but it is the church, it is ourselves that I am referring to." **We are his house.**

To make sure they know whom he is referring to, he adds this extra description of them: **if we hold on to our courage and the hope of which we boast.**

So, **we are his house** refers to believers who worship Christ according to his Gospel. Believers are Christ's house in three ways.

First, because Christ lives in them by his Spirit. Hence they are called "living stones," and on him they are built into a "spiritual house" (1 Peter 2:5). Christ dwells in them in this way (see John 14:17; 1 Corinthians 3:16; 2 Corinthians 6:16; Ephesians 2:20-22).

Second, they are cemented and united like the temple long ago (Ephesians 4:16; Colossians 2:19).

Third, Christ lives among them as they worship together (Matthew 28:20; Revelation 21:3).

If we hold on to our courage and the hope of which we boast. Two things are seen here: first, what the apostle requires of those who are in Christ's house, namely, **courage** and **hope;** second, how we achieve this—**if we hold on.**

Courage. Although this word often comes in the New Testament, it is never used to signify that trust in God that is a result of faith.

Hope. It is not our **hope** in itself but the **boasting** or "rejoicing" in it that the apostle means here.

The meaning of these words is seen from the Hebrews' condition and from what the apostle encourages them to do. They were being persecuted and were in danger of backsliding. The remedy for this lay in a bold and open profession of the truth that our hope is built on. For we know that this hope will never make us ashamed (Romans 5:5). This is the **courage and the hope** mentioned here: a confident, open profession of our hope. Peter gives us this command: "Always be prepared to give an answer to everyone who asks you to give a reason for the hope that you have" (1 Peter 3:15).

Hold on. This word signifies a careful, powerful holding on to anything in the face of opposition. So, this word shows that great opposition will face those who are firm in their profession. It also shows that great care, diligence, and endeavor are needed in this matter if we are not to fail. Because of the violent opposition we are to **hold on.**

Verses 7-11

So, as the Holy Spirit says: "Today, if you hear his voice, do not harden your hearts as you did in the rebellion, during the time of testing in the desert, where your fathers tested and tried me and for forty years saw what I did. That is why I was angry with that generation, and I said, 'Their hearts are always going astray, and they have not known my ways.' So I declared on oath in my anger, 'They shall never enter my rest.'"

The exhortation begun at the beginning of the chapter is pursued here. The Hebrews are warned not to follow the disobedience of others. The Hebrews were familiar with the example used, as it was recorded in the Scriptures, with which they were familiar. The evil ways of their own forefathers were used as examples not to follow. After these events had been recorded in Numbers 14, it had been recommended to them for their urgent consideration in Psalm 95.

7. So. This denotes both the deduction of the exhortation from the previous verses and its application, which follows in verse 12. **So,** that is, "Seeing that the Lord Christ, who is the author of the Gospel, is far superior to Moses in his prophetic office in God's house, as he is son and lord over that house, whereas Moses was only a servant, let us consider what our duty is. We should be particularly careful not to disobey anything he says."

As the Holy Spirit says. The words are the words of the psalmist, but are here ascribed to the Holy Spirit: **as the Holy Spirit says.** Our apostle, like other divine writers of the New Testament, uses his liberty in this matter. Sometimes they ascribe the words they cite from the Old Testament to individual authors, such as Moses, David, Isaiah, Jeremiah, and the like (see Matthew 2:17; 4:14; Luke 24:27; John 12:41; Acts 2:25). Sometimes they refer to the books where their quotations come from, saying, "it is written in the Book of Psalms" (Acts 1:20). At other times they ascribe to their quotations the principal author, namely, the Holy Spirit, as here. While they used their freedom here, it should not be supposed that they chose the words they used without some special reason. The apostle ascribes the words of the psalmist here to the Holy Spirit, through whom he was inspired and acted, to remind the Hebrews of his authority. His intention from these words was to press a practical duty on them. The mind immediately thinks about the authority of the person who is making such demands. "Consider," says the apostle, "that these are the words of the Holy Spirit" (that is, God himself), "so that you may submit yourselves to his authority."

If you will hear his voice. This means, "It is your duty to do this; and this is what you are exhorted to do."

The **voice** of God is usually the word of his command, the voice of his will. This is the rule of all our duty and obedience. In this instance, as is common elsewhere, it is not the word of command in general that is meant, but the special call or voice of God with reference to some special duty at some special season. Such was God's voice to the people in the wilderness when the law was given: the people heard it and saw its effects. Hence the *command* of God is translated as the *voice* of God in giving the Gospel through the ministry of his Son Jesus Christ. The psalmist speaks to the people as if the voice of God was sounding in their ears.

This, then, is the object of the duty exhorted, God's voice. The apostle uses this word to apply to the whole teaching of the Gospel, but with special reference to the revelation of it through Jesus Christ. In the same way, in the psalm the word "voice" applies to the whole teaching of the law but has special reference to it being given to Moses on Mount Sinai. **If you hear his voice** is an act of the whole soul, in understanding, choosing, and resolving to do God's will as declared by his voice. This is also seen by the next charge, **do not harden your hearts.** That is, "If you think it fitting to obey God's voice, and if you choose to do this, beware of what will hinder you in this."

Do not harden your hearts. The apostle enforces his exhortation, using the words of the psalmist, with a word of caution, **"Harden not your hearts."** We ask what is meant by **hearts,** and what is meant by **harden.**

The heart in Scripture, with reference to moral obedience, does not always denote the same faculty of the soul. Sometimes one is intended, on other occasions another faculty is intended. What is specifically intended is found from the words linked to the word *heart.* Thus, sometimes the heart is said to be "wise," "understanding," to "plot," to have its "plans" succeed; and, on the other hand, to be "ignorant," "dark," "foolish," and the like. In all of these instances it is clear that the mind is the guiding faculty intended. Sometimes the heart is said to be "soft," "tender," "humble," "melting"; and on the other hand, "hard," "stubborn," "obstinate," and the like. Here the will and the affections are dominant. Therefore, the word *heart* is the principle of all our moral actions, and the influence of all the faculties of our souls in them is expressed.

"Do not harden." This is a metaphorical expression signifying the inability of anything to receive an impression from what is applied to it. To be hardened is to be like wax that has gone hard and so cannot receive an impression from a seal that is set into it; or it is to be like cement that has set on a trowel. Obedience is applied to men's souls through God's Spirit, through his commands, his promises, and warnings. This is his voice, the whole revelation of his mind and will. When the due impression is not made in this way on the soul, people are said to resist the Spirit (see Acts 7:51).

"Today." The time and season for carrying out this duty is given as "Today." "Today, if you hear his voice." The apostle exhorts the Hebrews, in the psalmist's words, to make use of the present time, through faith and obedience, to be preserved from hardness of heart and final unbelief.

We now move on to the example given here, which comes in two parts: first, the *sin*, and, second, the *punishment* of the people long ago.

The sin is seen in the following words, "as you did in the rebellion, during the time of testing in the desert, where your fathers tested and tried me and for forty years saw what I did." Your fathers are the people who sinned. Verse 10 declares, "I was angry with that generation." Their fathers are the people who came out of Egypt with Moses. On account of their many sins, all who were more than twenty years old when they went into the desert died there, except for Caleb and Joshua. So the Lord said to Moses and Aaron, "How long will this wicked community grumble against me? I have heard the complaints of these grumbling Israelites. So tell them, 'As surely as I live, declares the LORD, I will do to you the very things I heard you say: In this desert your bodies will fall—every one of you twenty years old or more who was counted in the census and who has grumbled against me. Not one of you will enter the land I swore with uplifted hand to make your home, except Caleb son of Jephunneh and Joshua son of Nun'" (Numbers 14:26-30). And so it happened. For when the people were numbered again in the plains of Moab, it is said, "Not one of them was among those counted by Moses and Aaron the priest when they counted the Israelites in the Desert of Sinai" (Numbers 26:64)—that is, except for Caleb and Joshua.

Because the Hebrews were very prone to boast about their fathers, the apostle focuses on their sin in the desert. In this way the psalmist and the apostle remind the Hebrews that many of those in whom they glorified sinfully provoked God. The Hebrews were also reminded about their fathers in this way to warn them about their own danger. The Holy Spirit shows them how prone they are to fall into disobedience as they are reminded about the sinful ways of their **fathers.**

In the rebellion. Their sin was a **rebellion.** It would appear that one particular sin is not in mind here, but the whole way of life of those people is intended. And it is not for any particular time, but for their whole lives. The word **rebellion** in the original means "chide," "strive," "contend," as in the words of Isaiah, "Woe to him who quarrels with his Maker" (Isaiah 45:9). How does he do this? "Does the clay say to the potter, 'What are you making?'" (Isaiah 45:9). It is by "saying," by speaking against him, that he may strive with him. Here the apostle used a word that denotes the effect of that chiding—that is, exacerbation, provocation, or rebellion. This is clearly seen in Numbers 20:13, "the Israelites quarreled with the LORD." It was an altercation in words. The expression **in the rebellion** in this verse includes all the sinful actions of that people against God under Moses' ministry.

The time of testing. Now, this provocation of God through their unbelief, showing itself in complaining, is amplified by the mention of when it happened: **the time of testing.** They first grumbled about water and tested God at Meribah. It was called Meribah because they provoked God. Their constant testing of God made their whole time in the desert a **time of testing.**

"For forty years saw what I did." This explains the nature of the sin of the fathers of the Hebrews. The fathers had witnessed God's deeds and from them God was revealed to them. Some of these deeds were works of *power*, as when he divided the sea; some of these deeds were *majestic* and terrifying, such as the frightening appearances in thunder, lightning, fire, smoke, and earthquake, when the law was given; some of these deeds showed God's *favor* toward his people and his love and care for them. In all such works God abundantly manifested his power, goodness, wisdom, grace, faithfulness, and warned them of the consequences if they rejected him because of their unbelief.

"I was angry with that generation." The last part of the apostle's example speaks of the punishment these people received for their sin. Their sin grieved God: **"I was angry with that generation."** These words show how God viewed these people in his heart. God took these emotions on himself for our instruction. He says that he will "rejoice in doing them good and will assuredly plant them in this land with all my heart and soul" (Jeremiah 32:41). Because of their sin it is said that, "the LORD was grieved that he had made man on the earth, and his heart was filled with pain" (Genesis 6:6). These words, such as "anger," "it grieved him," are indications of serious trouble. These words, with verse 11, show God's judgment on their sin.

10. **"Their hearts are always going astray, and they have not known my ways."** In this judgment that God passed on that sinful generation he declares three things: first, the basis of their sins—**going astray**; second, their obstinacy—**always**; and, third, the result of their evil—**they have not known my ways.**

"Their hearts . . . going astray." God identifies their wrongdoing as **going astray** in **their hearts.** An error of the heart in moral things is making wrong judgments about what is good or evil for people. So they, through the power of their lusts and darkness, their temptations and obstinacy, often judged that sin and rebellion were better for them than faith, submission, and obedience. They did not, generally speaking, reckon that sin, as sin, was better than obedience, but in particular cases they chose to do sinful things rather than to reject such things. So they went **astray** in **their hearts.**

"Always." They persisted in their error: **always.** Whenever they were tested they chose the wrong side. Although God exercised great patience with them for a long time, they would not change their minds and hearts.

"They have not known my ways." This terrible sin resulted in their not knowing God's ways. As they erred in their hearts because they liked the ways of sin, so they disliked the ways of God because they did not know them.

When God views people's sins he principally looks at their hearts.

11. God's punishment on these people is stated here: **"They shall never enter my rest."**

"They shall never enter." They will not so much as enter into God's rest. Doubtless many of the people during their wanderings in the desert had a great desire to view the Promised Land. Moses, in particular, wanted to live there. He prayed, "Let me go over and see the good land beyond the Jordan—that fine hill country and Lebanon" (Deuteronomy 3:25). Many others must have prayed and desired the same thing. But the sentence is passed. They will not now so much as set one foot within its borders.

"My rest." This indicates what they will be denied, **my rest.** He does not say that they will not enter into the land of Canaan, or even the Promised Land. But he describes it in such a way that they may see the greatness of their sin and their punishment and his displeasure. **They shall never,** he says, **enter my rest.** "It is my rest, the place where I will live, where I will make myself known: you will not enter into my rest."

65

Verses 12-14

See to it, brothers, that none of you has a sinful, unbelieving heart that turns away from the living God. But encourage one another daily, as long as it is called Today, so that none of you may be hardened by sin's deceitfulness. We have come to share in Christ if we hold firmly till the end the confidence we had at first.

The apostle proposes three things in these verses. First, he gives an exhortation to avoid evil (verse 12). Second, he suggests one useful way to avoid sin (verse 13). Third, he reinforces his exhortation (verse 14).

His exhortation is linked to the previous verses. It is as if the apostle says, "Seeing that our forefathers, who were our types and are given to us as an example, rejected God's dispensation, let us beware."

12. Brothers. The apostle addresses the Hebrews with the affectionate name of **brothers,** as he had previously done (verse 1). He repeats it here to show them that he had no harshness in his spirit against them, even though he had to insist on severe teaching. A minister must be meek, patient, not easily provoked, not quick-tempered with any of his flock (1 Timothy 3:3; Titus 1:7). Tenderness, gentleness, and acts of love and care toward people we speak with secretly softens them, and opens their ears and hearts to let in a word of instruction and exhortation.

See to it. "Take heed." This is the way the apostle tells them to carry out the duty he presses on them. This word originally meant "to see" and "behold." Then it came to mean "to take heed," or "beware." It is frequently used in this way in the New Testament (see 1 Corinthians 1:26; 10:18; Ephesians 5:15; Philippians 3:2; Colossians 2:8). This word warns us to take care over some imminent danger or opposition.

That none of you. The people who have to follow the apostle's exhortation are mentioned here: **none of you.** The apostle does not seem to have any particular individual in mind, as if he is saying, "Let every one of you look to himself and his own heart, in case it is like this with you." Rather, he speaks to them collectively, to take care that there are none among them who have an unbelieving heart. This, of course, applied to every individual. For where everyone is spoken to, every individual is addressed. The same kind of expression is used for the same kind of reason in 12:15-16: "See to it that no one misses the grace of God and that no bitter root grows up to cause trouble and defile many. See that no one is sexually immoral, or is godless like Esau." This warning is clearly given to the whole church. It is the same in these verses.

It is the duty for every believer to be alert on every occasion, in case at any time he should possess **a sinful, unbelieving heart.** This verse shows the principle of evil, **a sinful, unbelieving heart,** and the effect of that principle, turning **away from the living God.**

Unbelieving heart. The principle of the evil spoken about is **a sinful, unbelieving heart.** In particular, it is said to be an **unbelieving heart.** This means more than just defective belief, as in the case of Thomas, to whom Christ said, "Stop doubting and believe" (John 20:27). Although Thomas failed in his faith, he did not fail completely. There is, however, something special meant by the phrase **unbelieving heart** in this verse. This kind of heart is under the power of evil.

The root of all backsliding, whether it is gradual or total, lies in unbelief. Unbelief is the hinge on which these next two chapters turn. He sets out before the Hebrews the nature, prevalence, danger, and way to prevent it.

This is the only place in the New Testament where a heart is described as **sinful.** In other places it is called "stubborn" and "unrepentant" (Romans 2:5), but only here is it described as being **sinful.** In the Old Testament it is sometimes called "sinful" or "evil" (Jeremiah 3:17, 7:24, 11:8, 16:12, 18:12). This word originally denoted a person who is industriously wicked. So the devil was called "the wicked one" because of his industrious and malicious wickedness. "When anyone hears the message about the kingdom and does not understand it, the evil one . . ." (Matthew 13:19). So we are taught to pray, "deliver us from the evil one" (Matthew 6:13). And it is said that "the whole world is under the control of the evil one" (1 John 5:19). Therefore, any heart called **sinful** is full of evil and wickedness.

The next thing in this verse is the special evil that the apostle warns the Hebrews against. As unbelief tends to make the heart evil, so an evil heart has a tendency to **turn away from the living God.**

Turn away. This word can denote any kind of departure, physical or moral, from a person or thing, a place or a principle. Sometimes it expresses a duty: "Everyone who confesses the name of the Lord must turn away from wickedness" (2 Timothy 2:19; see also 1 Timothy 6:5). Sometimes it denotes the worst sin: "the Spirit clearly says that in later times some will abandon the faith" (1 Timothy 4:1). This word is used more by our apostle than all of the other sacred writers put together. It is once used in the Gospel about falling away: "they believe for a while, but in the time of testing they fall away" (Luke 8:13).

The apostle is specific in Hebrews 3:12 about who these people are turning away from: **the living God.** It is clear that it is apostasy from the profession of the Gospel that is in mind here. We need to ask why the apostle chooses this special phrase here, saying that they are turning away from **the living God.**

The living God. The Hebrews probably pleaded that they were returning to God. To expose their misunderstanding, the apostle tells them that after Christ has been revealed to them and they have professed

belief in him, they turn away from the living God if they turn away from
Christ. John declares this: "Anyone who runs ahead and does not continue in the teaching of Christ does not have God; whoever continues in
the teaching has both the Father and the Son" (2 John 9). Turning away
from the Gospel or from Christ's teaching is to forsake God himself. He
who has not have the Son does not have the Father. Continuing in the
teaching of the Gospel secures an interest not only in the Son, but in the
Father also. So a person who rejects Christ, while still pretending to be
doing God's will, has forsaken the living God and clings to an idol in his
own heart. For the Father is always with the Son, and he is a God to us
only by Christ and in Christ.

The words **the living God** are also used to warn the Hebrews against
the sin he is cautioning them against. Should they **turn away**, they would
be leaving him who is the great, terrible, and dreadful God, the living God,
who is able to punish and avenge their sin for all eternity. He insists on the
same argument afterwards: "It is a dreadful thing to fall into the hands of
the living God" (Hebrews 10:31). God frequently prefaces expressions of
his severity against stubborn sinners with the words, "I live," says the
Lord, as if he was telling them what they were to expect. It seems to me
that the principal reason why the apostle thus states the sin of their apostasy is that it is turning away from **the living God.**

**13. But encourage one another daily, as long as it is called Today, so
that none of you may be hardened by sin's deceitfulness.** When a heart
is made evil through unbelief it is engaged in rebellion against "the living
God." Verse 13 gives one way of preventing the evil of verse 12.

Encourage. The Hebrews are told what to do in this verse. They are to
encourage one another—to entreat, beseech, comfort, refresh, and bring
consolation (see Luke 2:25; Acts 9:31; 15:31; Romans 15:5; 2 Corinthians
1:3-5). Sometimes this encouragement is an exhortation (see Acts 13:15;
Romans 12:8; 2 Corinthians 8:4, 17; 1 Timothy 4:13).

The principal meaning of the word **encourage** is to exhort, desire, or
call in; and only as a secondary meaning does it denote "to comfort." But
there is a close affinity between these two things. The way to bring consolation is through exhortation. "Therefore encourage each other with these
words" (1 Thessalonians 4:18). That is, "exhort each other, and through
these words bring mutual consolation." All exhortation should be only
through consoling words and ways. So it is observed of Barnabas, who
was "a son of consolation," that he excelled in exhorting people. "When he
arrived and saw the evidence of the grace of God, he was glad and encouraged them all to remain true to the Lord with all their hearts. He was a
good man, full of the Holy Spirit and faith" (Acts 11:23-24). This demonstrates how Barnabas exhorted people. It was because he was "a good
man," not in the ordinary sense of being holy and just; but one who was

kind, able to comfort and refresh people he met. So to **encourage** is to persuade people with humble, comforting words, consoling them so that they may be comforted. Some people have a ministry of encouragement. Speaking of such a ministry the apostle says, "if it is encouraging, let him encourage" (Romans 12:8). And all believers are sometimes required to exercise this duty, as the next words make clear.

One another. It is incumbent on all believers mutually to exhort and to bear the word of exhortation.

Today. The occasion when this duty is to be performed is indicated next. It is to be **Today,** or every day. A day is often used to indicate a period of time, so to do a thing daily is to do it at the right time. Although the expression denotes every day as a separate and distinct day, its sense does not mean that a day should never go by when we do not discharge this duty to each other.

Clearly, two things are intended. First, there should be a constant inclination of the mind to carry out this duty. Second, this duty should be actually carried out on all necessary occasions, which one should keep on the lookout for and be willing to embrace. In this way, we are commanded to "pray continually" (1 Thessalonians 5:17). We are told that we "should always pray" (Luke 18:1), and that we should "devote" ourselves "to prayer" (Colossians 4:2). The Hebrews were in particular need of being habitually on the alert as they continually faced their temptations.

As long as it is called Today. That is, "be careful to discharge this duty while the season lasts." The people of old had been given a day, a season that was called Today. The apostle now tells the Hebrews that the great day, the great season, had now arrived. It was rightly called **Today** to them. It was the day they enjoyed the Gospel. Thus it was a day of opportunity. But a limitation to this day is included in the words, **as long as it is called Today.** This means, "while the time in which you live is such a season as is called a day, that is, a day of grace." The apostle saw that the day or season for these Hebrews was nearly at an end. It continued only a few years after this letter was written. He reminds them of this, and, at the same time, exhorts them to make the best use of the present moment, especially in giving mutual exhortations.

Sin. The source of the evil that is to be feared in the neglect under discussion is **sin.** This is a general name for all or any sin. Our apostle often uses it to signify original sin, the sin of our nature, the root on which all other sins grow. This is the sin intended here. This is the sin that lives in us by nature, that is present with us when we try to do good. This sin constantly works to puts its venomous nature into actual sins and transgressions. This he calls a "bitter root" (12:15), which springs up to defile us.

Deceitfulness. The way this sin works is through **deceitfulness.** This word includes the ability to deceive and the deception itself. The word is derived from a word meaning to "draw anyone out of the right way," away from a path. So it came to mean "to lead astray" or "seduce." The word principally denotes an innate faculty of deceiving rather than the deceit itself. We read about the "deceitfulness of wealth" (Matthew 13:22) and "every sort of evil that deceives" (2 Thessalonians 2:10). This refers to an aptitude in riches and unrighteousness that seduces men into wicked paths.

That none of you may be hardened. The particular evil warned against is that they should not **be hardened.** So, this verse tells the Hebrews to be on their guard against being hardened by the deceitfulness of sin. The way to gain victory over this is through mutual exhortation.

14. We have come to share in Christ if we hold firmly till the end the confidence we had at first. This verse is linked to the previous verses as it gives a general exhortation to persevere, to avoid apostasy, as well as specific ways in which this can be achieved. The apostle tells the Hebrews that all their interest in Christ, and all the benefits they expect from him, depend on their obeying his command to persevere. In this verse the apostle states his argument, **we have come to share in Christ,** and how it can be applied to the Hebrews, **if we hold firmly till the end the confidence we had at first.**

Share in Christ. We were made **to share in Christ.** Nowhere else is this expression used. The word translated **share** is also used by Paul in 1 Corinthians 10:17 where he says that "we all partake of the one loaf." This is a sacramental expression of the same thing mentioned here.

The particular importance of these words is seen from the apostle's use of them when referring to Christ himself: "he too shared in their humanity" (2:14); that is, because those whom he would redeem were men, partakers of human nature, "he too shared their humanity." He was partaker of us; he partook of us. How? By taking flesh and blood, that is, complete human nature, to be his own. So are we partakers of him, partakers of Christ? This occurs through having an interest in his nature, through the fellowship of his Spirit, as he had in ours when he assumed our flesh. It is, then, our union with Christ that is intended, "for we are members of his body" (Ephesians 5:30). Chrysostom asks, "What is it to 'share in Christ'? It is when he and we are made one; he the head, we the body, co-heirs and incorporated in him. We are one body with him."

The evidence for this comes in the next words of this verse: **if we hold firmly till the end the confidence we had at first.** Everyone agrees that the same matter is referred to in verse 6, "if we hold on to our courage and the hope in which we boast." What is there called "the hope of which we boast" is here termed **the confidence we had at first.** In each instance they are to hold firmly to the end.

The confidence. Our partaking in Christ is being united with him; and the **confidence** that we are called to maintain is our remaining in Christ, as the branch remains in the vine. This is the meaning of **confidence** in this verse.

At first. This refers to the usual things that accompany the beginning of our faith and Christian profession. When we start with Christ we do so with much love, affection, and courage. If we do not take great care we move away from what **we had at first.** This is the sense of these words.

Verses 15-19

15. As has just been said: "Today, if you hear his voice, do not harden your hearts as you did in the rebellion."

As has just been said. These words introduce the following discourse. They indicate a repetition of the previous evidence and its additional explanations (see exposition of verses 7-8).

16. Who were they who heard and rebelled? Were they not all those Moses led out of Egypt? The apostle's intention here and in verses 17-19 is to confirm his previous exhortation from the example he had given them. From the various events that their forefathers went through in the desert, with God's promises and warnings on the one hand, and their own faith and disobedience on the other, they were to take careful note. To this end the apostle focuses on the people who came out of Egypt under Moses' leadership. They all were **led out of Egypt,** they all **heard** God's voice. However, everyone did not rebel, only some rebelled. The few words **Moses led out of Egypt** are a massive story. They speak of the work where God was glorified exceedingly, when that people took part in greater mercies and privileges than there had been since the foundation of the world. To press this teaching home is the whole purpose of the book of Deuteronomy. Moses sums up much of it in these words, "Has any god ever tried to take for himself one nation out of another nation, by testings, by miraculous signs and wonders, by war, by a mighty hand and an outstretched arm, or by great and awesome deeds, like all the things the LORD your God did for you in Egypt before your very eyes?" (Deuteronomy 4:34).

In addition to the other circumstances that the apostle insists on, this is mentioned here to remind this people how they were obliged to listen to God's voice, to the God who had brought them out of Egypt. This is why God prefaced his whole law with the words, "I am the LORD your God, who brought you out of Egypt" (Exodus 20:2).

Were they not all those Moses led out of Egypt? They came out through Moses, through the hand of Moses. That is, either under his guidance, or through the miraculous works that God performed through him. Both these senses are seen in the words of the prophet Isaiah: "Then his people recalled the days of old, the days of Moses and his people—where is he who brought them through the sea, with the shepherd of his flock? Where is he who set his Holy Spirit among them, who sent his glorious arm of power to be at Moses' right hand, who divided the waters before them, to gain for himself everlasting renown?" (Isaiah 63:11-12). Both Moses' conduct and the miracles performed through him are included in the words, **Were they not all those Moses led out of Egypt?**

Who were they who heard and rebelled? When it says, **who heard and rebelled,** it does not mean that all who heard also rebelled, but, rather, that of those who heard, only some rebelled.

What they **heard** was God's voice. As it says in verse 15, "Today, if you hear his voice." This can refer to hearing God's voice when the law was given on Mount Sinai, when the whole congregation heard God's voice in the thunder. What they heard might also have a more general reference to all the instructions that God gave them in the desert. This, then, was the voice of God that they heard.

Rebelled. The sin that is laid on some of those who were **led out of Egypt** and who **heard** is rebellion: **they . . . rebelled.** This word is illustrated by words found in Hosea the prophet: "But Ephraim has bitterly provoked him to anger" (Hosea 12:14). Great rebellion has a bitterness in it, which God hates.

Through this argument the apostle stresses his previous exhortation and shows how necessary it is. He is speaking to those who wish to listen carefully to the word of the Gospel and who wish to persevere in this. "For," he says, "when the people of old heard God's voice when his law was given and when the grace they needed was given, some of them rebelled against God. In the dispensation of the Gospel, people can easily do the same. So take great care that this is not how you are behaving."

17-18. And with whom was he angry for forty years? Was it not with those who sinned, whose bodies fell in the desert? And to whom did God swear that they would never enter his rest if not to those who disobeyed?

In verses 17-18 the apostle drives home his previous exhortation through details of the example he had given. He does this by means of questions. He poses a question and then answers it from what he had already told them or from what is clearly included in his words.

The kind of argument the apostle engages in here in not just a matter of asking questions. Rather, he asks questions, and from these questions he draws out the answers. This is the way great Roman orators went about convincing people. This method of reasoning is especially applicable when the proposed question is an inquiry into a matter of fact. Then the reply given comes in the form of a question, but is really an answer. This is the apostle's method of arguing here. The first question in verse 17 is, **And with whom was he angry for forty years?** The second question is really the answer to the first question, **Was it not with those who sinned, whose bodies fell in the desert?**

These words are a repetition of those in verse 10. The apostle repeats them here to remind the Hebrews about the people's sin, and how God dealt with them. The answer to the first question comes in a double description of those whom God is not pleased with. First, their sin is mentioned, **Was it not with those who sinned?** Second, their punishment is stated, **whose bodies fell in the desert.** From this it is clear that God was not displeased with them *all.*

Those who sinned. God was displeased with **those who sinned.** Their sin, in general, is stated, and this is followed by a description of its nature. These people were guilty of three kinds of sin in the wilderness. First, they were guilty of *personal sins.* They were all sinful of what the psalmist refers to, in the following words, "If you, O Lord, kept a record of sins, O Lord, who could stand?" (Psalm 130:3). But these are not the sins intended here. Second, they were guilty of *special rebellions,* in which large numbers of the people were involved but not the whole congregation. One such example was the rebellion of Korah, Dathan, and Abiram, who with their accomplices numbered "250 Israelite men, well-known community leaders who had been appointed members of the council" (Numbers 16:2). Third, they were guilty of *general sins* that involved the whole congregation. This was made up of frequent murmurings and rebellions, which came to a head like a great rebellion when the spies returned. They not only provoked God with their own unbelief, but they encouraged the people to kill Joshua and Caleb, who would not concur in their disobedience: "the whole assembly talked about stoning them" (Numbers 14:10).

Whose bodies fell in the desert. The apostle describes these people in terms of the punishment they were given. Their **bodies fell in the desert.** This is referred to in the book of Numbers: "In this desert your bodies will fall" (Numbers 14:29). Elias Levita supposes that this only refers to wicked people. This is true in most cases, but not in every case (see Isaiah 14:19; 34:3; Jeremiah 33:5; 41:9; Amos 8:3). A mass killing of people is a representation of hell: "And they will go out and look upon the dead bodies of those who rebelled against me; their worm will not die, nor will their fire be quenched, and they will be loathsome to all mankind" (Isaiah 66:24). The casting out of these bodies, which are to be looked on and abhorred, is a solemn judgment.

Fell. The apostle does not say that they died but that they **fell.** This indicates contempt and indignation, which is backed up by the story itself.

God was displeased with them because of their sin, so their **bodies fell in the desert.**

18. And to whom did God swear that they would never enter his rest if not to those who disobeyed? The apostle continues applying his illustration to the Hebrews with one further question. The answer he gives is self-evident from the story itself. He reveals their particular sin, which was the foundation of all their other trespasses, and will conclude in verse 19, "so we see that they were not able to enter, because of their unbelief."

Disobeyed. This word is translated as obeyed not, believed not, assented not, and acquiesced not. If the word is used of neglecting God's command it should be translated as disobeying or disobedience; if it is used of ignoring God's promise, it should be translated as unbelief. But since these things are so close to each other, wherever one is meant, the other is also understood. And this is the case in this verse. Their **unbelief** referred mainly to the promise that God would give them the land of Canaan. So their unbelief was that God would not bring them into that land. They were commanded by God to go and possess the land, but their unbelief was accompanied by disobedience and rebellion. This is the meaning of the words here, **to whom did God swear that they would never enter his rest?** It was made to those to whom the promise had been made, who had been commanded to go up and take the land. Because they refused to accept God's faithfulness and power, and because they would not believe his word, they would not obey his command. This justly provoked God's judgment on them.

19. So we see that they were not able to enter, because of their unbelief. This verse is a summary conclusion of the apostle's previous arguments about the example of their forefathers, as recorded by Moses and later by David. He makes it a foundation for the exhortation he intends to give in the next chapter.

So we see. That is, "it is evident from what has been laid down and proved"; or, "This we have demonstrated before your eyes."

So we see is an obvious conclusion with two parts. First, it asserts **that they were not able to enter.** Second, it supplies the reason for this, **because of their unbelief.** In the first the apostle declares the event: they did not enter, they died in the desert, their bodies fell there. He also explains that they **were not able.** That is, they lost all right to any entrance through God's promise. No matter how much they desired to enter, expressed in their mourning over Moses' exclusion (Numbers 14:39), they could not enter. "In things moral our ability is commensurate with our right." This was lost, so **they were not able to enter.** The expression is elliptical, and "God's rest" is to be supplied from the previous verse. "God swore that they would never enter his rest."

Because of their unbelief. The reason for them being unable to enter is given at the end of this verse: **because of their unbelief.** People who look at the complete catalogue of these people's sins might suggest other reasons for their exclusion from God's rest, as Jews do to this day. They might say, "It was because of their idolatry when they made the golden calf." This was such a serious sin that the Jews have a saying, that "no trouble befalls Israel which does not have in it an ounce of the golden calf." Or, they might conclude that they are excluded because of several other sins: mixing with the Midianites and Moabites, worshiping Baal-peor, eating the sacrifices of the dead, and giving themselves up to uncleanness. Their frequent grumbling could come to their minds. But our apostle states that they did not enter **because of their unbelief.** People very rarely say they have committed the sin of unbelief, but God accuses people of this sin more than any other. Here this charge is laid against this people quite justly. **So we see that they were not able to enter, because of their unbelief.**

Hebrews
Chapter 4

This chapter carries on the same plan as chapter 3. That chapter exhorted faith, obedience, and perseverance, and gave an example of the punishment that fell on those who sinned by not carrying out their duty.

In this chapter the apostle sets before the Hebrews the duty they should carry out. He reminds them about the sin and punishment that fell on those who ignored God's message (verses 1-2). He then supports his exhortation by saying that the rest which the psalmist speaks of, and which he urges them to try to attain, is something yet to come (verse 3). This rest is not the rest God had after creation, and it is not the Sabbath rest (verses 4-6); it is not the rest of Canaan, which Joshua brought the people into (verses 7-8). He explains that this rest is a spiritual rest, which remains for believers to enjoy (verses 8-10). He then reverts to his exhortation in verse 11. In verses 12-13 he teaches them about the Word of God as a warning. Verses 14-16 are words of encouragement about Christ's priesthood, through which this rest was procured for believers.

Verses 1-2

Therefore, since the promise of entering his rest still stands, let us be careful that none of you be found to have fallen short of it. For we also have had the gospel preached to us, just as they did; but the message they heard was of no value to them, because those who heard did not combine it with faith.

In these verses the apostle states how important it is for the Hebrews to heed the example he has referred to in the previous chapter. They were likely to say, "What have we to do with the people in the desert, with the promise of entering into Canaan, or with what the psalmist exhorts the people of old to do?" But the apostle replies, "These things are for you to take special note of. From their example you can see how God views you if you fall into the same sin. So the things mentioned in the psalm are prophetic and especially apply to your present condition."

1. Therefore. As in many other places, the apostle here delivers new exhortations from the teaching he had just given.

Let us be careful. This is derived from a word meaning "fear": Let us fear. It can be correctly applied to natural, civil, or religious fear. Here the fear intended is religious, relating to God, his worship, and our obedience.

An example of God's severity against unbelievers was given by the apostle in the previous verses. In this example the apostle declares that God will deal with all other people in the same way, who fall into the sin of unbelief. No one should flatter himself that he has any special privileges that will exempt him from this. Unbelievers will never enter into God's rest. The apostle confirms this in these two verses, although his present exhortation is an immediate inference from what went before: **Therefore ... let us be careful.** How are we to do this? What kind of fear is involved? It is not a fear of diffidence, or doubting, or wavering, or uncertainty about our obedience. This happens to many people, but no one is commanded to be like this. It is the fruit of unbelief, so it cannot be our duty. Neither can it mean fearfulness about difficulties, opposition, or danger. It is the fear of a sluggard who cries out, "There is a lion outside, I shall be killed in the streets." To cast out this fear, as the fear that weakens people's Christian profession, is one of the main purposes of this letter. The fear referred to in this verse does not mean that general reverence that ought to be with us all the time, whenever we have anything to do with God. For this is not particularly influenced by warnings from God, since we are always bound to "fear the Lord and his goodness."

The fear intended in this verse is a combination of two things. First, it is a reverent understanding of God's holiness and greatness, and his severity against sin. Second, it is using the means of grace carefully to avoid the evil of unbelief and disobedience.

Since the promise of entering his rest still stands. Some interpret these words to mean, "seeing God has left a promise to us now under the Gospel." These people add the words "to us" to the text. Then the warning in the text is applied to the end of the verse and the sin that is warned against there. Others take these words to mean the evil of the sin we are warned against, so that the next clause states the punishment that will follow. It is as if the apostle had said, "We ought to fear, lest, the promise being left, we should seem to come short of entering into God's rest." For this was the punishment experienced by those who rejected the promise. This is the way most expositors understand this verse. The difference comes in this, whether **still stands** refers to God's act in giving the promise, or if **still stands** refers to man's refusal of God's promise. Each of these interpretations gives a sense which is true to the subject under discussion, though it is not obvious which of them expresses the meaning of the words. I will therefore explain them in both ways.

In the first way, this is the summary of the apostle's exhortation: "The promise that was made to the people of old about their entering into God's rest did not belong absolutely and universally to them only. This is clear from the psalm that is quoted in verse 3. This promise, as far as they were concerned, they disbelieved, and so did not enter into the promised rest. The same promise, or rather a promise of the same nature, about entering into God's rest, remaining there and continuing in it, is offered to us, and we are required to show the same faith and obedience as was demanded from them. Therefore, since they missed out through unbelief, let us be careful not to fall into the same sins and not to enter into the rest we are now offered."

In the second interpretation of these words, what is said in the first interpretation is taken for granted; namely, that a promise of entering into God's rest is given to us no less than it was to those of old, which is further confirmed in the next verse. On this supposition, the present Hebrews are warned in case by neglecting, rejecting, and despising that promise, through unbelief, they fall short of God's rest because of his righteous judgment. It is as if the apostle had only said, "Take heed, lest, by your unbelief in rejecting the promise, you fall short of God's rest."

I will not state categorically which interpretation is correct. However, I incline to the first one for three reasons. First, because the apostle seems in these words to lay down the foundation for all his following arguments and exhortations in this chapter. That is, that a promise of entering into God's rest is left to us now under the Gospel. On this supposition he proceeds in all his following discourses, which are therefore asserted here. Second, the last clause, **that none of you be found to have fallen short of it,** does primarily and directly mean the sin and not the punishment of the unbelievers. The promise, and not God's rest, is therefore the object under consideration. Third, the apostle, after various arguments, gathers everything up into a conclusion, "there remains, then, a Sabbath-rest for the people of God" (verse 9). The root of the word "remains" there has the same root as the word **still stands** and is used in the sense that the first interpretation maintains.

So, I suggest that these words mean, "There is yet on God's part a promise left to believers of entering into his rest."

Of entering his rest. What is this rest, this rest of God, which is promised to **us,** that is, to those to whom the Gospel is preached?

Most expositors agree that it is the rest of glory that is intended here. This is the *ultimate rest* that is promised to believers under the Gospel. So those who are in glory are said to "rest from their labor" (Revelation 14:13) and to have "relief" (2 Thessalonians 1:7). This is the rest of believers in heaven, after they have passed through their course of trials, sufferings, faith, and obedience in this world. This rest such expositors take for granted that the apostle insists on throughout this chapter, and they make it the basis and controlling factor for the interpretation of the rest of this passage. I must be free to disagree with this interpretation for the following reasons.

First, the **rest** here proposed is *peculiar to the Gospel* and is distinct from what was proposed to the people in Moses' day. The people in the wilderness failed to enter into the rest, but the apostle shows, from the psalmist, that there is a different rest, distinct from that, a rest proposed under the Gospel. This cannot be the eternal rest of glory, because the people under the old testament had that promise as much as we have it under the Gospel. So the apostle affirms in the next verse, "the gospel preached to them, as it is to us." It was preached no less truly, though less clearly and evidently. Into this rest multitudes of people entered. For they were both "justified by faith" (Romans 4:3, 7, 8,) and "adopted as sons" (Romans 9:4). And when they died, they entered into God's rest. This means that at their death they went to a place of refreshment under God's favor. For whatever may be thought about their condition, since their souls were only in a place of refreshment and not enjoying the immediate presence of God, it cannot be denied that they entered into peace and rested (Isaiah 57:2). So, this cannot be that other rest that is provided under the Gospel, in contrast to the one given under the law or to the people in the desert.

Second, the apostle continues his argument in the form of an antithesis, which has many parts. The main subject is the *two people*; those who were in the desert and those Hebrews who now have the Gospel preached to them. About these two groups of people, the apostle contrasts numerous things: the *promises* made to them, the *things promised*, and the *means or people* through whom they were made partakers of God's rest. These people were, on the one hand, Moses and Joshua, and, on the other hand, Jesus Christ. Notice, then, God's rest that the people of old did not enter into, and see how it contrasts with the rest now proposed. This proposed rest, into which they did not enter, was the quiet, settled state of God's solemn worship in Canaan, or a peaceful church-state for the worship of God in the land and place chosen for that purpose.

Now, it is not to the rest of heaven that, in this antithesis between the *law* and the *Gospel*, a contrast is made, but the rest that believers have in Christ. Christ led the believers into this rest in the same way that Joshua led the people of old into the rest of Canaan.

Third, the apostle states his intention clearly in verse 3, "They shall never enter my rest." It is into this rest that true believers do enter in this world. This is the rest that we have through Christ in the grace and worship of the Gospel and no other. So, the rest that was proposed of old for the people to enter into, which some received and failed to enter because of unbelief, was a rest in this world, where the effects of their faith and unbelief were visible.

Fourth, Christ and the Gospel were promised of old to the people as a *means* and *state of rest*. In fulfillment of these promises they are here actually proposed for their enjoyment (see Genesis 5:29; Psalm 72:7-8; Isaiah 2:2-4; 9:6-7; 11:1-10; 28:12; Matthew 11:28; Luke 1:70-75). This was the main idea the church had from the foundation of the world about the kingdom of the Messiah, or the state of the Gospel, namely, that it was a state of spiritual rest and deliverance from everything that was burdensome to the souls and consciences of believers. This is what the people of God in all ages looked for and which in the preaching of the Gospel was proposed to them.

Fifth, the true nature of this rest is seen from the promise that was made about it. For a promise is said *to remain of entering into this rest*. This promise is nothing other than the Gospel itself as it was preached to us. The apostle specifically states this in the next verse. Expositors have made wrong interpretations because they have not given this consideration due weight. For they think of only the promise of eternal life given in the Gospel, which is but part of it.

Let us be careful that none of you be found to have fallen short of it. This is a warning, backing up the exhortation.

Be found. The apostle warns them against failing or falling. He wants them to be alert so that none of them, through abandoning their previous zeal, gives any appearance of desertion in their Christian profession. This is the apostle's intention in the words, **be careful that none of you be found to have fallen short.**

To have fallen short. This means to be left behind or to have been left behind. It refers to the work of first receiving the promise. If people fail in the beginning, they will most probably lag behind when they should be making progress.

Many expositors think that this alludes to running a race. People who run slowly, who do not stir themselves up diligently, fail, come behind, and so fall short of the prize. This is a thing that the apostle alludes to in 1 Corinthians 9:24-25.

But I think that the allusion is taken from the people in the wilderness and their traveling into the land of Canaan. Most of them were loaded down through unbelief, they lagged behind in their journey, and were, as it were, left behind in the desert, where they perished and failed to enter the Promised Land. These words, therefore, **let us be careful that none of you be found to have fallen short of it,** are as if he had said, "Lest it fall out with you in reference to the promise left to you, as it did with the people in the wilderness about the promise that was preached and proposed to them. Because of their unbelief they fell short and did not enjoy the promise, nor did they enter into the Promised Land, or God's rest. So take heed, in case you fall short in the same way concerning the promise that is now preached to you of entering into God's rest in the Gospel." The word, therefore, directly refers to the promise, **have fallen short of it,** and consequently the things promised, or God's rest in the Gospel.

2. For we also have had the gospel preached to us, just as they did; but the message they heard was of no value to them, because those who heard did not combine it with faith.

Those who did not mix the promises of the Gospel with faith will completely fail to enter God's rest. The apostle explains this in verse 2.

For . . . also. The conjunction of these particles links the reader to what has gone before and introduces a new reason to support the argument.

The gospel preached. Sometimes this word is used passively, as in 1 Peter 4:6 and Matthew 11:5 where the poor are evangelized, or "have the Gospel preached to them." This is the case in this verse. Nowhere does the use of the word mean the receiving of the Gospel by those who are evangelized. That is, it does not include the faith of the hearers, but only denotes the act of preaching and the outer enjoyment of it. The Gospel, and included in it, the promise of entering into God's rest, is preached to us.

Just as they did. This directs our attention to the fathers in the desert who were previously mentioned. They had disbelieved and rejected God's promise and so failed to enter into his rest.

It is taken for granted that the Gospel was preached to the people in the desert. The apostle does not directly assert this here, for it was not his intention to demonstrate this. He had in mind our privilege and duty, not theirs.

But the message they heard was of no value to them. The Gospel is, and always was, the only way to come to God. To imagine that there is any other way of coming to God is exceedingly derogatory to the glory of God's wisdom, faithfulness, and holiness. This part of this verse contains an absolute assertion that the word preached to them **was of no value to them.** To ensure that this in no way reflected badly on God, the reason for this is also given. **Those who heard did not combine it with faith.**

The message they heard. The subject of what **was of no value to them** is given here. It was **the message they heard.** Hearing is the only way through which the benefits of any word may be communicated to us. This is the intention of this expression. "Faith comes from hearing the message, and the message is heard through the word of Christ" (Romans 10:17). The purpose of God's Word is to plant faith in the hearts of men. It does not do this directly but through the means of hearing. People must hear what they are to believe, so that they may believe.

Was of no value to them. They gained no advantage from the message that they listened to. Despite the promise about entering God's rest, we find that they did not enter in. Far from benefiting them, it became their ruin. It is as if he said, "Consider what happened to them, how they died in the desert under God's judgment, and you will see how far they were from deriving any benefit from the Word they heard. This will be the same for everyone who neglects the Word in this way."

Did not combine it. This word is sometimes taken in a natural sense for "to mix or mingle one thing with another," like water and wine, or to mix different ingredients in cordials or poisons. This mixture was put in cups so that it could be drunk. This mixture was sometimes made in such a way that it had special strength and efficacy. This is seen when "In the hand of the LORD is a cup full of foaming wine mixed with spices" (Psalm 75:8). A cup sometimes signifies divine vengeance, as in Jeremiah 51:7; and wine often stands for God's judgment. "Babylon was a gold cup in the LORD's hand; she made the whole earth drunk. The nations drank her wine; therefore they have now gone mad" (Jeremiah 51:7). The vengeance threatened here, which will be very severe, is called a cup, and a cup containing wine. Sometimes the mixture was made to alleviate, as water mixed with strong wine. Hence a cup of "full strength" expresses great indignation (see Revelation 14:10).

The Word of God, especially the word of promise, is the food of people's souls. Our apostle talks about God's Word and the way people receive it as strong meat and milk (Hebrews 5:13-14; see also 1 Peter 2:1-2).

Sometimes **faith** is expressed by the word tasting, as it is used in eating food. "Now that you have tasted that the Lord is good," writes Peter (1 Peter 2:3). How do we taste God's grace? In his word, declares the psalmist: "How sweet are your words to my taste" (Psalm 119:103)! The metaphor is used again to declare that the word is sweet: "sweeter than honey to my mouth" (Psalm 119:103).

Faith is also often said to be *eating*, from which comes the sacramental idea of eating the body and drinking the blood of Christ, through which the special act of faith on that special promise expresses Christ crucified for us.

The summary of all this is that *spiritual truths*, if believed, are united with faith that receives them. When they have been incorporated with faith in the soul, the person receives God's new nature. The people in the desert had the Gospel preached to them, but they did not respond with faith. The words in this verse do not say that they failed to believe in a general way. Rather, these hearers did not receive the word of promise with faith and so they derived no benefit from the words heard. They *tasted* sometimes a little sweetness in these words, but they did not *digest* them. So the word did them no good and they did not enter God's rest. The apostle emphasizes this event both to the Hebrews and to us.

3. Now we who have believed enter that rest, just as God has said, "So I declared on oath in my anger, 'They shall never enter my rest.'" And yet his work has been finished since the creation of the world. This verse states three things. First, an *assertion*: **we who have believed enter that rest.** Second, evidence for that assertion from the psalmist: **just as God has said, "So I declared on oath in my anger, 'They shall never enter my rest.'"** Third, *an additional confirmation* of his assertion: **And yet his work has been finished since the creation of the world.**

We who have believed. The apostle states the subject of his assertion as those **who have believed.** In the New Testament people are frequently called "believers" or "unbelievers." "We have believed in Jesus Christ through the preaching of the gospel."

Enter that rest. This is the promised rest. This rest is principally that spiritual rest of God that believers receive entry into through Jesus Christ, in the faith and worship of the Gospel. This rest is not to be restricted to their eternal rest in heaven. This is the sense and importance of the apostle's assertion in this verse: "We who believe in Jesus Christ, through the gospel, have through this entrance given to us that blessed state of rest in the worship of God which of old was promised" (see Luke 1:69-73).

This apostle has been asserting this and providing evidence to back this up throughout his letter. His whole purpose is to show, through testimonies and examples, that unbelief cuts off from, and faith gives entrance to, God's rest. The entrance itself depends on faith alone. Negatively, this means that no entry can be made without faith, no matter what else people may plead. Positively, this means that faith alone, without the assistance of any other grace, makes entry possible. This is not like buying something with silver or gold, as people seek to buy a rest from purgatory. Works of the law and any other kind of works will not open this way for us. It is faith alone that opens the way to us. **We who have believed enter that rest,** asserts the apostle.

Just as God said, "So I declared on oath in my anger, 'They shall never enter my rest.'" These words confirm the apostle's assertion in the first part of the verse. However, this may not seem to be the case at first sight. For how is it that **we who have believed enter that rest,** because God stated on oath about others that **they shall never enter my rest**? This difficulty we must remove by a correct application of these words to the apostle's purpose.

First, the apostle's argument depends on a known rule, namely, that contrary attributes may be positively affirmed. So he affirms one thing, while he at the same time denies the other thing. And he denies one thing, and at the same time affirms another thing. He says, "It is day," meaning that it is not night, as if he had actually stated the words about the night. Now, the proposition laid down by the apostle to support his assertion is this: "Those who did not believe did not enter God's rest. For God declared on oath that they would not, because they did not believe. Hence it follows inevitably and rationally that those who do believe do enter into that rest." He takes for granted what he had already proved. His intention is to further confirm that the promise belongs to us as well as to them. The promise is the same, only the rest has changed. He also takes as read what he has already fully proved, namely, that the enjoying of the promise, or entering into rest, depends on combining it with faith, or believing. In this way he gives his evidence that those who do believe enter the rest, because God has declared on oath that those who do not believe shall not enter the rest. For the promise remains the same: if there is unbelief, there is exclusion; if there is faith, entrance is allowed. What is denied about one is affirmed about the other.

Second, the words may be considered theologically; that is, by other rules of Scripture, according to the analogy of faith. Thus, the force of the apostle's proof springs out of another root. It comes from the nature of God's covenant with us and its purpose. When God's covenant is given to us through promises and warnings, we all have the same thing given to us and the same grace to make it effective. Hence every warning includes a promise in it, and every promise includes a warning. This is true about God's covenant. The first covenant was given through a word of warning: "the day you eat it you will die." But no one doubts that there was also a promise of life included here for those who were obedient. Indeed that was the principal idea intended. In the same way, there is a warning included in every promise of the Gospel. So, although there is a great warning, confirmed by God declaring it on oath, in these words, that those who do not believe would not enter into his rest, there is a promise included in the same words, no less solemnly confirmed, that those who do believe should enter into rest. In this way the apostle confirms the truth of his assertion.

And yet his work has been finished since the creation of the world. The apostle here illustrates and confirms the truth of the evidence he had produced by maintaining that he had made a correct application of the testimony he had used for that purpose. He argued that those who believe in the Gospel enter into rest. Now he had to show that this rest refers to the Gospel, which was now preached to all the Hebrews and entered into by all who believe. The apostle now moves on to consider the different rests that are called "the rests of God" in the Scripture. From this he concludes that after all the other rests previously enjoyed by God's people, there still remains rest for them under the Messiah, which was the chief intention of

David's prophetic words in his psalm. This is the purpose of the following discourse. He introduces this somewhat abruptly, or at least with an elliptical phrase, **And yet his work has been finished since the creation of the world.**

His work. This is God's work of creation, the works of the creation, translated by the Syriac version as "the works of God himself"; that is, "all his work that God created and made," or that he designed to make in that first creation.

Has been finished. These works were made, perfected, completed, as in Genesis 2:1, which says they were "finished."

Since the creation of the world. We are then told when these works were finished—**since the creation of the world.** The root meaning of the word **creation,** or "foundation," is casting anything from above so that it abides where it is placed. Hence Chrysostom, commenting on Ephesians 1:4 says, "the founding of the word comes from above, from the power of God over all." The word is only used once in the New Testament to mean anything else (see Hebrews 11:11). It is often linked with the word **world** (see Matthew 13:35; 25:34; Luke 11:50; John 17:24; Ephesians 1:4; Hebrews 9:26; 1 Peter 1:20; Revelation 13:8; 17:8). It is twice linked with the word "before," Ephesians 1:4; 1 Peter 1:20, "before the creation of the world."

4. For somewhere he has spoken about the seventh day in these words: "And on the seventh day God rested from all his work."

This verse has two parts. One expresses the manner of the introduction of the following testimony; the other contains the testimony itself. The first part of this verse states, **For somewhere he has spoken about the seventh day in these words.**

Somewhere. The apostle only refers the Hebrews to Scripture, which was the commonly acknowledged source of truth for them both, and in which they were expert.

The seventh day. This is the subject about which the testimony is produced. Usually the words are translated "of the seventh day." **Seventh** means from the beginning of creation, after which one reverts to the first day again. It may also mean the name of a day of the week. At that time **the seventh** was the name the Hellenists gave to the Sabbath day. So in the Gospel, "one," or "the first day of the week," is the name given to the Lord's day. It is the Sabbath that the apostle is speaking about here. This refers to both God's rest and the rest that was given to us then. He now sets about demonstrating this. He shows that, under the law of creation, God rested when he finished his work, and he made way for his creatures to enter into his rest, and he gave them a day as a pledge of this.

"And on the seventh day God rested from all his work." These words are the testimony itself, taken from Genesis 2:2. The apostle uses not just the words of his quotation, but the whole passage from which they come, to lend weight to his argument. For it would not help his argument merely to state that God rested from his work, which is what these words affirm. The apostle's aim is to show that there was a rest provided for us to enter into, and a day of rest appointed as a pledge of this. This is fully expressed in the words, "God blessed the seventh day and made it holy" (Genesis 2:3).

"God rested." A *cessation* from work, and not *refreshment* from weariness, is intended. God is not weary. He was no more tired in the works of creation than he is in the works of providence. "The LORD is the everlasting God, the Creator of the ends of the earth. He will not grow tired or weary" (Isaiah 40:28). God labors not in working; and therefore there is nothing in this word except for a cessation from work. And this fully satisfies the meaning of the word.

Yet, the rest mentioned in Exodus 20:11, "but he rested on the seventh day," does signify the kind of rest that brings refreshment to the weary. We may, therefore, allow the word **rest** to be viewed anthropomorphically and say that God "rested" and found refreshment after his labor.

From the foundation of the world God was at work, then a rest came, and it was proposed that men should enter into this rest, and a day of rest was given as a pledge of this. However, this is not the rest the psalmist refers to in the next verse.

5. And again in the passage above he says, "They shall never enter my rest." The apostle's purpose in repeating this testimony is to show that the rest mentioned there was not the rest that was appointed from the beginning of the world, but another, still to come. So there was another rest of God besides that upon the creation of all.

6. It still remains that some will enter that rest, and those who formerly had the gospel preached to them did not go in, because of their disobedience.

These words contain an *assertion* and a particular *assumption* from it. The assertion is that *some will enter that rest.* This the apostle deduces from the previous arguments and evidence he has brought. The sense of these words is, "From what has been spoken, it is clear that some must yet enter into another rest of God besides that which was in the Sabbath appointed from the foundation of the world."

The apostle assumes that those to whom that rest was first preached **did not go in, because of their disobedience.** It is clear whom the apostle is referring to in these words, namely, those who came out of Egypt under Moses' command, whose sin and punishment he had detailed in chapter 3. These are the people God's rest was first proclaimed to. Here the apostle shows what kind of rest he means. It was definitely not the spiritual rest of the promise, for this was preached to believers from the creation of the world. Rather, it was the *church rest* of the land of Canaan that was first preached to them. So the fulfillment of the promise, based on their faith and obedience, was first offered to them. They did not enter into this rest because of their unbelief and disobedience.

So the substance of this verse is: Besides the rest of God from the creation of the world, and the institution of the seventh-day Sabbath as a pledge of this, there was another rest for men to enter into, namely, the rest of God and his worship in the land of Canaan. God's people of old were offered this, but they failed to enter into it because of their unbelief.

7. Therefore God again set a certain day, calling it Today, when a long time later he spoke through David, as was said before: "Today, if you hear his voice, do not harden your hearts." The apostle here confirms what he had previously asserted about a new rest, and a new day of rest, which remains for God's people to enter and possess.

The apostle argues that after the constitution of the sabbatical rest since the creation of the world, and the proposition of the rest of Canaan to the people in the desert, God, in addition to these, has determined another **certain day,** which was neither of the former two. This must be another day, and it can be no other day but the day of the Gospel. The apostle not only calls it a "rest," but a **day.** In this way it is comparable to the previous rests, which were types and shadows of it.

The apostle supports this argument by repeating the divine testimony on which it is built: **"Today, if you hear his voice, do not harden your hearts."** The apostle has often used these words in this chapter. It is just one of these words he now singles out: **Today.** From the word **Today** he deduces the great mysteries of a Gospel rest, and the rest under the old testament, and the day that it expresses.

8. For if Joshua had given them rest, God would not have spoken later about another day. The apostle is still insisting on the confirmation of his principal assertion from the words of David concerning the rest prepared in the Gospel for believers. He bases his whole exhortation to the Hebrews on this. On this same truth all his arguments rested. It was necessary for this to be established and clearly vindicated. So, the apostle now has to remove an objection that the Jews had in their minds about his line of argument. The implied objection raised can be stated thus: "Although the people who came out of Egypt did not enter into God's promised rest because of their unbelief and disobedience, as you have shown, yet the next generation, under the leadership of Joshua, went into and enjoyed the rest that the others had been excluded from. This, therefore, was the intended rest, which we now enjoy. So, how can you propose another rest for us?" This is the force of the objection. Two things are mentioned by the apostle in his reply. First, he denies their supposition. This is seen from the words, **For if Joshua had given them rest.** That is, no matter what may be said, Joshua did not give them rest; that is, he did not give them that ultimate rest. Second, the apostle gives a reason for this denial. It is this: after five hundred years, God in David, and through him, proposed another rest, or another day of rest, and invites the people to enter in, after they had already possessed all that Joshua had led them into. There was no new rest for the people to enter into in the days of David, for the psalm that records these words is prophetic about the days of the Messiah. So it must follow from this that there is still a rest a day of rest for God's people. He refers to this, in his conclusion, in verse 9, "There remains, then, a Sabbath-rest for the people of God."

9. There remains, then, a Sabbath-rest for the people of God. The apostle completes his analogy between the several rests of God and his people, which he has been expounding in this chapter. At the beginning of the world God performed his *work* after which he *rested*. This made a way for God's people to rest in God and to worship him by contemplating the works he had made. This day was special, was blessed and sanctified to express God's rest. This was the Sabbath-rest for God's people from the creation of the world. When the law was given, it was a great work of God, after which he rested. In the completion of this work his worship was established in the land of Canaan. This made way for the people to enter into his rest in that country, and they were given a day to experience this rest and to help them to enter completely into God's rest. These were all types and shadows of the rest mentioned by David. This was their Sabbath-rest, or sabbatizing rest. Now, under the Gospel, there is a Sabbath that includes all of this.

10. For anyone who enters God's rest also rests from his own work, just as God did from his. Expositors generally apply these words to believers, as they enter God's rest. But I do not believe this is the apostle's purpose. For, if believers are referred to here, what are the works they are said to rest from? Their sins, their labors, their sorrows, their sufferings? But how can it be said that they rest from these works **just as God did from his own?** For God rested from his works in order to take the greatest delight and satisfaction in them, to be refreshed by them: "in six days the LORD made the heavens and the earth, and on the seventh day he abstained from work and rested" (Exodus 31:17). He rested from them in that he rested in them and blessed them, and blessed and sanctified the time when they were finished. Indeed, God's rest from and upon his works, besides a mere cessation from working, consisted principally in the satisfaction that he had in them. But now, if those mentioned are the works intended here, people cannot rest from them in the same way that God did from his. Men cease from their works and detest them insofar as they are sinful and enjoy deliverance from them since they bring such sorrow. Now, this is not to rest as God rested. Again, when are men supposed to

89

rest from these works? It cannot be in this world, for here we are not free from temptations, sufferings, and sorrows. As we seek to attain mortification of sin we fight continually, "resisting even unto blood." So, it must be in heaven that they rest. But this completely excludes the rest in and of the Gospel from the apostle's discourse.

It appears, therefore, that it is another kind of rest that is intended here, that is, the rest of Christ from his works, which is compared with the rest of God from his at the creation of the world. The person of Jesus Christ is the theme of this verse.

11. Let us, therefore, make every effort to enter that rest, so that no one will fall by following their example of disobedience. In these words three things may be observed. First, the illative particle, **therefore,** denoting an inference from and dependence upon the previous discussion. What he now mentions arises from what he has already demonstrated, especially the part of the example where the people of old sinned and were punished. Second, this verse issues a command. Third, a reason is given for obeying this command. The exhortation is to **enter that rest,** and this is to be carried out diligently, **make every effort.**

To enter that rest. The exhortation is expressed in the same way as before: **enter that rest.** The duty intended here is faith and obedience to the Gospel. These were represented of old when the people entered the Promised Land of Canaan. Here, therefore, the apostle exhorts them to their present duty using these terms. The result of obeying this command is participation in God's rest.

There are glorious advantages in all Gospel duties. To know God in Christ is "eternal life" (John 17:3); to believe is to enter into God's rest. The apostle in verse 11 changes the word he uses for "rest" from the word he used in verse 9. In verse 9 he tells us that "there remains a Sabbath-rest" (a "sabbatism") "for the people of God." He does not tell them to enter into that Sabbath-rest. He did this because by using the word "Sabbath-rest" he meant the rest of the Gospel as a pledge of the day of rest. In verse 11 the apostle returns to exhort the Hebrews to pursue their participation in the whole rest of God in the Gospel, with all the privileges and advantages contained in it. So he uses the word for rest that he had used before to express the rest of God in general. He does not use the word for "Sabbath-rest" used in verse 9.

Make every effort. The apostle states how this duty is to be performed: **make every effort.** Let us "diligently study," "endeavor," or "labor," he commands. If we use the word "labor" (although I prefer "endeavor"), such a laboring includes the mind and the whole soul. Both go through intense exercise because of the difficulties they meet as they carry out this command. The apostle speaks of our faith and Gospel obedience so that we will manage to enter God's rest. This reminds the Hebrews about the people entering into the land of Canaan. Like them, the Hebrews are to expect great opposition as they enter their rest. It is well known that the people in the desert met many difficulties, storms, and contrary winds. These were so great that they became discouraged and then acted in unbelief, which led to their downfall. Sometimes their lack of water and food, sometimes the weariness and tediousness of the journey, sometimes the reports they received about giants and fortified towns, stirred up their unbelief so that they murmured and hastened their destruction. The apostle warns us to be on our guard because we are bound to meet similar opposition to faith and Christian profession. The apostle does this by using the words, **enter that rest.**

So that no one will fall by following their example of disobedience. The last part of this verse either indicates the sin to be avoided or the punishment that should deter us from sinning.

Fall. The word "to fall" is ambiguous and can be used in two senses. It is used about men who may *fall into sin* and who may fall into the punishment due *because of their sin*. This is when the word is used in a moral sense. "They are blind guides. If a blind man leads a blind man, both will fall into a pit" (Matthew 15:14). Both fall into a pit of sin or trouble (see Romans 11:22; James 5:12). But the prime use of the word is in things natural and is only metaphorically translated to express moral things.

Following their example. This word is most commonly "a teaching example," meaning "to teach," or "to instruct" by showing. "You brood of vipers! Who warned [that is taught, instructed] you?" (Matthew 3:7). I take this verse to mean, "You have the Gospel, and the rest of Christ in it, preached and proposed to you. Some of you have already professed this faith, as the people did of old at Mount Sinai when they said, 'All that the Lord our God will command, that we will do.' Your condition is now like theirs and was represented therein. Therefore, consider how things ended up with them and what event caused their sin and God's dealings with them. They did not believe, they did not persist in their profession, but were disobedient and stubborn, and God destroyed them. They 'fell in the desert' and perished, not entering into God's rest, as had been declared. Now, if you, or any among you, are found to be guilty of their sin, of a similar sin, you should not think or hope that you will avoid a similar punishment. An example of God's severity is set before you in their destruction. If you do not want to fall into it, or fall under it, labor by faith and obedience to enter into Christ's rest."

This I take to be the true meaning and importance of these words. For the words **Let us make every effort to enter that rest** are no more but, "Let us sincerely believe and obey; wherein we will find, through Jesus Christ, rest for our souls." This clause in this verse gives us the motive for this: **so that no one will fall by following their example of disobedience.**

91

Verses 12-13

These verses contain a new confirmation of the previous exhortation, taken from the event warned against in the case of unbelief. Two things are likely to arise in people's minds to allay such fears. First, that their own failings in this area will not be noticed. For they will make sure that any such transgressions are not visible to everyone. They hope that what they do in secret may be overlooked or not observed. Second, the warnings that are given are only to make people stand in awe and will never be carried out. Our apostle counters both such vain pretenses in these verses. For he tells them that men will be judged by the One who discovers all the secrets of our hearts and deals with men accordingly. He tells them that mere outward observance is not enough.

12-13. The word of God is living and active. Sharper than any double-edged sword, it penetrates even to dividing soul and spirit, joints and marrow; it judges the thoughts and attitudes of the heart. Nothing in all creation is hidden from God's sight. Everything is uncovered and laid bare before the eyes of him to whom we must give an account.

The word of God. The exposition of these words depends on the subject spoken about in verse 12. This is **the word of God.** Sometimes in the Scripture this denotes the *essential Word of God* and sometimes the *word spoken by him.* Among the old commentators, Ambrose, with many others, contends that it is the *essential and eternal Word of God* that is spoken about here. Chrysostom, however, inclines to the view that it means the *written word.*

The *name* used here, **the word of God,** is sometimes ascribed to the essential Word of God and sometimes to the inspired or written word, or the Scripture. (Later I will show that the Son of God is called by this name.) I concede that there are many examples in Scripture where the words **the word of God** do not refer to Jesus Christ. "The people crowding around him and listening to the word of God" (Luke 5:1). There the Word of God is clearly different from Jesus Christ who spoke it. "The seed is the word of God" (Luke 8:11), and here this is the Word preached by Jesus Christ, the good sower of the seed, as the whole chapter states. "Blessed rather are those who hear the word of God and obey it" (Luke 11:28); that is, preserve it in their hearts, and obey what they hear. "Thus you nullify the word of God by your tradition that you have handed down" (Mark 7:13). The Word of God, that is, in his commands, is directly contrasted with the traditions and commands of men, and so is of the same general nature. "And they were all filled with the Holy Spirit and spoke the word of God boldly" (Acts 4:31). The Word of God was the Word that they preached, declaring Jesus Christ to be the Son of God. When Philip had preached the Gospel at Samaria and many believed, it is said, "when the apostles in Jerusalem heard that Samaria had accepted the word of God" (Acts 8:14). There, the Word of God is equated with believing the teaching of the Gospel that was preached. "But the word of God continued to increase and spread" (Acts 12:24); that is, on Herod's death the Word of God was preached and received more. I give these examples to show how wrong people are who say that **the word of God** cannot mean the Scripture, or the preached Gospel. "The word," and "the word of the Gospel," "the word preached," "the word of Christ," are common ways of referring to the declared Word of God.

I agree that the *attributes and effects* that are ascribed to the Word of God, in a number of instances, may be applied to the things mentioned. It is clear that in some sense they may be applied to the written word and in other places to the Scripture. To confirm this assertion, Grotius cites Psalms 45:5; 105:19; 107:20; 147:15, 18; Isaiah 40:8; 49:2; 55:11. For though the Word of God is mentioned in them, yet in some places the essential Word of God, in most places his providential Word, the Word of his power, is unquestionably intended (but see Hosea 6:5; 1 Corinthians 14:24-25).

It must be acknowledged that if the things mentioned here are ascribed to the written Word, they do not *primarily* and absolutely belong to it. They only belong to it by virtue of its relation to Jesus Christ, whose Word it is, and because of the power and efficacy that are through him communicated to it. Also, if it is the Son, or the eternal Word of God, that is intended here, the things that are here ascribed to him are the things that, for the most part, he effects by his Word in and on the hearts and consciences of men.

I judge that the *eternal Word of God*, or the *person of Christ*, is the subject of this verse.

For "the word," or **the word of God,** is the correct name of Christ for his divine nature as the eternal Son of God. He is called by this name (John 1:1-2), and "his name is the Word of God" (Revelation 19:13). Therefore, since this is Christ's name, where this name appears, and where there is no cogent reason from the context to the contrary, Christ is spoken of. No rule of interpretation can allow us to embrace any other sense.

Whatever may be said of this phrase in other places and in other letters by this apostle, there is a special reason for its use here. In writing this letter to the Hebrews, our apostle accommodates himself to the expressions that were then used by the Hebrews whenever they agreed with the truth, rectifying them when they were mistaken. At that time, there was nothing more common among the Hebrews than to speak of the second person of the Trinity by the name **the word of God.**

The word is introduced here to provide an admonition. For its purpose is to bring a reverence or fear in people's minds as they live under the profession of the Gospel. They are reminded that disobedience will lead to punishment. Now the Lord Christ is particularly called "the Word of God" with reference to the judgment he exercises over his church and his Gospel (Revelation 19:13). Having this administration in mind, it gives special weight to his name here, **the word of God**, as he will destroy all who oppose or forsake the Gospel.

No one does, or can, deny that the person of the Son, or of the Father, is intended in verse 13. We will show later that it refers directly to the Son, but all agree that God is intended. Nor can the expressions **everything is uncovered** and **laid bare before his eyes** be applied to anyone other than God. The last words of this verse, **to whom we must give account,** show that it is the Son who is especially intended.

The *attributes* ascribed to **the word** in verse 12 all correctly apply to the person of Christ and cannot firstly and directly be ascribed to the Gospel. This is manifested in the exposition of the following individual words.

Living. "Living" is applied to God himself, as expressing a characteristic of his nature (Matthew 16:16; 1 Timothy 4:10; Hebrews 3:12). It is also especially ascribed to Christ the mediator (Revelation 1:18). Christ is also "the living one." As "the living one," he "has life in himself" (John 5:26). As "the living one" he is "the author of life" (Acts 3:15). He can convey life on all, and all our concerns about earthly life and eternal life belong to him (see John 1:4). It is clear how relevant mentioning **living** here is to the apostle's purpose. The apostle reminds the Hebrews that the Person with whom they relate to in this matter is "the living one." In a similar way he had previously exhorted them to beware of turning "away from the living God" (3:12). Later on, he warns them that "it is a dreadful thing to fall into the hands of the living God" (10:31). So here, to dissuade them from the one and to ensure that they had reverence for the other, he reminds them that the Word of God, whom they relate to in a special way, is **living.**

This word cannot correctly be ascribed to the word of the Gospel. It is, indeed, the instrumental means of quickening the souls of men with spiritual life, or it is the instrument that the Lord Christ uses for that purpose. But, in itself, it is not absolutely **living.** It does not have life in itself, nor in its power. But Christ has this. For "in him was life, and that life was the light of men" (John 1:4). This characteristic of Christ gives us two motives for obeying him. On the one hand, Christ is able to support us and reward us forever; on the other hand, he will avenge all disobedience. One will not go unrewarded, while the other will not be unavenged. For he is "the living one" whom we have to deal with in these things.

Active. This word is often translated "powerful," meaning power for work, as in the act of life. These things, **living and active,** relate to each other. This power signifies actual power in action or exerted, effective in actual operation. Having already assigned life to the Word of God, that is, the principle of all power, life in himself, as being "the living one," our apostle now adds that he exerts that power of life in actual operation, and that it is **active** when, where, and how he pleases.

I agree that **active** is a common word, meaning the efficacy of anything in operation according to its principle of power. But our apostle also uses it frequently to express the almighty, effectual, operating power of God in and about spiritual things (1 Corinthians 12:6, 11; Galatians 2:8; 3:5; Ephesians 1:11, 19; Philippians 2:13; Colossians 2:12; 1 Thessalonians 2:13). This had to be added to the characteristic of **living** to show that the Lord Christ, the Word of God, would use his power in dealing with people who profess Christian faith according to how they live. The apostle tells the Hebrews that Christ's power is not idle or useless, but is continually exercising itself us in the necessary way.

I also acknowledge that there is an energy, an operative power, in the Word of God as it is written or preached. But this is only as a consequence of being his word who is "the living one," or "as it is indeed the word of the living God."

Sharper. One of the characteristics of the Word in connection with Christ's power is that it is **sharper than any double-edged sword.** **Sharper** means to "cut" or "divide."

Double-edged. This word means "cutting in every way," or "double-edged or mouthed." As a Hebraism, it means "the mouth of the sword." The metaphor comes from wild beasts, which mankind first feared, that devour with their mouths. When the sword was used to kill, its edge was called its "mouth." So, "double-mouthed" meant cutting each way, which left nothing uncut. Christ, in the exercise of his power, is said to be **sharper than any double-edged sword.** God often depicts himself and his power with an allusion to things we feel, to help us in our understanding. So he is said to be "a consuming fire," and "like a lion." Both such things were very frightening for men. A "sword" is often linked to the Lord Christ (Isaiah 49:2). "Out of his mouth came a sharp double-edged sword" (Revelation 1:16). It is principally assigned to him concerning his power in using his word. This is called "the sword of the Spirit" (Ephesians 6:17); the "sword upon your side" (Psalm 45:3), which he held in readiness when he went to subdue people's souls to himself.

But it is Christ himself who makes the word **active** and sharp. The main efficiency is in himself, acting in and with it. So what is meant in this verse is the spiritual, almighty, penetrating efficacy of the Lord Christ as he deals with people's souls and consciences by his Word and Spirit. The sword is used in two senses. In the natural sense, it cuts through or pierces all opposition and all armor. In the moral sense, it executes judgments and punishments. From this sense the sword is taken to mean the right and authority to punish, and often for the punishment itself. "For he is God's servant to do you good. But if you do wrong, be afraid, for he does not bear the sword for nothing. He is God's servant, an agent of wrath to bring punishment on the wrongdoer" (Romans 13:4). Here is an allusion to the sword in both senses. The Lord Christ, through his Word and Spirit, pierces into people's souls (as we shall see in the next clause) despite all the defense of pride, obstinacy, and unbelief that they wrap themselves in. This is taking the sense of the sword in its natural way. But Christ also executes judgment on wicked people, hypocrites, and apostates. "He will strike the earth with the rod of his mouth; with the breath of his lips he will slay the wicked" (Isaiah 11:4). He cuts off the life of their earthly hopes, false peace, worldly security, and whatever else they trust in, by the **double-edged sword** that comes out of his mouth.

This power of the Word is described by its effects. **It penetrates even to dividing soul and spirit, joints and marrow; it judges the thoughts and attitudes of the heart.** The act itself that is meant is seen in the word **penetrates.** The object of this action is described by two words being linked together: **soul and spirit,** and, **joints and marrow.**

It penetrates even to dividing. This sword **penetrates** or "pierces," since it is so sharp. It is used to show Christ's power, as a sword piercing into the soul. It goes into the inner recesses, the secret rooms of the mind and heart.

Soul and spirit. The aim of this sword is to penetrate even to dividing the **soul and spirit.** Some think that **soul** refers to the natural and unregenerate part of the soul, and **spirit** to the renewed and regenerate part of a person. There are some grounds for making this distinction. The natural person is the "man without the Spirit" (1 Corinthians 2:14). The "body" is opposed to the "spirit." The spiritual part of a person is often called the "spirit": "the Spirit gives birth to spirit" (John 3:6). The regenerate person is called "the spiritual man" (1 Corinthians 2:15). According to this interpretation, these words mean that the Word of God, the Lord Christ, through his Word and Spirit, penetrate into the state of the soul to show who or what is regenerate among us or in us, and who or what is not. These things are often hidden from human view. But the Lord Christ **penetrates even to dividing soul and spirit.**

Other commentators think that although the apostle does make a distinction between **soul and spirit,** the distinction he makes means that the **soul** refers to the affections and desires; and the **spirit** refers to the mind or understanding. They think that it is most probable that the apostle means this here. For by showing the penetrating power of the Word of God with reference to people's souls, he shows the soul in its constituent parts, or faculties; namely, the mind that leads, conducts, and guides it.

Joints and marrow. This meaning is confirmed from the words **joints**

and marrow, where the same thing is asserted using a different illustration. What in the soul answers the **joints and marrow** in the body is what is intended here, by way of allusion. **Joints and marrow** in themselves are sensual and bodily things that have no concern in this matter; but in the body they are important for two reasons.

They are important, first, because of their use. They are the ligaments for the whole body, the principal means of communication for the parts of the body to the head. This is used to illustrate spiritual truths: "From him the whole body, joined and held together by every supporting ligament, grows and builds itself up in love, as each part does its work" (Ephesians 4:16). If the joints are dislocated, the whole body breaks down.

Joints and marrow are important, secondly, because they are hidden and secret. They are invisible to human sight, and a sharp instrument or sword is needed to penetrate into them and so divide them, by which action natural life is destroyed. The apostle uses this to illustrate our souls. The most useful and secret parts of our souls are pierced and divided by Christ's power. If this is done in judgment, spiritual death follows.

It judges the thoughts and attitudes of the heart. The apostle confirms his illustration with these last words of this verse. The apostle describes the effects of the Word of God. Christ **judges the thoughts and attitudes of the heart.** This highlights Christ's absolute power and ability to judge people's crooked ways, which includes both their outward actions and their inner thoughts. This expression, **judges the thoughts and attitudes of the heart,** is similar to the assertion that God "knows and searches the hearts of men." This is one of God's special characteristics (1 Samuel 16:7; Psalm 7:9; Jeremiah 17:10). It is a characteristic that is especially ascribed to the Lord Christ (John 2:24-25; 21:17; Revelation 2:23). This is particularly well expressed in Peter's confession, "Lord, you know all things; you know that I love you" (John 21:17). That is, "By virtue of your omniscience, through which you know everything, you know my heart and the love it has for you."

Judges. This word refers to someone who can make an accurate inspection, judge the situation, and then give sentence in the matter.

Heart. The **heart** includes the whole soul and all its faculties, making up one rational principle. It includes the **soul and spirit.**

Thoughts. In this verse the **heart** has two things ascribed to it: **thoughts and attitudes. Thoughts** are whatever is inwardly conceived in the mind: "The LORD saw how great man's wickedness on the earth had become, and that every inclination of the thoughts of his heart was only evil all the time" (Genesis 6:5). Here the thoughts are suggested by the inclinations of the heart.

Attitudes. These are "designs" or "purposes," inwardly framed in the understanding. Sometimes this word means the moral principles of the mind, by which it is guided in its actions. Here it denotes the principles that guide people's intentions.

The apostle is teaching here the intimate and absolute acquaintance that the Word of God has with the inner purposes, designs, resolutions, and decisions of the mind of professing Christians. He also stresses the unerring judgment that Christ will make on them through his penetrating power.

13. This verse confirms what has just been taught. The apostle has just declared how the Word of God penetrates people's hearts, minds, and souls, to discern and judge them. To ensure that his readers would not doubt this, the apostle confirms this by showing the basis of his assertion, which is the natural omniscience of the Word of God: "It cannot be otherwise than as I have declared, because the person we have to give account to, the 'Word of God,' sees and knows everything."

In all creation. That is, every person and every created thing, including angels, men, devils, persecutors, every sort of person. Nothing about them, their inner thoughts, affections, temptations, or secret inclinations, are hidden from God. This confirms and continues the previous attributes of the Word of God.

Hidden. This is the opposite of "to appear," "to shine forth." This word stands in contrast to what is perspicuous and eminently manifest. So it is **hidden,** "obscure," and not open to view. It is more than being out of sight (see Luke 24:31). It is deliberately hidden and obscure.

From God's sight. Every creature is continually under his view.

Everything is uncovered and laid bare. This may be an allusion to a wrestling bout in which the naked men fought until one was thrown on his back and had his neck and face held and exposed for all to see. Or this may be an allusion to animals that had been killed, which were then skinned and hung up by their necks, so that everyone could see them. Or the illustration here is more probably to sacrificial animals. The carcasses were, first of all, flayed by the priests. In this way the carcass of the beast was **uncovered** and laid open to everyone to view. Then all its entrails were opened up, from the neck down to the stomach, before the body was cut up into pieces. So every part of it was exposed to view. The apostle is emphasizing that **everything,** whatever it may be, including the hearts of people professing the Christian faith, is **uncovered and laid bare** before him.

The eyes of him. The apostle continues his previous allusion. He has ascribed everything to the omniscience of the Word, and now he mentions his eyes which view what is **uncovered and laid bare** in front of him. Both expressions are metaphorical, and both emphasize Christ's omniscience.

To whom we must give account. This is in line with the apostle's teaching in these two verses. He has supplied evidence of the efficacy and omniscience of the Word of God, who judges everything and discerns everything. Now he brings this message home by reminding the Hebrews that they must give a final account to him who is intimately acquainted with who they are and what they do in the world.

Verses 14-16

As this chapter ends the apostle summarizes his previous teaching and arguments. He particularly insists that they should put into practice those things that they profess to believe. He focuses on two. One is more general—that they should **hold firmly to the faith** (verse 14). This is the third time the apostle has ordered this (see 3:6, 14). The second thing the apostle insists on is to go to the Lord Jesus Christ, our **high priest,** for the necessary assistance in this matter (verses 15-16). For without special grace we will not be able to carry out our duty.

With this double duty the apostle proposes a double encouragement. And various motives, reasons, and directions are included in this. The first encouragement is made up of several things that all help us to persevere to the end (verse 14). The second encouragement assures us of the ground on which we stand (verse 15) and also of the helpfulness of the commands we are exhorted to obey (verse 16).

Moreover, the apostle here moves on from his general discourse to the main purpose of his letter. This would destroy the life and soul of Judaism. He had declared that Jesus Christ was "the apostle and high priest we confess" (3:1). The apostle declares that Christ was the apostle, legate, and ambassador of God, to reveal and declare his will to the church. Because this was Moses' office with respect to the church of the Jews in the giving of the law, the apostle compares them with each other. This was necessary because the Hebrews almost worshiped Moses. Through all these arguments the apostle declared that the Lord Christ was "the apostle . . . whom we confess." Then he moved on to illustrate how Christ was their "high priest." This was the principal thing he emphasized in his teaching throughout the letter. He pursues this theme until the end of chapter 10. He explains the nature of Christ's priesthood, how excellent it was, and how superior it was to Aaron's. He details the nature of the sacrifice he offered, its purpose, its use, and its efficacy. Often he demonstrates how the priesthood, sacrifices, and laws of old are types of Christ's priesthood. This ocean of spiritual truth and heavenly mysteries we are now launching into.

14. Therefore, since we have a great high priest who has gone through the heavens, Jesus the Son of God, let us hold firmly to the

faith we profess. The **high priest** is the center of attention in this verse. He is described in two ways. First, his quality and condition are shown, **who has gone through the heavens.** Second, he is called by a special name, **Jesus the Son of God.** We are in need of the high priest's assistance. And we have a high priest who is able to help us. We have a high priest, as the people of old had one, but ours has **gone through the heavens, Jesus the Son of God.**

A high priest. This refers to Aaron, the most eminent of all high priests. In the Old Testament he is called "the great priest." This phrase was used to denote those who were the main heads, rulers, or leaders of any of the twenty-four orders that the priests were split up into for temple service (1 Chronicles 24). In the Gospel they are frequently called "chief priests" (Matthew 2:4; 16:21, 20:18, 21:15). We correctly call them "chief priests" to distinguish them from the "high priest," who was set over them all, the special successor of Aaron.

Who has gone through the heavens. The **heavens** are understood in two ways. First, and most frequently, **the heavens** denote the place of God's glorious residence, the holy habitation of God, the resting place of blessed souls and palace of the great King, where his throne is, and where thousands of his holy ones stand before him, serving him. This heaven the Lord Christ did not pass through, but into, when he "was taken up into glory" (1 Timothy 3:16). There he sits, on the right hand of the majesty on high; and "he must remain in heaven until the time comes for God to restore everything, as he promised long ago through his holy prophets" (Acts 3:21).

Secondly, **heavens** are taken to mean the air, as in the phrase "birds of heaven." That is, the birds that "fly above the earth" (Genesis 1:20). **Heavens** also stands for the ethereal regions, the sun, the moon, the stars, which are "lights in the expanse of the sky" (Genesis 1:15). These are the **heavens** that "declare the glory of God," and "the skies" that "proclaim the work of his hands" (Psalm 19:1). These are the **heavens** intended here. Our apostle says that **we have a great high priest who has gone through the heavens** and is exalted above them. When Christ was taken up into glory (Acts 1:9-10) the disciples looked up into these heavens. Christ passed through them and ascended above them into what is called "the third heaven," or the "heaven of heavens," where is is blessed residence.

Now that we have understood the meaning of these words, we ask what the apostle's purpose is in using them. This becomes clear from considering what the apostle is alluding to. He makes special reference to the high priest. He explains what was typically represented in and by him to the church of old. Everyone knew he was the principal officer of the church for the things immediately pertaining to the worship of God. The chief or most important part of his duty was to discharge his office. This consisted in his annual entry into the Most Holy Place, on the day of expiation, with the necessary services. This is described in detail in Leviticus 16.

Three things were very important. First, he went *out of the sight of the people*, including all the ministering priests. The people were outside in the courtyard. The priests who ministered in the tabernacle, when the high priest opened the veil to enter the holy place, left the tabernacle, so that they were unable to look into where he was going. "No one is to be in the Tent of Meeting from the time Aaron goes in to make atonement in the Most Holy Place until he comes out, having made atonement for himself, his household and the whole community of Israel" (Leviticus 16:17).

Second, the high priest had to enter into the Most Holy Place by *passing through the second curtain* of the Tent of Meeting. This received him and hid him by closing the curtain behind him so no one could see him. Third, the place the high priest went to had *special pledges* of the presence of God's covenant. "The LORD said to Moses: 'Tell your brother Aaron not to come whenever he chooses into the Most Holy Place behind the curtain in front of the atonement cover on the ark, or else he will die, because I appear in the cloud over the atonement cover'" (Leviticus 16:2). Our apostle proceeds to explain how all these things were really and gloriously accomplished in and by our high priest.

For first, Christ had a holy place to pass into. He entered into the holy place not made with hands, even "heaven itself, now to appear for us in God's presence" (9:24). This is the heaven of heavens, the place of the glorious residence of God's majesty. Second, Christ passed through these heavens, which the apostle compares with the second curtain in the temple, because they are a veil between us and the holy sanctuary he entered into. Hence, when in his great trial and testimony he miraculously enabled Stephen to see into the heavenly place, where he is in glory on the right hand of God, these heavens were opened (Acts 7:55-56). The curtains were drawn apart so that he might see the glory behind them. Third, these heavens took him and hid him from everyone's sight (Acts 1:9-10). Thus, in answer to the type of old, he passed through the curtain of these heavens into the glorious presence of God, to appear there as our intercessor.

Jesus the Son of God. This "Son" is especially *that* **Son of God;** that is, the only-begotten Son of the Father. Two things about the person of our high priest are mentioned here. First, we are given his name; second, we are told his relationship to God.

First, there is his name; that is, **Jesus.** This name was given to him to indicate what work he had to do. The angel said, "you are to give him the name Jesus, because he will save his people from their sins" (Matthew 1:21). So our apostle calls him "Jesus, who rescues us" (1 Thessalonians 1:10), that is, "Jesus the deliverer." Our high priest is our Savior. He was also born of a virgin. "The virgin will be with child and will give birth to a son, and they will call him Immanuel" (Matthew 1:23). This merciful high priest took part in our human nature.

Second, our apostle describes him as **Son of God,** that is, by his relationship to God. He is the **Son of God,** the eternal Son of God. His divine nature is included in this name. For in his one person, comprising human and divine nature, he is our high priest, God and man in one. The following words encourage us to carry out our duty.

Let us hold firmly to the faith we profess. We need to ask what **profess** means, and what is meant by **let us hold firmly.**

The faith we profess. Christ the Lord is called "the apostle and high priest whom we confess" (3:1). What we **profess** is our "confession of the Gospel of Christ" (2 Corinthians 9:13). In this we submit our souls by acknowledging the power and authority of Jesus Christ in the Gospel. This contains both our *secret subjection* to the Gospel and our *solemn declaration* of it. The former is "the pledge of a good conscience toward God" (1 Peter 3:21), by virtue of the resurrection of Jesus Christ "who has gone into heaven and is at God's right hand—with angels, authorities and powers in submission to him." This has two parts: faith in Christ; and obeying him, "the obedience that comes from faith" (Romans 1:5). *Faith* is the root, and obedience the fruit of our profession. And that faith that constitutes evangelical profession focuses on Christ, the Son of God, the mediator of the covenant, the king, priest, and prophet of his church. This Christ specifically commands: "Trust in God; trust also in me" (John 14:1; see also John 3:18, 36; 7:38). This, I say, makes our profession formally evangelical, distinguishing it from that of believers under the old testament. Their faith was directly in God as one (see Deuteronomy 6:4), and consequently in the Messiah, as promised. Ours is directly in Christ also (see John 17:3) and in the Father through him (see 1 Peter 1:21).

To faith is added *obedience,* which is indeed inseparable from it. Here is a full description of it: "but now that you have been set free from sin and have become slaves of God, the benefit you reap leads to holiness, and the result is eternal life" (Romans 6:22). This obedience is internal and absolutely spiritual, or the constant acting of all the graces of the Spirit of God, for purification and holiness (Acts 15:9; 2 Corinthians 7:1; 1 Thessalonians 5:23). This belongs to our profession of faith, and this we must hold on to firmly. Obedience is also external, as it diligently puts into practice all that the Gospel commands. These include *moral* duties of holy behavior (Philippians 1:27; Titus 2:10-13). Failure here can lead to the complete overthrow of our profession (Philippians 3:17-18; 2 Timothy 2:19; Titus 1:16). External obedience also includes observing institutional duties, such as Gospel worship (Matthew 28:20). It is this aspect of our profession that the apostle particularly emphasizes in his letter.

To make sure that we are **holding firmly to the faith we profess** we must ensure that we subject ourselves to the Gospel in these things. We do this by actions and by words.

Our correct Christian behavior is constantly commanded by Christ and particularly refers to Gospel worship (Matthew 28:20; John 14:15; 15:14). We should carry out this duty with prudence. We should not needlessly provoke the world because of our misguided zeal (Matthew 10:16; 1 Corinthians 10:32; 2 Corinthians 6:3). Nor should we put ourselves into danger needlessly (Matthew 10:23). We should behave consistently and confidently, so that we are not terrified by any troubles or persecutions that come on us on account of the Gospel (Philippians 1:28; 1 Peter 3:14). We should never stop meeting for worship (Hebrews 10:25).

Our Christian profession should be clear from our words. "It is with your mouth that you confess and are saved" (Romans 10:10). This relates to all times in general: "Always be prepared to give an answer to everyone who asks you to give the reason for the hope that you have" (1 Peter 3:15). We are on all occasions to declare whose servants we are, and whom we own as our Lord and Master. This also relates to specific situations. First, it relates to temptation. People may praise us or despise us so that we do not witness to the Gospel as we should. This happened to Peter in the worst possible way (see Matthew 26:70). Second, it relates to persecution. If we do not witness to our Christian faith under persecution, we will lose it. The oral, open confession of the Lord Christ, in and under persecution, is the touchstone of all Christian profession: "Whoever acknowledges me before men, I will also acknowledge him before my Father in heaven. But whoever disowns me before men, I will disown him before my Father in heaven" (Matthew 10:32-33; see also 1 Corinthians 3:13.)

Let us hold firmly. The root of this word means to hold a thing "strongly," "firmly," "with all our strength," by all lawful means, with resolution (see 3:11; Revelation 2:25). **Hold firmly,** that is, with all your might, as you would hold on to your crown if someone attempted to deprive you of it. This word is used about the Pharisees concerning their traditions. They adhered to them so firmly and resolutely that nothing could make them change their minds about them. "Holding to the traditions of the elders" (Mark 7:3) means that they held tenaciously to these traditions (see also Revelation 2:15). So this means that we should **hold firmly** against all opposition and take care that we do not lose our profession after we have started it.

So this verse has a duty to be carried out, and it provides us with a motive for doing it. The duty is clear from the words, **let us hold firmly to the faith we profess.** We are encouraged to do this with the words, **since we have a great high priest who has gone through the heavens, Jesus the Son of God.** This is expanded in verse 15, where Christ's qualifications are declared, and we are exhorted to seek Christ's assistance in this matter in verse 16.

It might be thought that this description of our high priest included a discouragement in it about us. For if Christ is himself so great and glorious, if he is exalted beyond the heavens, how can we understand that he is concerned about us in our weak, frail, and sinful condition? How can we be bold or confident in approaching him for help? For the apostle Peter, when he realized that he was witnessing a miracle, thought that he was unfit to be in Christ's presence. So Peter cried out to Christ, when he was on earth, "Go away from me, Lord; I am a sinful man" (Luke 5:8). How much more should we be frightened to approach Christ now that he is in glory? How can we imagine that we should receive compassion since we are such sinful worms? "Yes," the apostle says, "we may, because of Christ's office, 'approach the throne of grace boldly.'" The reason for this is given in verse 15, along with an answer to an objection and with a new kind of encouragement.

15. For we do not have a high priest who is unable to sympathize with our weakness, but we have one who has been tempted in every way, just as we are—yet was without sin. This verse has a further description of our high priest. We are encouraged to put our trust in Christ because of his greatness and his power, declares verse 14, for he has "gone through the heavens." This verse gives us a reason for trusting Christ because of his goodness and love.

For. This is not so much a connecting word as an introduction to an additional reason for trusting Christ, which the apostle now gives. He had exhorted them to hold firmly to the faith they professed (verse 14) on account of their high priest. In verse 16 he tells them to go to Christ for the necessary grace and strength to carry this out. In verse 15 the apostle gives the qualifications of the high priest that should encourage us to go to Christ.

For we do not have a high priest. This is a common kind of expression. A double negative produces a strong affirmation. It is so with our high priest, even the opposite of what is thus denied. He is a person who can be moved.

But we have one. "We also," says the apostle, "have a high priest." In his person, office, and usefulness to the church, he exceeds the high priest under the law that the apostle has already described. The apostle points out that the people of God are not left without a high priest. He is also the life and glory of their profession, worship, and obedience.

Our apostle treats the Gentiles differently from the Jews in this matter. When talking to the Gentiles he reminds them of their miserable condition before they were called to the knowledge of Christ by the Gospel, as in Ephesians 2:11-13. But when talking to the Jews, he assures them that they are not at any disadvantage, since all their previous privileges are increased and heightened beyond imagination. God has appointed Christ and given him to us, and he is ours. All the purposes of his office are for our benefit, and we are to take advantage of them in every possible spiritual way. The church has never lost any of the privileges it has been given through any of the changes that God has made to his ordinances for worship. Rather, it kept what it previously had and these ordinances were completed in Jesus Christ. God instituted sacrifices so they could have fellowship with him. This was a privilege for those who believed. Today, we have not lost the sacrifice or the high priest, as we have them in an even superior way. Under the old covenant the church was granted special favor and spiritual privilege. It would be derogatory to Christ's glory and to the Gospel's honor to suppose that the church has been deprived of these privileges. For God has ordained better things for us, and that without us, they should not be made perfect. So the apostle does not say, "There is a high priest," but, **we have** "a high priest."

Unable to sympathize. "That cannot be touched with a feeling," "who cannot be affected with a sense," "who cannot suffer with."

Sympathize. This word is translated in different ways: "To suffer," "to suffer with," "to have compassion," "to be touched with a feeling," "to be affected with a sense," "to condole" or "bewail." The word is used once more in this letter but nowhere else in the New Testament. It comes in chapter 10, verse 34: "You sympathized with those in prison."

This word **sympathize** includes a concern in the troubles, sufferings, or evils of others, so that the two people are united. Sometimes part of the body is affected with a disease. Then another part of the body may be affected, although that part is not actually infected by the disease. That part of the body is not really sick, because it does not have the disease. But it may be said to **sympathize**; that is, it is not free from the infection. This kind of suffering comes about through the harmony between two individuals.

This word also includes the idea of an ability to relieve those who are suffering. So David, in the deep feeling he had about Absalom's death, wished that he had died for him, or relieved him from suffering by dying in his place. Where this is not the case, there is no sympathy. In some circumstances we may not be able to relieve the situation. In some cases it may not be possible or appropriate for us to give the succor and help that our compassion urges on us. But if there is no inclination to do this, there is no sympathy.

This word also contains a collection of affections. In Arabic the word is thus translated, "who can mourn with us." So the Hebrew used in Psalms 69, verse 20 may be translated, "I looked for any to be grieved with me"; "to be affected with sorrow on my behalf"; "to take pity"; "to lament with me" through movement of the affections, as the word signifies. This belongs to this sympathy, to have our emotions moved by other people's sufferings.

And these things are here ascribed to our high priest because of his union with us; so we become members of his body, one with him. He is deeply concerned about all our infirmities, sorrows, and sufferings. This comes with an inclination to relieve us, according to the nature of the covenant. During our trials he has a real movement of affection in his holy nature, which he received or took on himself for that very purpose (see 2:16-18).

In this sense of the word, to sympathize, "to be affected with a sense," ascribes this ability in a moral and natural sense to our Lord Christ, our high priest, as he is man, in contrast to just being God, whose nature is incapable of compassion in this sense. There are, indeed, in the Scripture assignations of these kinds of affections to God: "In all their distress he too was distressed" (Isaiah 63:9). God was afflicted by their afflictions. This is as anthropomorphic expression, where things are assigned to God after the likeness of men. The real purpose of such ascriptions is not merely to assist our weakness and help our understanding of the things themselves, but to show what God does and will do in the human nature that he has assumed. This is the foundation of his dealing with us in Scripture. Thus it is said that he is able to be affected with a sense of our infirmities, because in his human nature he is capable of such affections and, as he is our high priest, is graciously inclined to act according to them.

With our weaknesses. "Our infirmities." This word is used, both in the Scripture and by all Greek authors, for any debility, weakness, or infirmity of body or mind. Frequently bodily diseases are expressed by it, "to be sick," "to be diseased," concerning the weakness or illness that is being introduced (see Matthew 10:8, 25:43; Luke 4:40; John 5:3, 5.) At other times this word means the weakness of mind or spirit that is unable, or scarcely able, to bear the difficulties or troubles that are so pressing. "I came to you in weakness and fear, and with much trembling" (1 Corinthians 2:3). Sometimes this word conveys weakness in judgment: "One man's faith allows him to eat everything, but another man, whose faith is weak, eats only vegetables" (Romans 14:2). On other occasions, this word expresses spiritual weakness, weakness about life, grace, and power: "You see, at just the right time, when we were still powerless, Christ died for the ungodly" (Romans 5:6); "the Spirit helps us in our weakness. We do not know what we ought to pray for" (Romans 8:26). Thus this work is used to express every kind of weakness that may happen to us, including difficulties, troubles, and perplexities. In this verse it is mentioned in a general sense, without reference to a particular infirmity; so it may be used to refer to any kind of weakness or pressure we are under. However, in the second half of this verse the reason that Christ, our high priest, can be touched with a sense of our infirmities is linked to his being tempted. So it is clear that the **weaknesses** that are especially meant here are those related to afflictions and temptations, which being persecuted for the Gospel brings. Our high priest is intimately involved in our infirmities and weaknesses, and in wrestling with them and removing them and, consequently, in our troubles, sorrows, suffering, and danger. Since we are members of his mystical body, we are united with him, and he is concerned with our troubles. From his own heart and affections he gives us help and relief as is necessary. He is inwardly moved during our sufferings and trials with a sense of empathy.

The following words give a special reason for our merciful high priest's ability to **sympathize with our weaknesses.** For he was **tempted in every way, just as we are—yet was without sin.** The basis for this argument rests on the fact that Christ **has been tempted,** and that he was tempted **in every way,** and that he was tempted **just as we are,** but with the limitation that he **yet was without sin.**

But. The particle, **but,** is in contrast to what has just been denied. "He is not like a person who is unaffected, but one who was himself tempted." This clearly shows that was is now introduced is the principal proof of the previous assertion: "It is evident that he can be "affected with a sense of our weaknesses," because he was "tempted.""

Tempted. That is, "tried," "exercised," for the word does not mean more than this in the original. Whatever the moral evil of temptation is, it stems from the depraved intention of the tempter, or from the weakness and sin of the tempted. In itself it is but a trial, which may have a positive or a negative result.

In every way. "In all things"; that is, from all means and instruments of temptation, and in all things with which as a man, or as our high priest, he was concerned.

Just as we are. "In like manner." There is a clear allusion to other people's temptations. This refers to the trials and temptations of those who believe and to the things that press on them as a result of their weakness.

Yet without sin. Sin, in relation to temptation, may be considered in two ways: first, its principle; second, its effect. First, sin is sometimes the principle of temptation. People are tempted by sin into sin, to actual sin by habitual sin, to outward sin by indwelling sin: "each one is tempted when, by his own evil desire, he is dragged away and enticed. Then, after desire has conceived it, it gives birth to sin; and sin, when it is full-grown, gives birth to death" (James 1:14-15). This is the greatest spring and source of temptation in us who are sinners. Second, sin sometimes results from temptation.

It may be asked which of these two relate to our high priest, who was tempted **without sin.** If it is the former, then it means that he was tried and tempted by every means, from all directions, just as we are, except that he did not sin. For he did not sin because sin had no part in him, so that it has no basis on which it could make suggestions to him. Here the apostle is making us observe Christ's purity and holiness, so that we will not imagine that he was liable to any temptations to sin from within, as we find ourselves prone to, and which defile us and make us guilty.

If the latter is intended, then our high priest was never successful in defeating temptation. We are tried and tempted by Satan, and the world, and by our own evil desires. The purpose of these temptations is to make us sin. In this state sin is often the result, and temptation has its effect in us and on us. Indeed, when any temptation is strong and pressing, we are nearly always affected by it and sin. It is not like this at all with our high priest. Whatever temptation he was exposed to, as he was by all kinds that come from outside, none of them affected him in the least degree. He was still in all things absolutely **without sin.** He was not tempted by sin, such was the holiness of his nature. When he was tempted it never resulted in sin, such was the perfection of his obedience.

16. The last verse of this chapter contains an inference from the previous two verses, which is clear from the way in which these words are woven together with the previous ones. The exhortation is insisted on that we should "hold firmly to the faith we profess" (verse 14). The motive for this is derived from Christ's priesthood. Now verse 16 adds a further word of encouragement, aimed at the same end. It is taken for granted that we will meet many difficulties, much opposition, and numerous temptations as we carry out this command. By ourselves we are not capable of succeeding in this conflict. So we are encouraged to seek help against all this from everything that has been said about the Son of God's priesthood.

Let us then approach the throne of grace with confidence, so that we may receive mercy and find grace to help us in our time of need.

Then. "Therefore." "Seeing we have a high priest, and one who has been described in such a way." This is aimed to encourage, guide, and influence us to carry out the command in all its aspects. Without this help we have no strength or ability to be successful in this sphere.

Let us approach. "Let us come." But this word means more than just "let us come." It means "let us draw near." "Let us approach in a sacred manner," or, "let us draw near for a sacred purpose." It is translated this way, "let us draw near," in 10:22. It is used in connection with coming to God in worship in 7:25, and in 10:1, "those who draw near to worship"; and in 11:6. So this word especially signifies the solemn approach made to God in order to worship him. It also means "to offer sacrifices and offerings." So this word may refer either to the access the people of old had to the altar in the temple when they brought their sacrifices, or to the priests' approach to this holy place, as the following words specifically declare.

The apostle has asserted that the Lord Jesus Christ, the Son of God, is our high priest. The high priest among the Jews was a type of Christ. "**Let us approach,** in a holy, sacred way, as he has instructed"; that is, with prayers and supplications.

With confidence. Our apostle uses this phrase in connection with worshiping God both here and in 10:19: "Therefore, brothers, since we have confidence to enter the Most Holy Place . . ." This is a new aspect in the new covenant which is not found in the old covenant. Elsewhere, the apostle refers to this as "liberty": "Where the Spirit of the Lord is, there is freedom" (2 Corinthians 3:17). This is a freedom that the Holy Spirit gives to believers under the new covenant, which was not shared by people who were still in slavery to the letter of the old covenant. He refers to "unveiled faces" (2 Corinthians 3:18). This contrasts with the veils that covered the face of the Jews and that fills them with darkness and fear to this day. The "liberty" of "unveiled faces" denotes boldness and a freedom from fear, shame, and discouragement.

Therefore, there are two things that the apostle intends to remove and to have us delivered from as we draw near to the throne of grace with our prayers and supplications, on account of the intervention of our high priest. The first is to remove our slavery to fear and the second is to remove our belief that we are not accepted.

First, a spirit of slavery to fear was on the people under the old testament as they worshiped God. The apostle often ascribes this to them but not to us: "For you did not receive a spirit that makes you a slave again to fear, but you received the Spirit of sonship. And by him we cry, 'Abba, Father'" (Romans 8:14); "Therefore, since we have such a hope, we are very bold. We are not like Moses, who would put a veil over his face to keep the Israelites from gazing at it while the radiance was fading away. But their minds were made dull, for to this day the same veil remains when the old covenant is read. It has not been removed, because only in Christ is it taken away. Even to this day when Moses is read, a veil covers their hearts. But whenever anyone turns to the Lord, the veil is taken away. Now the Lord is the Spirit, and where the Spirit of the Lord is, there is freedom. And we, who with unveiled faces all reflect the Lord's glory, are being transformed into his likeness with ever-increasing glory, which comes from the Lord, who is the Spirit" (2 Corinthians 3:12-18).

When God gave the law and the ordinances about worship he surrounded himself with fire to instill awe in the minds of the people. This made them stand far away, wishing that God would not come close to them. They would not go close to God, but everything was done at a distance. "When the people saw the thunder and lightning and heard the trumpet and saw the mountain in smoke, they trembled with fear. They stayed at a distance and said to Moses, 'Speak to us yourself and we will listen. But do not have God speak to us or we will die'" (Exodus 20:18-19). This diffidence in approaching God closes the heart, cramps the spirit, and takes away the freedom of treating God as a father. All this is now removed by Christ (see Galatians 4:4-6). Christ was "born under the law" to deliver us from its slavery. Christ's Spirit adopts us as God's children, so we have the liberty, boldness, to cry in a childlike way, "Abba, Father," as we act in faith and love.

Second, we must remove the thought that we are not accepted. This stems from a sense of our own unworthiness in God's presence. A fear and dread of God's greatness comes to people who live under the law. When they reflect on their own vileness they begin to doubt and become fearful and despondent. They feel that there is no hope for them. The apostle wants this to be removed on account of Christ's high priesthood. How we are instructed to approach God encompasses all this. We are to do this **with confidence.**

This freedom is internal and spiritual, in contrast with the legal diffidence and slavery just described. This **confidence** is our spiritual freedom, accompanied by a holy boldness in our approach to God as we make our requests known to him, stating our needs and desires freely and with confidence.

Our confident approach includes the conviction that we will be accepted. "In him [Christ] and through faith in him we may approach God with freedom and confidence" (Ephesians 3:12).

 The throne of grace. We **approach the throne of grace with confidence.** The correct and immediate object of our approach is and must be a person. Who that is, is not stated here, but we know from this expression who is intended. A throne is a seat of majesty and is ascribed to God and men. God is often referred to as the "great king" over all. Isaiah saw him "seated on a throne, high and exalted" (Isaiah 6:1); and Ezekiel saw him "high above on the throne" (Ezekiel 1:26). "Righteousness and justice" are said to be "the foundation of your throne" (Psalm 89:14). In general, heaven is called God's throne (Matthew 5:34), a the place where he principally shows his glory and majesty. But as this is a metaphorical expression, it is not confined to one particular thing. The Hebrews say that God has a double throne, "a throne of judgment" and "a throne of compassion" and tender mercy—that is, a **throne of grace.** A throne, then, is the place where and from where judgment is exercised and mercy administered. So when we come to God in worship for mercy and grace, we say we are coming to his throne.

There may also be an allusion here to the mercy-seat in the tabernacle. It was laid on the ark with a coronet of gold around it, in the shadow of the cherubim. It was like God's throne or seat, as a most solemn representation of his presence among the people. What the apostle refers to here as "approaching the throne of grace with confidence" he describes in 10:19 as having "confidence to enter the Most Holy Place by the blood of Jesus." This is a clear reference to the place where the ark and mercy-seat were placed. The love and grace of God in Christ is represented here.

We next ask which person is specifically on this throne. Some reply, "it is the Lord Christ as our mediator and high priest who is intended: for the previous and following discourse is about him." He is also described here as our merciful, faithful, and caring high priest. These are all encouragements to come to him, which we are told to do with confidence. A throne is specifically applied to him in this letter: "About the Son he says, 'Your throne, O God, will last for ever and ever'" (1:8). He sits on God's throne (Revelation 3:21), and at his throne of grace we may be sure of acceptance.

However, this does not seem to be the particular intention here. For first, a throne, rule, and government are ascribed to the Lord Christ about his kingly rather than his priestly office. While it is true that it is said of him that he should be "a priest on his throne" (Zechariah 6:13), this shows that his kingly power is inseparable from his person. So he will be a priest, even though he is sitting, or, while he sits as a king on his throne.

Second, wherever the Lord Christ is spoken about, as on his throne, exalted in the glory and majesty of his kingdom, it is always in reference to his power and authority over his church, giving laws and rules for it for his worship, or over his enemies for their ruin and destruction.

Third, the context demands another meaning. For the Lord Christ, in his office and intervention on our behalf, is not proposed as the object of our coming, but as the means of it, and a great encouragement to it; "for through him we both have access to the Father by one Spirit" (Ephesians 2:18). Because he has undertaken this for us, appeared before God on our behalf and made atonement, we may come in his name with confidence of acceptance to God's throne (see 7:25; Revelation 4:2-3; 5:6-7). So **the throne of grace** is God, exalted, exercising grace and mercy toward those who through the Lord Jesus believe in him and come to him.

This is a duty we are commanded to do. It has a double result. First, it has a general and immediate result. Second, it has a particular effect. The general result has two parts: **that we may receive mercy,** and **find grace to help.** The particular result is to find help **in our time of need.**

That we may receive mercy. The first thing intended, as part of the goal of this duty we are to carry out, is **that we may receive mercy.** Some translate this as "obtain" mercy, others translate it as "receive" mercy. I see no reason why "receive" mercy is not the correct meaning here. For the apostle seems to indicate that mercy is prepared for us, but that our access to God through Christ with confidence is required if we are to participate in this. And this links up with his words that it is "with confidence," that is, spiritual confidence, that we are to approach the throne of grace to receive that mercy which in and through Christ is prepared for us.

Mercy. This word often means that "mercy" in God from which we receive pardon for our sins—mercy in pardoning. Most commentators expound it in this way here, that we may obtain mercy for our sins, that we may be pardoned. But this interpretation does not seem to support the present purpose of the apostle. For he is not talking about sin and its guilt but about temptations, afflictions, and persecutions. So the **mercy** meant here must be the cause for our deliverance—namely, in its consequences. The Septuagint often translates the word "mercy" as "kindness" rather than pardoning grace. In addition to this, the apostle is not here referring to the initial approach of sinners to God through Christ for mercy and pardon, but about the daily access of believers to him for grace and assistance. To **receive mercy,** therefore, is to be made to participate in the gracious help and support of the kindness of God in Christ, when we are in distress. This springs from the same root as pardoning grace and is therefore called "mercy."

And find grace. "And that we may find grace." That is the next general purpose of our access to the throne of grace. The word "find," or, "obtain," is used in two ways.

First, it is used to mean "to find" or "obtain favor," or favorable acceptance with God. When God is pleased to make us acceptable to himself in Christ, then we find **grace** or "favor" with him. This is the foundation of all the graces given to us. This phrase often occurs in the Old Testament. "Let me find grace in your eyes," or "favor in your sight," that is, "be accepted by you." This corresponds exactly with **find grace,** that is, "to be accepted" (see Genesis 6:8; 18:3; 39:4; Ephesians 1:6). It is the same with the Greek phrase, "who enjoyed God's favor" (Acts 7:46), and, "you have found favor with God" (Luke 1:30). Instead of the word "grace," the Greek is sometimes translated "favor."

This meaning is reverent and matches the analogy of faith; for our free, gracious acceptance with God is the foundation of all that grace and assistance that we participate in.

But, second, the apostle is not referring to the personal acceptance of sinners or believers in or through Christ here, but of that special assistance which, on particular occasions, we receive. When our apostle in his distress asked God for relief, he received this answer: "My grace is sufficient for you, for my power is made perfect in weakness" (2 Corinthian 12:9). The apostle received God's gracious care, as well as the actual, powerful assistance he needed for his temptation.

To help us. The kind of **help** intended here is "succor"; that is, assistance to people who cry for help. "To run to assist someone's cry for help" is the meaning here.

In our time of need. "Seasonable;" that is, help "in its time," its proper time or season. "How good is a timely word" (Proverbs 15:23). Help that matches our need—that is, on God's part who gives it, to the people who receive it, at the time when it is given, for the purpose that it is given—is all help **in our time of need.** This is the kind of help that God in his greatness and wisdom gives. The psalmist refers to this kind of help in the words, "God is our refuge and strength, an ever-present help in trouble" (Psalm 46:1). What is meant here is the grace that is given in answer to our cry to God in Christ for help **in our time of need.**

Hebrews
Chapter 5

This chapter divides into three parts. First, there is a description of the office and duties of a high priest (verses 1-4). Second, this general description is applied to the person and priesthood of Jesus Christ in particular (verses 5-10). Third, there is a reproof of the Hebrews for their backwardness in learning the mysteries of the Gospel (verses 11-14, and continuing into the next chapter).

In the first part, the general description of the high priest is given.

1. His origin is stated: he is "selected from among men."

2. The nature of his office is given: "he is appointed to represent them in matters relating to God."

3. The special purpose of this is stated: "to offer gifts and sacrifices for sins" (verse 1).

4. The qualifications needed to carry out this office are given: he must be one who "is able to deal gently with those who are ignorant and are going astray." Linked to this is the basis of his qualification: "he himself is subject to weakness" (verse 2).

5. The constant duty stemming from his office and personal qualifications for this, in respect of others and himself, is stated: "he has to offer sacrifices for his own sins, as well as for the sins of the people" (verse 3).

6. His call to his office is from God: "No one takes this honor upon himself; he must be called by God"; and his call is exemplified by Aaron's call: "just as Aaron was" (verse 4).

The second part of this chapter is the application of this description to the person of Jesus Christ. It is not exactly like this description in every detail, as if everything had to match up perfectly. This is not the apostle's intention. The description he has given is that of a high priest who was under the law. The apostle's purpose is to show them how much more excellent a priest Christ is than that. So there must be certain differences between them. So in applying this description of a high priest under the law to the person and office of Christ, the apostle aims to show three things.

1. To demonstrate that there was nothing that was essential to a high priest that was not found in the Lord Jesus Christ.

2. All the weaknesses in the former high priests, due to their frail conditions, are absent in Christ.

3. Christ had several advantages over the old high priest.

So the apostle's application of the description of the old high priest does not correspond exactly with Christ's high priesthood.

1. He applies the call of the high priest to Christ: negatively, "Christ . . . did not take upon himself the glory of becoming a high priest" (verse 5); positively, the calling was from God, which he demonstrates with a double testimony from Psalm 2:7 and Psalm 110:4-6.

2. The apostle applies the discharge of the office of the high priest to Christ. He states when it happened: "During the days of Jesus' life on earth"; how he carried this out: "he offered up prayers and petitions with loud cries and tears"; and the general result of this: "he was heard" (verse 7).

3. The apostle anticipates an objection and so states the special preeminence Christ had above all other priests, and the love and humility that accompanied his office, as well as the great benefit that followed: "he learned obedience from what he suffered" (verse 8).

4. The apostle shows the glorious purpose of Christ's priesthood, showing how it was superior to Aaron's (verse 9).

5. The apostle then gives a summary of Christ's call and office (verse 10).

The third division of the chapter has a diversion. It is a reproof of and expostulation with the Hebrews about the things he is writing about. The things he refers to "are hard to explain." This is their fault because they are "slow to learn" (verse 11). This is made worse because of what they were lacking (verses 12-14).

Verses 1-4

1. Every high priest is selected from among men and is appointed to represent them in matters related to God, to offer gifts and sacrifices for sins.

Every high priest. That is, "every chief" or "great priest." Or, as the Syriac says, "prince" or "chief of priests." A high priest is first mentioned in Leviticus 21:10, "The high priest, the one among his brothers who has had the anointing oil poured on his head and who has been ordained to wear the priestly garments." The males of Aaron's family were equal as far as the priesthood was concerned. But there was one who was head of the

116

rest, whose office was not distinct from theirs, but did many special things in carrying out his duties and in preparing for them. These things are enumerated in several places. The whole office was primarily vested in him, the rest of the priests being regarded as his assistants. The whole nature of the type was preserved in him alone. In one place our apostle tells us about these high priests themselves, that through the law they "were many." This means that there were many because they succeeded each other: "Now there were many of those priests, since death prevented them from continuing in office" (7:23). One single high priest would have been enough to have represented Christ's high priesthood, but because they kept on dying there was a succession of them. Similarly, because of their weakness no single man was able to discharge the whole office, so others were added to the high priest for the time being as his assistants; they also were types of Christ as they participated in his work. But because the work was principally centered on the high priest, and because many of the important parts of the duty were given over to him, he alone is singled out as the principal representative of the Lord Christ in this office.

The high priest was a single person—there was only one at a time, as a type of Christ's work.

Is selected from among men. This is one of the things that is attributed to every high priest. He is **selected from among men.** This is the first characteristic of a high priest. Two things are worthy of note here: first, he is **from** men; and, second, he is **selected** from men.

From among men. The high priest has, and must participate in, common human nature with the rest of mankind, or he is not, for many reasons, suited to carry out his work. Divine nature and angelic nature cannot carry out this work. This is what is principally meant here.

Is selected. He is separated from other men. Once he is made a high priest, he no longer holds the same position as other men.

To represent them. He is selected to represent people. The word used means to be "in the stead." "I am the good shepherd. The good shepherd lays down his life for the sheep" (John 10:11); "I lay down my life for the sheep" (John 10:15; see also John 13:38). The high priest stands and acts in the place of others, appears on their behalf, represents them, pleads their cause, and confesses their sins. "He is to lay both hands on the head of the live goat and confess over it all the wickedness and rebellion of the Israelites—all their sins—and put them on the goat's head" (Leviticus 16:21). And "on their behalf," or "for their good, to perform what on their part is with God to be performed," is clearly intended here.

Appointed. The apostle explains himself in this way: "Every high priest is appointed to offer both gifts and sacrifices" (8:3). Two things are indicated by this word **appointed.** First, God's designation and appointment;

second, the actual consecration as specified in the law. This was so in Aaron's case.

First, God commanded that he should be set apart for the office of priesthood. "Have Aaron your brother brought to you from among the Israelites, along with his sons . . . so they may serve me as priests" (Exodus 28:1). This separation was the foundation of his call.

Second, he was actually consecrated to his office by various sacrifices, which are described in Exodus 29. He could not be consecrated without the sacrifice of other things. But the Lord Jesus Christ, being both priest and sacrifice himself, did not need such an ordination. His ordination consisted in divine appointment. This was the difference between the priests who were made high priests by the law, and him who was made high priest by God's word, who is the Son. "For the law appoints as high priests men who are weak; but the oath, which came after the law, appointed the Son, who has been made perfect forever" (7:28).

In matters related to God. These are the things that were to be done with God, or toward God, in his worship, by which God might be appeased, atoned, reconciled, pacified, and have his anger turned away (see 10:17).

To offer gifts and sacrifices for sins. To offer gifts comprises the whole priestly work, from first to last, in bringing, killing, and burning the sacrifice, according to the law (see Leviticus 1—5). If any distinction is to be made between **gifts** and **sacrifices** I think that **gifts** refer to all freewill offerings and **sacrifices** those that the law commands at certain seasons. But I judge that the apostle uses these two words to express all sorts of sacrifices for sin. So the expression **for sins** may refer to **gifts** as well as to **sacrifices**.

2. The apostle expands on two things in the following verses. First, he describes the high priest according to the law. Second, he shows that whatever was useful or excellent in such a high priest was to be found in a better way in Jesus Christ, the only real and proper high priest of the church, and whatever was weak and lacking in a human high priest on account of his weakness and sin was totally absent in Jesus Christ. As Chrysostom commented, "First, he sets out the things that are common to both, then declares where Christ is superior."

He is able to deal gently with those who are ignorant and are going astray, since he himself is subject to weakness. This discourse began with the words "every high priest" in verse 1, and they still apply to verse 2. "Every high priest" is one who is **able to deal gently** with people. There are three things to note about these words. First, a great and necessary qualification or endowment of a high priest: he is, he was to be, one who is **able to deal gently.** Second, the special object of his office stems from that qualification, that he deals with **those who are ignorant and are**

going astray. Third, a special reason is attached to his qualification, that **he himself is subject to weakness.**

First, **he is able to deal gently. Deal gently,** in the first place, signifies natural ability, a power that affects something. It is applied to both God and man. The word also implies a moral power concerning what we can do according to the law. Men are capable of doing many things naturally that they cannot do morally. (See 1 Corinthians 10:21, "You cannot drink of the cup of the Lord and the cup of demons"; and 2 Corinthians 13:8, "we cannot do anything against the truth.")

To deal gently. This word is not found elsewhere in the New Testament. It means to bear anything without becoming angry. Moses displayed this characteristic: "Now Moses was a very humble man, more humble than anyone else on the face of the earth" (Numbers 12:3). He is referred to as being "a very humble man" in the face of exasperating provocations when Miriam and Aaron opposed him. He dealt with them gently. But even Moses did not manage to be like this all the time. "Moses said to them, 'Listen, you rebels, must we bring you water out of this rock?' Then Moses raised his arm and struck the rock twice with his staff. Water gushed out . . ." (Numbers 20:10-11). Only Christ could **deal gently** with people all the time. A high priest can quietly bear with the weaknesses and sinful provocations of those who are ignorant and can commiserate with those who need help.

Second, this compassion is shown to **those who are ignorant and are going astray.** All God's people may be included in these words. So, here, the Holy Spirit endows the high priest with the ability to assist in this situation. All God's people are under the care of the high priest. But they do not go for help until they are aware of the danger they are in.

Those who are ignorant. That is, those who sin because of the ignorance and darkness of their minds. The law provided a sacrifice for those who sinned in a state of ignorance (Leviticus 4). "If just one person sins unintentionally, he must bring a year-old female goat for a sin offering. The priest is to make atonement before the LORD for the one who erred by sinning unintentionally, and when the atonement has been made for him, he will be forgiven. . . . But anyone who sins defiantly . . . must be cut off" (Numbers 15:27-29). It is the same under the Gospel. For after we put our trust in Christ's sacrifice for our justification and sanctification there are sins that we may defiantly engage in, for which there is no forgiveness. "If we deliberately keep on sinning after we have received the knowledge of the truth, no sacrifice for sins is left, but only a fearful expectation of judgment and of raging fire that will consume the enemies of God" (Hebrews 10:26-27). But those who are **ignorant** are those who sin unintentionally.

He adds, **and are going astray.** Our sins are often expressed like this. "I have strayed like a lost sheep" (Psalm 119:176); "we all, like sheep, have gone astray, each of us has turned to his own way" (Isaiah 53:6). We have erred, or wandered astray from God's way, and turned to our own ways. "You were like sheep going astray" (1 Peter 2:25).

Third, **he himself is subject to weakness.** This **weakness** is both natural and moral. This **weakness** is inseparable from our human nature. This our Lord himself was surrounded by. Had it been otherwise he could not have been such a merciful high priest whom we need. The moral weakness is our inclination to sin. "When we were still powerless, Christ died for the ungodly" (Romans 5:6). Our powerlessness was caused by our sin.

3. The apostle illustrates how the high priest is "subject to weakness" from the necessary consequence of this, that he was to offer sacrifices for his own sins. In verse 2 he had described, in general terms, the purpose of his office as "to offer gifts and sacrifices for sins," and then he mentioned his own frailty. He did this so that he might give an account of these institutions of the law in which he was appointed to offer sacrifices for his own sins.

This is why he has to offer sacrifices for his own sins, as well as for the sins of the people. Had the high priest under the law been sinless, as the Lord Jesus was, he would have had nothing to do but to offer sacrifices for the sins of the people. But this is not the case with him, since he, as well as they, were surrounded by the disease of sin.

He has to. He ought to offer sacrifices for his own sins, for two reasons. First, because of the condition in which he was in. He sinned in many things and would have ruined his office if he had not offered up sacrifices for himself. It was absolutely necessary that sacrifices should be offered up for him and for his sin, and yet no one else could do this for him, so he had to do it himself. Second, there was God's command. He had to do this because God had ordained it.

Of the people. The great annual sacrifice that the high priest himself celebrated is principally intended here (see Leviticus 16:16, 24). In addition to this, the daily sacrifice in the temple was offered and the whole church was equally involved in this.

For his own sins. He offered sacrifices for his own sins, just as he offered sacrifices for the sins of the people. He had the same interest as they had in the daily sacrifice, which was the public worship of the whole church. In addition to this, there were three kinds of offerings that particularly concerned him, which he offered especially for himself.

First was the solemn offering that followed his inauguration, "He [Moses] said to Aaron, 'Take a bull calf for your sin offering and a ram for your burnt offering, both without defect, and present them before the LORD'" (Leviticus 9:2). This offering was for himself, as is stated in verse 8: "so Aaron came to the altar and slaughtered the calf as a sin offering for himself." After this, he made a different offering for the people (Leviticus 9:3, 15).

Second was an occasional offering or sacrifice, which he offered especially for himself, when he broke any of God's commands unintentionally, or for any actual sin. "If the anointed priest sins, bringing guilt on the people, he must bring to the LORD a young bull without defect as a sin offering for the sin he has committed" (that is, just as any of the people do for sin); "he is to present the bull at the entrance of the Tent of Meeting before the LORD" (Leviticus 4:3-4). After this there is a sacrifice for the sin of all the people (verse 13); and then a sacrifice for the sin of individual people (verse 27). This prefigures Christ's death pardoning us for our sin.

Third was another solemn offering, on the annual feast, or Day of Atonement. "This is how Aaron is to enter the sanctuary area; with a young bull for a sin offering and a ram for a burnt offering" (Leviticus 16:3). "Aaron shall bring the bull for his own sin offering to make atonement for himself and his household, and he is to slaughter the bull for his own sin offering" (Leviticus 16:11). After this, he offers also on the same day, for the sins of the people, verse 15, a bullock for himself, and a goat for the people. This solemn sacrifice for all their sins, known and unknown, great and small, in general and in particular, represents our coming to Christ for pardon and sanctification, which may be frequently renewed. The Jews affirm that the high priest when he offered this sacrifice used the following prayer: "O Lord, I have done perversely, I have transgressed, I have sinned before you; I and my house, and the children of Aaron, and your holy people. O Lord, pardon the iniquities, transgressions and sins of me and my house and the children of Aaron, and your holy people, as it is written in the law of your servant Moses, that on this day you may pardon and purify us from all our sins" (Mishnaioth, Tract iv). And all these different kinds of sacrifices for himself were, as our apostle states here, **for . . . sins.** And this was necessary because he was surrounded by the disease of sin and stood in need of expiation and atonement as much as the rest of the people.

Expositors generally agree that this refers to the high priest and that the Lord Christ is neither intended nor included in the expression. For Christ had no sin of his own to offer a sacrifice for, for he was "just as we are—yet was without sin" (4:15). It is specifically stated that "unlike the other high priests, he does not need to offer sacrifices day after day, first for his own sins, and then for the sins of the people" (7:27), for he himself was "holy, blameless, pure, set apart from sinners" (7:26). Therefore this belonged to the weakness and imperfection of the high priest according to the law.

4. The previous verses declare the personal qualifications of a high priest. But these alone are not enough to invest anyone with that office. It is necessary that he is lawfully called to this office. The former makes him suitable for the office, the latter gives him the right to hold the office. This is applied to Jesus Christ, and insisted on, in verse 4.

No one takes this honor upon himself; he must be called by God, just as Aaron was. Having laid down the qualifications a high priest needed, the apostle now declares what was necessary for his actual investiture for this office. He states this positively and negatively. Positively, he is to be called of God, which he exemplifies in the case of Aaron—**just as Aaron was**; and negatively, he is not to assume this honor to himself.

No one takes. That is, according to the law, no one does this. Men might do otherwise, and did do otherwise, but no one should do so, for it was against God's appointed law in his church.

This honor. Honor here refers either to the office itself or to the high esteem in which it was held. The office may be called **honor**, because it is honorable. This is how the word is used in 3:3: "just as the builder of the house has greater honor than the house itself." I think that the office itself is intended here. The office was most honorable for two reasons.

First, it was honorable because of its nature. It was especially designated by God (Exodus 27); it had a special drawing close to God (Leviticus 16); and it carried out all special divine services. These things made the office honorable and a high honor for those who were invested in this way. For what greater honor can a human being have than to come close to God?

Second, it was honorable because this was God's intention. It was partly for this reason that the high priest was to be dressed in clothes made for beauty and glory (see 1 Samuel 2:30).

He must be called by God. The person who is called by God is given the honor of holding this office. This call is here exemplified in the instance of Aaron: **just as Aaron was.**

Just as Aaron was. The comparison here concerns the general nature of a call. The apostle considers Aaron's call so that Christ's call will be seen more clearly. First, Aaron was **called by God.** By a word of command Aaron was set apart for his office of priesthood. "Have Aaron your brother brought to you from among the Israelites, with his sons . . . so that they may serve me as priests" (Exodus 28:1). Second, God's call was expressed in his actually being set apart for his office. He was given special clothes for this office. "Make sacred garments for your brother Aaron, to give him dignity and honor" (Exodus 28:2). In his consecration, holy, consecrated oil was used, and solemn sacrifice was offered in his name and for him (see Exodus 29). There was a great deal of glory in his consecration.

Verses 5-10

5. So Christ also did not take upon himself the glory of becoming a high priest. But God said to him, "You are my Son; today I have become your Father."

Christ. Christ, that is, the promised Messiah, the anointed one. In this letter the apostle sometimes calls him by significant names: the "Son" (1:2, 8); the "Son of God" (4:14); the "word of God" (4:12); "Jesus" (2:9; 3:1); and "Christ" (3:6). In this verse he uses this name of Christ in a way that is particularly appropriate for the occasion. He set out to demonstrate that the promised Messiah, the hope and expectation of the fathers, was to be the high priest forever and ever over God's house. So he calls him by the name by which he was known from the beginning and which indicated his anointing to his office—the anointed one. He was to be the anointed priest, that is, **Christ.**

Not take upon himself the glory. Christ was not called by men. He was made a priest by God himself. But he did not take this honor to himself, nor was it possible for him to do this, as the office and its implementation depended on a covenant or compact between him and his Father. As he undertook this office he received many promises from the Father and was to do his will and work. It was therefore impossible for him to **take upon himself the glory.**

But God said to him. These words are stated in order to confirm Christ's priesthood and his call to this office. The words originally signify the eternal relation between the Father and the Son, with their mutual love within this relationship. God declares Christ to be his Son and in this way accepts him to carry out the appointed mission. The Father himself showed this when Christ undertook the duties of his office. As the evangelist says, "We have seen his glory, the glory of the One and Only, who came from the Father, full of grace and truth" (John 1:14).

The relationship depends on Christ being the Son of God. Faith in him as the One and Only from the Father is the foundation of the church. In contrast to other opinions, Peter said about Christ Jesus, "You are the Christ, the Son of the living God" (Matthew 16:16), to which Christ replied, "on this rock I will build my church" (Matthew 16:18). For it is God's will that "all may honor the Son just as they honor the Father" (John 5:23).

The love from the Father to the Son is twofold. First, the love is the natural and eternal love of the Father to his Son and his delight in him, as he shares the same nature as himself. This is expressed in Proverbs 8:30-31: "Then I was the craftsman at his side. I was filled with delight day after day, rejoicing always in his presence, rejoicing in his whole world and delighting in mankind." Second, there was the actual love toward the Son for his infinite humility and grace in undertaking his work (see Philippians 2:6-11).

6. The next verse gives us a further confirmation of Christ's call to his office, by another testimony, taken from Psalm 110:4. There is, therefore, only one thing to ask of these words, and that is, how far do they bear witness to the apostle's assertion that Christ did not seek his own glory in becoming high priest but that he was appointed to this position by God, even the Father?

And he says in another place, "You are a priest forever, in the order of Melchizedek."

And he says in another place. In the previous verse he had said, "You are my Son; today I have become your Father." This truth is so great and important that it needed a solid confirmation.

He who **says** these words may be David. He wrote both Psalms 2 and 110. So both these words come from him. He who **says** these words may be the Holy Spirit, who in both places spoke in and through David. "Therefore God again set a certain day, calling it Today, when a long time later he spoke through David" (4:7). But what is said is what matters most here. And **he says** refers to God the Father himself. The apostle set out to show that Christ was appointed high priest on the authority of God the Father. The Holy Spirit, through the mouth of David, speaks these things to us. But he is only declaring what the Father said to the Son.

In another place means in another Psalm, that is, Psalm 110:4.

The words of the Father to the Son are, **"You are a priest forever, in the order of Melchizedek."** (See commentary on 5:10 for "Melchizedek.")

7. During the days of Jesus' life on earth, he offered up prayers and petitions with loud cries and tears to the one who could save him from death, and he was heard because of his reverent submission.

During the days of Jesus' life on earth. The first thing mentioned about Christ refers to the weakness that accompanied him as he undertook his work. It describes the time and place where he exercised his work as **the days . . . of life on earth.**

Offered up. Only this word, and no other, is used in the New Testament of gifts and sacrifices, or offerings, being made at an altar (see Matthew 2:11; 5:23-24; 8:4; Mark 1:44; Luke 5:14). Leviticus 1:2 says, "when any of you brings an offering," meaning, brings an offering to the altar. And in this letter the word constantly means a priestly act (see 5:1, 3; 8:3, 4; 9:7, 9, 14, 25, 28; 10:1, 2, 8, 11, 12; 11:4, 17).

Prayers and petitions. His offering is expressed through **prayers and petitions,** and these words have the same general meaning. In the great sacrifice of expiation, the high priest confessed over the head of the scapegoat's head "all the wickedness and rebellion of the Israelites—all their sins" (Leviticus 16:21). So **prayers and petitions** here do not just refer to the mere supplications of our blessed Savior, but as they accompanied the offering up of himself, his soul and body, a real propitiatory sacrifice to God. So, wherever our apostle elsewhere speaks of the "offering" of Christ, he calls it the "offering of himself," or of his "body" (Ephesians 5:2; Hebrews 9:14, 25, 28; 10:10). In this verse, therefore, he refers to the whole sacrifice of Christ as the **prayers and petitions** that accompanied the sacrifice.

With loud cries and tears. The manner of Christ offering these prayers and petitions is now mentioned. He did it with **loud cries and tears.** Chrysostom observes that the Gospels never mention these things. This is the only place where we learn that tears accompanied his priestly prayers.

In prophecy the prayers that are meant here are called his "groaning": "Why are you so far from saving me, so far from the words of my groaning?" (Psalm 22:1). This "roaring" or "groaning" is a strong and vehement outcry. Psalm 32:3 says, "When I kept silent, my bones wasted away through my groaning all day long." The vehemency of his complaints consumed his natural strength. So Job 3:24, "For sighing comes to me instead of food; my groans pour out like water." A sense of extreme pressure and distress is signified in the words, "I am feeble and utterly crushed; I groan in anguish of heart." This is, again, a strong cry. Psalm 22:9-21 has in nearly every sentence a spirit of roaring, groaning, or a strong cry. It is not just the outward noise, but the inner heart and soul that is principally intended.

It is the same with the evangelists in the Gospels. The prayers offered **with loud cries and tears** are those prayed to God during his passion, both in the garden and on the cross. Luke 22:44 declares, "And being in anguish, he prayed more earnestly, and his sweat was like drops of blood falling to the ground." This inner frame of mind here reflects what our apostle is referring to when he mentions **loud cries and tears.** Christ was totally possessed by an "agony" or "anguish," that is, a strong and vehement conflict of mind, in and about dreadful and terrible things, which has been called "a dread of utter ruin" by the commentator Nemes, and, as "a dread of evil to come upon us from outside" by Aquinas. Jesus prayed "more earnestly" with more vehement anguish of mind, spirit, and body. For the word denotes the highest degree of earnestness that the mind, spirit, and body are capable of. This produced that preternatural sweat, "like drops of blood," falling off him onto the ground. About this he says, in Psalm 22:14, "I am poured out like water."

Again, on the cross itself, it is said, "Jesus cried out in a loud voice" (Matthew 27:46). This is how Christ prayed his priestly prayers that related to his offering himself as a sacrifice, which the evangelists record.

To the one who could save him from death. The object of Christ's offering is described as **the one who could save him from death** and had the power to do this. God is intended here. The apostle does not call him God, or the Father of Christ, even though the Lord Jesus, in these prayers, calls upon him, using both of these names. So, in the garden, Christ calls him Father: "My Father, if it is possible, may this cup be taken from me" (Matthew 26:39). On the cross Christ called him God: "My God, my God, why have you forsaken me?" (Matthew 27:46). Christ calls him Father again as he places his life and soul into his hands: "Father, into your hands I commit my spirit" (Luke 23:46). But our apostle does not use these expressions here and only describes God as **the one who could save him from death.** He does this to show the Lord Christ's thoughts about God at this time as he faced death and reflected on its consequences. His purpose is to declare what frame of mind Christ was in during his suffering and offering of himself.

And he was heard because of his reverent submission. To be **heard** in Scripture means two things. First, it signifies to be accepted, even if the request we make is denied. "God will hear me," is equivalent to, "God will accept me, and is pleased with my supplications" (see Psalm 55:17). Second, to be **heard** means to have our request answered. To be heard is to be delivered. It is expressed like this in Psalm 22:24, "For he has not despised or disdained the suffering of the afflicted one; he has not hidden his face from him but has listened to his cry for help." In the first sense there is no doubt that the Father always heard the Son. As John 11:42 states, "I knew that you always hear me." Always, in all things, God the Father accepted the Lord Christ and was well pleased with him. But we ask here how far the Lord Christ was heard in the latter way. Was he so heard as to be delivered from what he prayed against?

Christ's prayers fall into two categories with regard to this: conditional and absolute. As far as his conditional prayers were concerned, Luke 22:42 is a prime example. "Father, if you are willing, take this cup from me; yet not my will, but yours be done." Christ would not have been human if he had not experienced extreme aversion to the things that were about to happen to him. This expression of his nature, in his mind and will and emotions, which were completely holy in him, our Savior expressed in that conditional prayer. This prayer was answered in the following ways. His mind was strengthened against the terror of the impending events. This enabled him to be perfectly composed to embrace God's will: "not my will, but yours be done." So Christ was heard to the extent he had wished to be heard. Although, by nature, he desired deliverance, since he was human, yet he did not desire this absolutely, as he was wholly given over to God's will.

We move on to Christ's prayers as absolute prayers. The main prayers he offered up to him who was able to save him from death were absolute; and in them he was absolutely heard and delivered. He hoped, trusted, and believed in God's deliverance, and therefore prayed absolutely for it. "Because the Sovereign LORD helps me, I will not be disgraced. Therefore have I set my face like flint, and I know I will not be put to shame. He who vindicates me is near. Who then will bring charges against me?" (Isaiah 50:7-8). Here he was heard absolutely; **he was heard.**

Reverent submission. The word for **reverent** comes in only one other place in the New Testament: Hebrews 12:28, "let us be thankful, and so worship God acceptably with reverence and awe." However, in its adjectival form it comes three times—in Luke 2:25, Acts 2:5; 8:2—where it is translated "devout," "God-fearing," and "godly." In Hebrews 11:7 the verb derived from this word is translated as "holy fear." Christ's soul was engaged in a conflict in the sense that his faith and trust in God were tried to the limit by the attacks of fear about what would happen to him during his passion. In all this Christ showed his **reverent submission** to God's will.

8. Although he was a son, he learned obedience from what he suffered.

Although. It may be supposed that some people raised an objection about what had just been stated, namely, "If he were **a son**, how did he come to pray and cry in a way that indicated that he needed help and relief?" The apostle may be saying here, "Although he was like this, yet these things were necessary."

He was a son. It was not unknown for a son or child adopted by God to be disciplined, to suffer, and so learn to be obedient. But we are not talking about a son or child of God here; we are talking about the Son of God, God's own Son (see John 1:14; Romans 8:3; Philippians 2:6). That the Son of God should go through the things spoken about here is indeed a wonder. Therefore it is said of him, **although he was a son . . .**

Three questions may be asked of this verse: first, what is the **obedience** referred to here? Second, how did Christ "learn" obedience? And third, by what means did Christ learn obedience?

Obedience. This word means to be obedient to someone else's command. The word has come to mean to "hear" or to "listen to." Hence, to "listen" or "hear" is often used in Scripture to mean obey. To disobey is to "refuse to listen." In Christ, this obedience may be said to be general and particular.

Christ's obedience is said to be general in that his whole life in this world was in line with God's will. This obedience to God was the life and beauty of Christ's holiness. Christ was obedient in particular events. "He became obedient to death—even death on a cross!" (Philippians 2:8). His Father had commanded him to lay down his life, and Christ did this in an obedient manner. In this verse the apostle is especially referring to Christ being obedient to God in his suffering and death. "Here I am, I have come—it is written about me in the scroll. I desire to do your will, O my God; your law is within my heart" (Psalm 40:7-8). This is a similar offering up of himself as a sacrifice for us, as our apostle declares in Hebrews 10:9-10. Far from being rebellious, he offered his back to those who beat him and his cheeks to those who pulled out his beard (see Isaiah 50:5-6).

Learned. Christ is said to have **learned obedience.** This kind of "learning" is what a humble disciple does as he receives instruction. Here it says about the Lord Christ that **he learned obedience,** not that he learned to obey. This sheds light on the whole subject. It is possible to talk about learning obedience in three senses. First, we can learn obedience through coming to know what our duty is. The psalmist says, "Before I was afflicted I went astray" (Psalm 119:67). In this way the psalmist was taught what duties God required of him. But our Lord Jesus did not learn obedience in this sense, nor could he do so. For he knew beforehand all he would have to go through. God's law was in his heart, and he never forgot God or his law.

It is possible to speak of "learning obedience" in the sense that one is instructed, guided, helped, and directed. In this way we "learn" obedience as we are gradually instructed in the knowledge and practice of it. But the Lord Christ did not learn obedience in this sense. He had fullness of grace always with him and in him, directing him and guiding him. Being full of grace, truth, and wisdom, he was never at a loss about what to do.

It is, however, possible to say that the Lord Christ **learned obedience** when he experienced it in practice. In the sense that a person knows the taste of meat by eating it, it may be said of our Savior that he "tasted death" when he experienced death. One special kind of obedience is intended here, namely, a submission to great, hard, and terrible things, accompanied by patience and quiet endurance, and faith for deliverance from them. This Christ could have not experience of, except by suffering the things he had to pass through, exercising God's grace in them all. Thus, Christ **learned obedience.**

From what he suffered. Here the way or means by which Christ learned obedience is stated: from the things that he suffered. And we cannot exclude from here anything Christ suffered, throughout his life on earth. But since the apostle is especially concerned with Christ as high priest, **what he suffered** refers to his death and the events leading up to his death. He "became obedient to death—even death on a cross!" (Philippians 2:8). Through his sufferings Christ learned obedience as he had occasion to exercise the graces of humility, meekness, patience, and faith. While these graces always lived in him, they were not capable of being exercised in this special way except through his sufferings. The Son of God is said to learn from his own sufferings in another special sense, because he was a sinless person suffering for sinners, the just for the unjust. The obedience was unique to him, and we can have no similar experience of this.

9. And, once made perfect, he became the source of eternal salvation for all who obey him.

Made perfect. This is very similar to 2:10, "should make the author of their salvation perfect through suffering." **Made perfect** means dedicated, consecrated, sanctified, and set apart, and this through some kind of suffering. So, under the law, the high priests were consecrated through the suffering and death of the animals that were offered in sacrifice at their consecration (Exodus 29). But it belonged to the perfection of Christ's priesthood to be consecrated in and by his own sufferings.

He became. Being consecrated, **made perfect**, Christ **became** the source of eternal salvation. Nothing was now lacking to achieve these things.

The source. Where Christ's consecration is previously mentioned (2:10) he is "the author" of their salvation. Here Christ is said to be **the source** or cause of their salvation. The apostle uses this word **source** to refer to all the ways and means by which the Lord Christ won salvation for us.

Eternal. This salvation is said to be **eternal.** In 9:12 the redemption purchased by this offering of Christ is said to be "eternal." It is eternal, endless, unchangeable, and permanent. We are made for an eternal duration. Through sin we deserved eternal damnation. If the salvation won for us was not eternal, it would not be perfect or suit our condition.

For all who obey him. Salvation is limited to those who **obey** the Lord Christ. Christ is the source of eternal salvation only for those **who obey him.** So Christ is not the author of salvation to everyone in the world.

Salvation is confined to believers; and those who look for salvation through Christ must secure it for themselves by faith and obedience. It is Christ alone who is the source of our salvation; but he will only save those who obey him. He came to save sinners but not those who choose to continue in their sins. Although the Gospel is full of love, grace, mercy, and pardon, yet it includes this warning: "whoever does not believe will be condemned" (Mark 16:16).

10. In this verse the apostle returns to the witness given of Christ's priesthood from Psalm 110. In this necessary digression he declares the special nature and preeminence of his priesthood, as prefigured in Melchizedek's priesthood. But no sooner does he mention Melchizedek than he diverts into a preparatory digression and does not return to Melchizedek until the beginning of chapter 7.

And was designated by God to be high priest in the order of Melchizedek.

Designated. We ask why the apostle uses this special expression **designated.** When we say that Phinehas and Eli and Zadok were high priests after the order of Aaron, we mean that they had the same priesthood as Aaron. But that is not the meaning of this expression. The priesthood of Christ and Melchizedek are not the same. For no mere man could possibly aspire to Christ's priesthood. Certain things that were special to Melchizedek prefigure Christ's priesthood. Christ's priesthood went beyond that of Aaron, and he is said to be **high priest in the order of**

Melchizedek. **Designated** does not signify a call to an office but the name of the person so called. So Christ's priesthood was named after Melchizedek rather than after Aaron.

High priest. Verse 6 says, "you are a priest," and it says no more. For where the **high priest** is intended to indicate a note of distinction he is called the "great" or "high priest." While every priest had the nature and privilege of a priest, not every priest was a high priest. Christ is called "priest," as he is invested with the office of priesthood, and he is called **high priest** by our apostle, as he was prefigured by Aaron the high priest.

In the order of Melchizedek. This does not restrict Christ's priesthood to a certain order, but is a reference to the priesthood that prefigured him most closely. This indicates that Christ was not a high priest according to the law or the Aaronical priesthood. It also demonstrates that there was a priesthood before and different from Aaron's, which was appointed by God to represent how he would call the Lord Christ to his work of priesthood. Note how Melchizedek became a priest and you will see why Christ is called a priest **in the order of Melchizedek.** As Melchizedek, without ceremony, without sacrifice, without visible consecration, was constituted a high priest, so was Christ, by the direct word of the Father, saying to him, "you are a priest forever." In this sense, Christ is called a high priest **in the order of Melchizedek.**

Verses 11-14

In this verse the apostle begins his digression.

11. We have much to say about this, but it is hard to explain because you are slow to learn. There are four things summarized in this verse: first, the subject he is to talk about—**about this**; second, the way he is going to treat it—he had **much to say**; third, the nature of these things, which are **hard to explain**; and, fourth, the reason why they are hard to explain, because they were **slow to learn.**

About this. The apostle is referring to Melchizedek here and not to Christ.

We have much to say. The apostle had much to say. But he did not just have a multitude of things to say but also weighty and important things to say, which is also emphasized here.

Hard to explain. It may be that the things that are here called **hard to explain** are the same as those things Peter calls "hard to understand" (2 Peter 3:16). There are some things that are in themselves sublime and mysterious. But the apostle does not must mean the nature of these things, but our understanding of them, which is weak and imperfect.

You are slow to learn. This is the reason why these things are **hard to explain.** The Hebrews were slothful, slow, dull of hearing. The word **slow** does not appear elsewhere in the New Testament, except in 6:12, where it is translated as "lazy." The apostle declares that these Hebrews are at fault here. "You are," he says, "in your listening to the Word, like lazy people, who do no work and achieve nothing because of their dull, inactive inclinations." These kind of people are graphically depicted by Solomon (see Proverbs 12:27; 15:19; 18:9; 19:24, 25; 22:13; 24:30-34; 26:13-15). In the reproach that Christ will issue on unfaithful ministers on the last day, there is nothing greater than that they were "lazy" (Matthew 25:26). The natural dullness of our minds to receive spiritual things may also be meant here, although it is our depraved affections that are condemned.

12-14. The next three verses belong together. They give the reasons for the reproof made in verse 11.

In fact, though by this time you ought to be teachers, you need someone to teach you the elementary truths of God's word all over again. You need milk, not solid food! Anyone who lives on milk, being still an infant, is not acquainted with the teaching about righteousness. But solid food is for the mature, who by constant use have trained themselves to distinguish good from evil.

12. Though by this time. "Considering the time you Hebrews have had, you might have been different a long time ago." They were "slow to learn."

You ought to have been teachers. The word for "teacher" is the word used by the New Testament writers for "Rabbi," which was the usual name for public teachers of the law among the Jews. He was one who was not only fit to teach others, but who also had disciples attached to him who depended on him for their learning. In the Gospel our Savior himself is called a rabbi or "teacher," and he called himself one in relationship to his own disciples (Mark 4:38; John 13:13).

You ought to be. The apostle does not only say that they had enjoyed such a time of instruction so they should have been capable of teaching others, but he declares that this was expected from them, as their duty. To understand this properly depends on knowing the state of the churches in those days. Otherwise this reproof may appear to be harsh. Our hearers do not consider it their duty to learn to be teachers, or at least not in the church. They think that it is enough for them to benefit themselves from what they hear. But this was not the position in the early times. Every church was then a seminary where provision was made for the continuation of the preaching of the Gospel as well as for the calling, gathering, and teaching of other churches. When, therefore, a church was planted through the ministry of the apostles, it continued under their care for some time before they usually committed this ministry to some evangelists. Through them they were instructed more and more so that they might grow in grace and knowledge. They continued like this until some were found from among their own number who were capable of instructing the others and becoming their overseers (see Acts 14:23; 2 Timothy 2; Titus 1:5).

People in those days did not only learn so that they could teach but also so that they could take the Gospel to other places. I do not say that this was the duty of every hearer. But in those days it might be the duty of many, especially in that church of the Hebrews. For they were the great seminary of preachers for the whole world. There were two reasons why the ministry of the Jews was so necessary and useful to the world, through which the Gentiles were in debt to them in their participation in spiritual things. First, as soon as they were converted to Christ, they at once increased greatly in knowledge. For they had already received the seeds and foundations of all evangelical truths in the Scriptures of the Old Testament. So, as soon as the light of the Gospel shined into their hearts, everything became clear to them. And our apostle at once blames these Hebrews for their lack of acquaintance with those principles. The Gentile converts, however, needed longer to become conversant with the mysteries of the Gospel, of which they had previously been complete strangers. This is not taking into account the extraordinary illumination, revelation, and inspiration through God's Spirit that many people in those days received.

Second, it was through the Jews' synagogues throughout the world, that the preachers of the Gospel began to spread their message. For God had ordained that in all places the Word of God was first preached to the Jews (see Acts 13:32-33, 46). Now this could only be done by Jews. For the Gentile converts, as they were uncircumcised, would not be allowed into the synagogues. For this reason it was imperative that these Hebrews should grow in knowledge, so that they could teach others when God called them to do so. This is what happened when the early Christian church was scattered by persecution. All its members preached the Gospel wherever they were driven (see Acts 7:4; 11:19-20). Then those who succeeded these scattered Christians, it seems, were remiss and neglected to learn, and so were unfit to be teachers. The apostle places the blame for this at their door.

You need someone to teach you the elementary truths of God's word. This is the second part of the apostolic rebuke, which follows on from their own negligence.

You need someone to teach you. They should have been teachers, but they needed someone to teach them.

The elementary truths. They needed to be taught about the first principles of Christian religion.

God's word. This is the "oracles of God." The words of God are the Scriptures. In the New Testament they often refer to the Old Testament. So, Moses "received living words to pass on to us" (Acts 7:38).

Third, it follows, as an illustration of what the Hebrews had been charged with, that they needed **milk, not solid food!**

You need. The apostle states their condition. Positively, they needed milk; negatively, they did not need strong meat. "This is the need you stand in." In this illustration the Word of God is compared with food, both in its usual physical sense, and also as food for our souls. The natural food is here put into two categories, **milk** and **meat**, which reflect two categories of the Word of God.

Milk. The whole Word of God is, and may be, sometimes compared with milk because of its purity and nourishment. "Like newborn babies, crave pure spiritual milk, so that by it you may grow up in your salvation" (1 Peter 2:2). The Apostle Peter warns us, "Rid yourselves of all malice and all deceit, hypocrisy, envy, and slander of every kind" (1 Peter 2:1). James has a similar warning, "Get rid of all moral filth and the evil that is so prevalent, and humbly accept the word planted in you, which can save you" (James 1:21). In these places the whole Word of God, the whole Gospel, which is food for our souls, is compared to milk. But even here I think that some particular parts or doctrines of the Word, relevant to the apostle's aims, are intended. He calls them "newborn babies"; that is, people who have been recently converted to Christ, whose faith may be weak. The apostle advises these people to search for suitable food in the Word, to nourish their souls, or to strengthen them in their faith and obedience. These straightforward teachings of truth are suitable for people who are not able to take in the higher mysteries. Therefore, it is just parts of the Word, and the things taught there, which are compared to milk, both in its nature and use.

Milk is the kind of food that is easy to digest, and so it is often given to babies, children, and sick people. The apostle used a similar metaphor when he wrote, "Brothers, I could not address you as spiritual but as worldly—mere infants in Christ. I gave you milk, not solid food, for you were not yet ready for it" (1 Corinthians 3:1-2). Babies are given milk because they do not have the strength to digest meat. So, says the apostle, they were able to imbibe milk but were not able to feed on strong, spiritual meat. Clearly, the apostle thinks that "the elementary truths of God's word" are **milk.** They can cope with plain, basic truths, but cannot take the great and deep mysteries of the Gospel.

Solid food! Negatively, the apostle says that they do not need **solid food.** That is, meat was not appropriate to their present condition. "A message of wisdom among the mature" (1 Corinthians 2:6) or adult, and those who have grown up in some good measure into the stature of Christ, are meant here. The apostle has in mind those things that belong to Christ's priesthood and sacrifice. This is **solid food** for the souls of mature believers. Here is a yardstick by which Christians can measure their spiritual maturity. If the solid doctrines about the work of Christ, especially his priesthood and sacrifice, are in their minds and emotions, and if they find spiritual nourishment in them, this is a sign of the progress they are making in understanding Christ and the Gospel.

13-14. These verses contain a further illustration and confirmation of what has just been stated. The Hebrews are told why they needed milk and not solid food. **Anyone who lives on milk, being still an infant, is not acquainted with the teaching about righteousness. But solid food is for the mature, who by constant use have trained themselves to distinguish good from evil.** The apostle again describes the two types of hearers he has just mentioned. First, those who use **milk**, that is, those who should take milk. Second, those who should feed on **solid food**. About the first he says, "you are **not acquainted with the teaching about righteousness.** It may appear that the apostle's reasoning would have been clearer if he had said, "Those who are not skilled in the word of righteousness need milk." In the next verse he talks about those who are **mature,** and **have trained themselves to distinguish between good and evil.** These people are said to need, or eat, **solid food.** But it all comes to the same thing. Having told them in the previous verse that they were in **need** of **milk,** he now describes their condition as those who are **not acquainted with the teaching about righteousness,** such as "infants."

13. Anyone who lives on milk. Everyone who is weak or ill should be fed milk.

Not acquainted with the teaching about righteousness. "One who has no experience." David would not wear Saul's armor, which was doubtless excellent in itself, because he was not experienced in using such equipment. He was unacquainted with it. This is not said of somebody who is totally ignorant about something, but of one who is not able to use it wisely. It is used in this way about **the teaching of righteousness.**

The teaching about righteousness. This **teaching about righteousness** is nothing other than the word or doctrine of the Gospel. It is the word of the cross (see 1 Corinthians 1:18). This is where the righteousness of God was revealed to us (see Romans 1:17).

Infant. The apostle gives the general reason for this whole condition: **being still an infant:** "it cannot be anything different with such a person, since he is an infant." Infants do not drink milk occasionally; it is their staple diet. Such are infants. The word either means the kind of children we call babies or people who are weak and foolish like them. The allusion here is to the first of these, to those who live on milk alone. There are many excellent characteristics about children, such as innocence and dependence. Believers are sometimes likened to such qualities. David says of himself that he was like "a weaned child" (Psalm 131:2) because of his submission to God's will. Our Savior tells us to receive the kingdom of God like little children (see Matthew 18:3; Luke 18:17). There are other characteristics of children we are told not to emulate (see 1 Corinthians 14:20; Ephesians 4:14). Here we are not to copy such infants. "Such," says Chrysostom, "as have to be fed with milk; for left to themselves, they will put dirt and straw into their mouths." It is clear what kind of people the apostle has in mind. These people enjoy listening to the Word, but because of their own indolence and neglect have made little spiritual progress. They are infants who need milk and are incapable of receiving instruction about the mysteries of the Gospel.

14. But solid food is for the mature, who by constant use have trained themselves to distinguish good from evil.

Trained. The mature have their senses **trained.** But this is not the case with infants. Infants are unable to make correct judgments about spiritual truths and cannot understand the mysteries of the Gospel because their minds are not trained in spiritual matters. This word **trained** does not refer to actual exercise but the readiness and ability and fitness of anything that is acquired through assiduous exercise. Such a person is like a soldier who trained for his duty or a wrestler striving for a prize. To have our minds exercised like this is to have our understandings and minds increasing in grace and knowledge through study, meditation, prayer, and listening to the Word. Then we become fit and able to receive spiritual truths, which then nourish our souls.

To distinguish good from evil. To **distinguish** is to make an exact judgment between two alternatives. The judgment to be made here is between **good** and **evil.**

By constant use. This ability is attained **by constant use.** It is a habit, and a habit is a firm, rooted disposition, acquired by use and exercise. The first principle or spring of spiritual light is infused by the Holy Spirit. This is turned into a habit by constant exercise. In this way the mind becomes accustomed to the Word of God and then makes correct judgments when necessary.

Hebrews
Chapter 6

This whole chapter continues the digression started at 5:11. The chapter divides into four parts. First, the apostle explains what he is going to talk about and what he will omit (verses 1-3). Second, he calls the Hebrews to special diligence about the teachings of Christianity and progress in the knowledge of Christ. He does this by considering the great sin and inevitable destruction of apostates. For this sort of error often comes from people who have received the truth and have made a profession of it but do not diligently strive for maturity, which is their duty (verses 4-8). Third, the apostle expresses the hope that this is not the case with the Hebrews and that this sin will not be found among them and so they will not receive the threatened punishment. He prays that they may continue in their faith and love (verses 9-12). Fourth, the apostle encourages them to persevere; he reminds them of the example of Abraham, who first received the promises, and of the nature of the promises themselves, their confirmation by God's oath, and the help we may obtain from our hope in Christ (verses 13-20).

Verses 1-3

1. Therefore let us leave the elementary teachings about Christ and go on to maturity. The apostle gives the Hebrews further instruction from which they should learn.

Let us leave. "Let us not always dwell on the teaching and learning of these **elementary** things, but omitting them for a time, as you know them well, let us proceed to what is now necessary for you."

It is the duty of ministers of the Gospel to make sure that the doctrine they teach is not only true but also appropriate to the condition of their hearers. Some important Christian truths may, in the preaching of the Gospel, be omitted for a time, but none should be permanently neglected or forgotten.

The elementary teachings about Christ. What these **teachings** are the apostle states at the end of this verse and in verse 2. They are the same as the "elementary truths of God's word" (5:12).

Go on to maturity. Having said what he would pass over, the apostle declares his present purpose, that they should **go on to maturity. Maturity** is their goal. This is a knowledge of the sublime doctrines of the Gospel that those who have been thoroughly instructed in them possess. Paul speaks about this when he writes, "We . . . speak a message of wisdom among the mature, but not the wisdom of this age or of the rulers of this age, who are coming to nothing. No, we speak of God's secret wisdom, a wisdom that has been hidden and that God destined for our glory before time began" (1 Corinthians 2:6-7). The apostle aims at **maturity.**

And go on to. These words picture the progress a ship makes under full sail. Let us **go on,** "be carried on," that is, with the full strength of our minds and emotions and the endeavor of our souls. "We have stayed long enough by the shore; let us now hoist our sails and launch into the deep."

1b-2. Not laying again the foundation of repentance from acts that lead to death, and of faith in God, instruction about baptisms, the laying on of hands, the resurrection of the dead, and eternal judgment. Here the apostle specifies what he meant by "the elementary teachings about Christ." We are told two things about these "elementary teachings." First, they are a **foundation;** second, he mentions particular examples of what they are.

Foundation. This is an architectural metaphor. The architect or builder first lays the foundation. Only a most foolish builder would then do no more. The teachings of Christ are called a **foundation** here. If they do not build on the foundation they make no progress.

A foundation has two characteristics. First, it is the first thing that is laid in every building. This is the natural sequence for every building. Second, it bears the whole weight of the superstructure, as the rest of the building is laid on it. Christ himself, and only Christ, is the foundation who bears the weight of the church (see Isaiah 28:16; Matthew 16:18; 1 Corinthians 3:10-11; Ephesians 2:20-22; 1 Peter 2:4-5). Christ is the life of the church, as each member is spiritually united to him (see 1 Corinthians 12:12). All Christian truth revolves around Christ; so in this sense Christ is the doctrinal foundation of the Christian church. "By the grace God has given me, I laid a foundation as an expert builder . . . each one should be careful how he builds. For no one can lay any foundation other than the one already laid, which is Jesus Christ" (1 Corinthians 3:10-11).

Not laying again. The apostle says that he will not be **laying** this foundation **again**. He is not here inferring that he himself had laid the original foundation among the Hebrews, but just that it had already been laid. The apostle often appeals to the churches whose foundations he had laid down (1 Corinthians 3:5-6, 10; 4:15), but he does not do this in the letter to the Hebrews. The apostle does not want to lay these foundations again, as they had already been instructed by other people in these things, and so the apostle would not merely repeat them.

The apostle proceeds to specify what part of this **foundation** consisted of.

Repentance from acts that lead to death. This was taught to everyone who wanted to give themselves over to the discipline of Christ and the Gospel. We shall consider what these acts were and what repentance from them means.

First, **acts that lead to death** is only used by our apostle in this letter. It only comes here and in 9:14—"cleanse our consciences from acts that lead to death, so that we may serve the living God." He uses it elsewhere about people being dead in sin by nature (Ephesians 2:1, 5; Colossians 2:13). Peter calls these our "past sins" (2 Peter 1:9): "has forgotten that he has been cleansed from his past sins." Before their conversion, they were taught to forsake their sins. "For you have spent enough time in the past doing what pagans choose to do—living in debauchery, lust, drunkenness, orgies, carousing and detestable idolatry" (1 Peter 4:3). To go back into the sins that had been publicly repented of was always viewed with great concern.

The sins of unregenerate people are called **acts that lead to death,** or "dead works." They proceed, by nature, from a principle that is under the power of spiritual death. They are the deeds of people who are dead in their trespasses and sins. All the moral actions of such people, as far as their supernatural purpose is concerned, are dead works, as they do not have any spiritual life. It is essential for a person to be spiritually alive before his actions can be of any value spiritually. Our walk in holy obedience is called "the life of God" (Ephesians 4:18); that is, the life that God requires, which by his special grace he works in us when we seek to work for him. Where this life is absent, people are dead, and so are their deeds, including all their actions which are linked to the living God.

These people are dead by nature, but their end is also death. For these **acts lead to death.** "Sin, when it is full-grown, gives birth to death" (James 1:15). They proceed from spiritual death and end in eternal death. They are called "the fruitless deeds of darkness" (Ephesians 5:11). From this we deduce that they were taught that these deeds are useless. They were taught that they were "dead in" their "transgressions and sins" and were "by nature objects of wrath" (Ephesians 2:1, 3). God's law condemned both them and their deeds.

Repentance from acts that lead to death. This is the first thing to do for people who want to profess the Gospel, and, consequently, it is the first principle of the teaching of Christ, as the apostle states here. Without this, whatever is attempted or attained only dishonors Christ and brings disappointment to people. This method of preaching was confirmed by the example and command of Christ himself: "Repent, for the kingdom of heaven is near" (Matthew 4:17); "Repent and believe the good news" (Mark 1:15). In almost all the sermons of the apostles we find the necessity for repentance is the first essential to be pressed home on their listeners (Acts 2:38; 3:19; 14:15). John the Baptist was the same as he prepared for the declaration of the Gospel (Matthew 3:2). So, as the Gospel was preached, it was said that "he commands all people everywhere to repent" (Acts 17:30). When the Gentiles received the Gospel, the church at Jerusalem praised God, saying, "God has granted even the Gentiles repentance unto life" (Acts 11:18).

And of faith in God. The second example of the doctrinal foundation that was supposed to have been laid down among the Hebrews was **faith in God.** This is linked by **and** to **repentance.** These should never, and never can be, separated. Where one is, there is the other; and where either is absent, neither are present, no matter how much people may pretend. If a person does not have faith in God he has not repented, and the person who has not repented does not have faith in God.

We now ask, What does it mean to have **faith in God** here? It cannot mean faith in the most general way, since it is a principle of the teaching of God. Once God is acknowledged it is then necessary for a person to believe in him as the first eternal truth. We have to submit to him and trust in him as the sovereign Lord, the Judge, and rewarder of all. In Judaism they had been taught about faith in God and did not need to be taught about this teaching of Christ. But our Savior makes a distinction between this faith in God that they had and the special faith in himself that is required: "Trust in God; trust also in me" (John 14:1). In addition to this, repentance and faith are elsewhere linked together, and this special sort of faith in God is intended (see Acts 19:4; 20:21).

2. The resurrection of the dead. The third principle, according to the sense of these words before us, is **the resurrection of the dead.** This was a fundamental principle of the Jewish church, as it is indeed of all proper religions in the world. The twelfth article of the creed of Jews today is "The days of the Messiah." That is, the time will come when God will send the Messiah and restore all things through him. In the days of the old testament this referred to faith in God. But the present Jews do not believe the fulfillment of this promise and so reject all faith in God about this promise. However, they still maintain that they profess faith in God. And their thirteenth article is "The revivification" or "resurrection from the dead." This is explained and confirmed in the Gospel and sealed by Christ's resurrection and is the chief principle of Christianity.

The resurrection of the dead is usually expressed as the "resurrection" only (Matthew 22:23, 28; Mark 12:18; Luke 20:27-28), though it is also sometimes referred to as "the resurrection of the dead" (Acts 4:2), that is, from the state of being dead. Our apostle uses a special expression in 11:35, "Women received back their dead, raised to life again." Sometimes it is called "the resurrection of the righteous" (Luke 14:14).

This truth is so important that nothing in religion can exist without it. The apostles diligently confirmed it in the first churches; and for the same reason it was attacked by Satan and denied and opposed by many. This was done in two ways: first, by an open denial of any such thing—"how can some of you say that there is no resurrection of the dead?" (1 Corinthians 15:12); and second, those who did not dare to attack it directly expounded it in an allegorical way, saying that "the resurrection has already taken place" (2 Timothy 2:18). Observe that our apostle in both cases does not only condemn these errors as false but declares positively that their admission overthrows the faith and makes the preaching of the Gospel vain and useless.

Eternal judgment. The fourth principle mentioned is **eternal judgment.** This is the immediate consequence of the resurrection of the dead. People will not be raised again to life in this world, as if they were starting on a new adventure, but they must give an account of what is past, "for we must all appear before the judgment seat of Christ, that each one may receive what is due him for the things done while in the body, whether good or bad" (2 Corinthians 5:10). Because there are no outward, visible transactions between God and people's souls once they have left this world, nor any alteration made to their eternal state, this judgment is spoken of as happening immediately after death itself: "Just as man is destined to die once, and after that to face judgment" (9:27). This judgment is certain, and there is nothing between death and it that it takes notice of.

Some think that this **judgment** is only the judgment of wicked and ungodly people. And indeed the Day of Judgment is most frequently spoken of in this way in Scripture (see 2 Thessalonians 1:7-10; 2 Peter 2:9; Jude 14-15). But the judgment is a general one, for all people, both good and bad. "For we will all stand before God's judgment seat. It is written: 'As surely as I live,' says the Lord, 'Every knee will bow before me; every tongue will confess to God'" (Romans 14:10-11). This is what is intended here. As the resurrection of the dead is for everyone, so is the judgment that follows it for everyone.

This **eternal judgment** is clearly taught in the Scriptures. First, its time is fixed: "For he has set a day when he will judge the world with justice by the man he has appointed" (Acts 17:31). This time is frequently called "the

141

day of judgment" (Matthew 10:15; 11:22, 24; 12:36; 2 Peter 2:9; 1 John 4:17). This day has been fixed in the foreknowledge of God and can be neither deferred nor brought forward except by God himself. As for its precise time, this is one of the main secrets of his sovereignty, which he has kept in his eternal heart. Hence our Savior said, "No one knows about that day or hour, not even the angels in heaven, nor the Son [that is, in and by his human nature], but only the Father" (Mark 13:32). This is a way of saying that this divine secret will not be revealed. All inquiries about it are not only sinfully curious but also foolish and impious.

Second, there is a judge. The judge is Jesus Christ. Originally and absolutely this is the judgment of God, of him who made the world. Therefore, it is often said that God will judge the world (Deuteronomy 32:35-36; Ecclesiastes 12:14); "God, the judge of all men" (Hebrews 12:23). The actual carrying out of the judgment is committed to Jesus Christ alone (Daniel 7:13; Matthew 16:27; 19:28; John 5:22-27; Acts 17:31; Romans 14:10; 2 Corinthians 5:10; 1 Thessalonians 4:16; 2 Thessalonians 1:7).

Third, the outward manner of this judgment will be with solemnity and great glory (Daniel 7:9-10; 2 Thessalonians 1:7-10; Jude 14-15; Revelation 20:11-12). The order of this judgment will be: first, all the elect will be acquitted and pronounced blessed; for they join in with the Lord Christ in the judgment of the world, which they could not do if they themselves were not freed in the first place and exalted. Next, the devil and all his angels will be judged, followed by the world of wicked people.

Instruction about baptisms, the laying on of hands. This summarizes the teaching they received when they were baptized and had hands laid on them.

Baptisms. The use of the word baptism in the plural **baptisms** has caused great difficulty. The word **baptisms** is not used in the New Testament elsewhere to refer to the baptism of the Gospel, whereas it was used to refer to Jewish washings. The most general interpretation is that although baptism can never be repeated, nor are any two baptisms identical, yet because many people are baptized, each taking part in the same special baptism, all of them are called **baptisms,** or the baptism of the many.

The laying on of hands. Some people think that **the laying on of hands** refers to a later ceremony in the church called confirmation. But there is no scriptural reference to the laying on of hands on people who had been baptized in these early days of the Christian church. Confirmation came much later on.

Scripture mentions a fourfold imposition of hands by our Lord and the apostles. The first was unique to our Lord, in that it was an authoritative blessing. So, he "took the children in his arms, put his hands on them and blessed them" (Mark 10:16). Second, laying on of hands was used in healing diseases. They laid their hands on sick and weak people, healing them in a miraculous way (Mark 16:18; Luke 4:40; Acts 28:8). This was the sign of healing virtue from the Lord Christ through their ministry. Thirdly, imposition of hands was used to set people apart for the work and office of the ministry (Acts 6:6; 1 Timothy 4:14; 5:22). The rite is derived from the Old Testament (see Numbers 8:10), where the whole congregation laid their hands on the Levites when they were consecrated. It was a normal way for the Jews to dedicate their rulers, rabbis, and teachers. Fourth, **laying on of hands** was used by the apostles in the giving of the supernatural spiritual gifts of the Holy Spirit to those who were baptized (Acts 8:17; 19:6). In no other religious duties was this ceremony used or mentioned in the New Testament or in the records of the early church. The first of these was only a personal action of our Lord Jesus Christ and is only recorded as happening once, so is not intended here. The second was also exceptional and did not include all Christians in general. There is no reason given why anything so extraordinary, occasional, and temporary should be inserted here. The third was a rite used in the church, but only one type of person was involved in it.

So **the laying on of hands** in the last sense is most probably what the apostle means here. This laying on of hands often took place in those days immediately after baptism (Acts 8:13-17; 19:6). Through this event the glory of the Gospel and its propagation were highlighted. When the Gospel was preached, and people were converted to Christ and professed their faith and repentance in baptism, the apostles laid their hands on them, and they received the Holy Spirit in the form of supernatural gifts. This, after the preaching of the Word, was the great means that the Lord Christ used in the spread of the Gospel. By the Word he performed this internally on people's minds and consciences; and through these miraculous gifts he made people think about what was preached, which they witnessed through their external senses. This was not confined to a few ministers of the Word but was common among all who were baptized, according to a number of places in the Scriptures (see 1 Corinthians 14; Galatians 3:5).

Verse 4 speaks of people who "have shared in the Holy Spirit"—that is, of his miraculous gifts and work, which were communicated through this laying on of hands, which must therefore refer to the same thing. After these times this rite was used on other occasions in the church, to imitate, no doubt, the extraordinary actions of the apostles. But there is no mention of this in the Scripture, nor was it in use in those days, and therefore cannot be intended here. This is the most genuine interpretation of these words. Those mentioned received "the elementary teachings about Christ" (verse 1), and, among others that were equally important, they were to be well instructed, baptized, have hands laid on them, through which the extraordinary gifts of the Holy Spirit would be communicated to them.

But we shall allow room also for another exposition of these words, which is more widely accepted. This interpretation says that "the teaching of laying on of hands" is a separate Christian principle. The thing signified is the communication of the Holy Spirit to believers in his gifts and graces, both normal and extraordinary, of which this rite is the external sign. This was special to the Gospel so it could be verified. It could be verified in four ways. First, because the promise of the Lord Christ about the sending of the Holy Spirit was eminently and visibly accomplished. When he was leaving the world he planted the expectation in his disciples that he would send them the Holy Spirit. He did this, not just to comfort them in his absence, but also so that they would be able to carry out the duties that he had given them. So he commanded them to wait quietly in Jerusalem, without taking part in any public ministry, until they had received the promise of the Spirit (Acts 1:4, 8). When this happened, it gave a full and glorious witness, not only about his truth in what he had told them in the world, but also about his present exaltation and acceptance with God. Peter declared this as follows: "Exalted to the right hand of God, he has received from the Father the promised Holy Spirit and has poured out what you now see and hear" (Acts 2:33). The second verification is that many of his gifts themselves were such that miraculous deeds were performed through which God himself bore immediate witness to the truth of the Gospel. "God also testified to it by signs, wonders and various miracles, and gifts of the Holy Spirit distributed according to his will" (2:4). This made the teaching about them of unimaginable importance to the believers in those days, since through them their faith and profession were eminently justified in the face of the world.

The third verification is that the dispensation of the Holy Spirit was special to the times of the Gospel and was in itself sufficient proof of the ending of all legal ordinances. For it was the principal prophecy and promise under the old testament that in the days of the Messiah the Holy Spirit would be poured out in this way. It was the result of Christ's glorification: "'Whoever believes in me, as the Scripture has said, streams of living water will flow from within him.' By this he meant the Spirit, whom those who believed in him were later to receive. Up to that time the Spirit had not been given, since Jesus had not yet been glorified" (John 7:38-39). Our apostle uses the argument of receiving the Holy Spirit to prove to the Galatians that they were freed from the law (Galatians 3:2). The fourth verification is that this dispensation of the Spirit was special to the Gospel and so might be esteemed a special principle of its doctrine. For although the Jews believed in the Holy Spirit as one person in the Trinity, they had no idea about this dispensation of the Spirit and his gifts. These things had been promised under the old covenant but were not to be fulfilled except under the new covenant. Even John the Baptist, who outshone all previous prophets, did not have this knowledge given to him. For those who were only baptized by him, and thereby initiated into the teaching of repentance for the forgiveness of sins, "had not even heard that there is a Holy Spirit" (Acts 19:2)—that is, had not heard about the dispensation of the Holy Spirit. So our apostle instructed them about the doctrine of the Gospel and performed this rite by the imposition of hands so that "the Holy Spirit came upon them, and they spoke in tongues and prophesied" (Acts 19:6). This was an important part of the Gospel, and this was the rite appointed to represent that it is among "the elementary teachings about Christ." This promise Christ made to send the Holy Spirit, with the nature, use, and purpose of the gifts that he performed in believers, was part of "the elementary teachings about Christ." The reader is free to follow either of these two interpretations.

People who are allowed to join the church and take part in all its holy ordinances need to be well instructed about the important principles of the Gospel. Here we have the apostle's rule and the example of the early church as the basis of this doctrine. Such people should be taught for their own sake and for the church's sake. They need this instruction for themselves because without this the ordinances will be of little use to them. For what benefit can anyone derive from something they know so little about? Their instruction is important for the church, as neglect in this area is the biggest reason for the collapse of most churches in the world. Once the care and diligence with which the first churches instructed people admitted into their fellowship was set aside, a vacuum replaced teaching and the churches themselves fell into apostasy.

It is not the outward sign but the inner grace that matters most in the ordinances of the church that are performed in rites and ceremonies. In the rite of imposition of hands what matters principally is the dispensation of the Holy Spirit.

3. And God permitting, we will do so. These words reflect the apostle's resolve, **we will do;** and the limitation of that resolve with a specific submission to God's will, **God permitting.**

We will do so. In verse 1 the apostle mentioned two very different things, "maturity," and "not laying again the foundation." Which does **We will do so** refer to? To "maturity," or to "not laying again the foundation"? I think it refers to "maturity." For Paul states that he is going to "leave" the elementary teachings of Christ, and that he is "not" going to lay again the foundation of repentance, verse 1.

And God permitting. This may refer to three aspects of God's will. First, it may refer to the unknown sovereign will and pleasure of God. If this is so, no more is intended other than our absolute dependence on him, which we should have in all our resolutions. This is our duty, and we should be always reminded of it. "Now listen, you who say, 'Today or tomorrow we will go to this or that city, spend a year there, carry on business and make money.' Why, you do not even know what will happen tomorrow. What is your life? You are a mist that appears for a little while and then vanishes. Instead, you ought to say, 'If it is the Lord's will, we will live and do this or that.' As it is, you boast and brag. All such boasting is evil" (James 4:13-16). If this is intended (as it is, even if more is intended as well), then it is as if he had said, "If God in whose hand is my life, and breath, and all my actions, whom I belong to, whom I serve, and to whom I willingly submit myself in all things, see good, and is pleased to continue my life, then his help is necessary in everything that I do, and I will proceed with my aim to teach you the great mysteries of Christ's priesthood and sacrifice" (see also 1 Corinthians 14:7).

Second, **and God permitting** may refer to the condition of the Hebrews. The apostle had rebuked them for their laziness. For the apostle seems to intimate to them that perhaps God may be so provoked by their previous neglect that he would not provide the means for their further instruction. This is a thing that God often threatens. It is the same as the Gospel being turned away from any person or people. "When they came to the border of Mysia, they tried to enter Bithynia, but the Spirit of Jesus would not allow them to" (Acts 16:7). God did not allow them to enter. This is the same as being forbidden to preach the word in Asia, "having been kept by the Holy Spirit from preaching the word in the province of Asia" (Acts 16:6). So the sense here amounts to, "If God, whom I fear you have provoked so much by your neglect and contempt of his Word, will still be patient and long-suffering toward you, and not throw you out of his care by forbidding me to proceed with my intention, or deprive me of my opportunity—if God does not obstruct me because of your unworthiness, but is graciously pleased to be with me in my proposed work. . ."

Third, **and God permitting** may include the continuance of God's help and presence with the apostle. He often declared that he could neither undertake nor accomplish anything without God's assistance. God can, at the start or in the middle of a letter or sermon, take us aside when he pleases, if he withdraws his assistance from us. All these aspects of God's will are consistent with each other and may all be included in the apostle's thinking here.

Verses 4-8

4-6. It is impossible for those who have once been enlightened, who have tasted the heavenly gift, who have shared in the Holy Spirit, who

146

have tasted the goodness of the word of God and the powers of the coming age, if they fall away, to be brought back to repentance, because to their loss they are crucifying the Son of God all over again and subjecting him to public disgrace.

The people described in these verses had participated in five privileges of the Gospel. Despite all these, it is presumed that they wholly deserted the Gospel itself. We observe some things about their general description. First, the apostle, as he describes the fearful state of these people, says that this was unavoidable, in the sense that it was a righteous judgment on them. They had participated in the privileges and advantages of the Gospel. In their apostasy they despised these, so they deserved God's destruction. Second, all these privileges were linked to the special work of the Holy Spirit, which was unique to the dispensation of the Gospel and which they could not have participated in under Judaism. For the Spirit, in this sense, was not received by the works of the law, but by believing what was heard (see Galatians 3:2). It was a great privilege of the Gospel for them to be delivered from the slavery of the law and to participate in the Spirit. Third, nothing is mentioned here of any covenant grace or mercy in them or toward them, nor of any faith and obedience on their part. Justification, sanctification, or adoption are not specifically attributed to them. Later, when the apostle comes to express his hope and conviction about the Hebrews, that they were not like those he had described previously, nor among those who fall into perdition, he does so on three grounds by which they can be distinguished from them. First, they had things "that accompany salvation" (6:9), along with their salvation, from which salvation was inseparable. None of these things are ascribed to the people described in verses 4-6. Second, the apostle describes the Hebrews (not those mentioned in verses 4-6) by their obedience and fruits of faith. This was their "work" and "love" (verse 10). The apostle differentiates these people who had saving faith and sincere love from those others whom he supposes may perish eternally. Third, the apostle adds that in the preservation of those mentioned, the faithfulness of God was concerned: "God is not unjust. He will not forget" (verse 10). These people were interested in the covenant of grace, which is the only place where God's faithfulness and righteousness can preserve men from ruin and apostasy. This is the case for all who are taken into the covenant. But the apostle does not suppose this to be the case with those mentioned in verses 4-6. He does not intimate that either the righteousness or faithfulness of God was in any way engaged for their preservation, but rather the contrary. The whole description, therefore, refers to some special Gospel privileges, which people claimed to have in those days in a most mixed-up and irregular way.

4. Once been enlightened. The first way in which these people are described is that they had **once been enlightened**. In the whole of

Scripture **enlightened** denotes the inner working of the Spirit and not the outward act of an ordinance, such as baptism. For it was after the New Testament had been written that this word was used mystically to express baptism.

Enlightened means "to give light or knowledge by teaching." Our apostle uses it to mean, "bring to light" (1 Corinthians 4:5). To be **enlightened** is to be instructed in the teaching of the Gospel and so to understand it spiritually: "For God, who said, 'Let light shine out of darkness,' made his light shine in our hearts to give us the light of the knowledge of the glory of God in the face of Christ" (2 Corinthians 4:6). A complete measure of the knowledge of the most fundamental teachings of the Gospel is required for anyone to be **enlightened** (see 2 Peter 1:19-21).

This is the first characteristic of the people described here. They were **enlightened** by the instruction they had received in the doctrine of the Gospel and the impression made on their minds by the Holy Spirit. This is the normal work of the Spirit.

Who have tasted the heavenly gift. The second thing asserted about these people is that they had **tasted the heavenly gift.**

Gift. The "gift of God" sometimes refers to the giving itself and sometimes to the thing given (see John 4:10; Romans 5:15-17; 2 Corinthians 9:15; Ephesians 4:7; James 1:17). As far as I can observe "the gift," when referring to God, denoting the thing given, is only used to signify the Holy Spirit. Under the new covenant "the gift of God" is the Holy Spirit.

Heavenly. The Holy Spirit is said to be **heavenly,** or from heaven. This refers principally to his mission through Christ after his ascension into heaven: "Exalted to the right hand of God, he has received from the Father the promised Holy Spirit and has poured out what you now see and hear" (Acts 2:33). Being exalted, and having received the promise of the Father, Christ sent the Spirit. He was to be "from above," or "from heaven," which is the same as **heavenly.** (See Deuteronomy 4:39; 2 Chronicles 6:23; Job 31:28; Isaiah 24:18; 32:15.) When he came on the Lord Christ to anoint him for his work, "heaven was opened" (Matthew 3:16).

Who have tasted the heavenly gift. We now ask what it is to **taste** this heavenly gift. The metaphorical expression means no more than to make a trial or experiment, for this is what we do by tasting what is offered to us for eating. We taste such a thing to see if we want to receive or refuse it. Therefore, it does not include eating, much less digesting something and being nourished by it. "Now that you have tasted that the Lord is good" (1 Peter 2:3) or found out by experience. So, these people had had an experience of the power of the Holy Spirit, that gift of God, in the dispensation of the Gospel, the revelation of the truth, and spiritual worship. In this state they had made a trial and had some experience—a privilege in which all people do not participate. So, tasting, when compared to spiritual eating and drinking, is small, but in itself it denotes an experience of the excellency of the Gospel given by the Spirit. This is a great privilege and to express contempt for it would be an unimaginable sin, leaving an apostate without remedy.

Shared in the Holy Spirit. The third way in which these people are described is that they **shared in the Holy Spirit.** This is placed in the middle of the list of privileges, two preceding it and two following it. They are all about the work of the Holy Spirit, his gifts and graces, and so depend on sharing in him. People share in the Holy Spirit as they receive him. The world cannot receive him in a personal way (John 14:17). His work is linked to his gifts. So, Peter told Simon the sorcerer that he had no part in spiritual gifts and did not share in the Holy Spirit (Acts 8:21). So to share in the Holy Spirit is to benefit from his spiritual work.

5. Who have tasted the goodness of the word of God. Fourth, these people are described as having **tasted the goodness of the word of God.**

Word of God. This is God's Word preached and declared (see John 6:68; Romans 10:17). The **word of God,** that is, the Word of the Gospel as preached, is what they **tasted.** But it may be said that they enjoyed the Word of God as Jews. They did so, for it is written that they "have been entrusted with the very words of God" (Romans 3:2). But it is the Word of God as preached in the dispensation of the Gospel that is primarily given this name, about which such excellent things are declared (see Acts 20:32; Romans 1:16; James 1:21).

Goodness. The Word is said to be good and desirable as it contains the whole system of truths that are to be declared to fulfill the promise of sending Jesus Christ for the redemption of the church (see 1 Peter 1:25). The Gospel is "good news [good tidings]" (Isaiah 52:7).

Taste. They were to **taste** the goodness of the Word of God, just as they were to "taste" the heavenly gift. The apostle seems to keep studiously to this expression to show that he does not refer to those people who by faith really do receive, feed, and live on Jesus Christ, as pictured in the word of the Gospel (John 6:49-51, 54-56). It is as if he had said, "I am not speaking about those who have received and digested spiritual food for their souls and turned it into spiritual nourishment. I am speaking about those who have tasted it enough to desire to grow by this milk."

The powers of the coming age. Lastly, the apostle says that these people have tasted **the powers of the coming age,** the mighty, great, miraculous work of the Holy Spirit. By **the coming age** the apostle means the days of the Messiah; this was the usual name for it in the church at that time. So, **the powers of the coming age** were the gifts by which those signs, wonders, and mighty deeds were performed by the Holy Spirit, as the prophets had foretold (compare Joel 2 and Acts 2). The people referred to in verse 5 are supposed to have **tasted.** They had an experience of the glorious and powerful working of the Holy Spirit in the confirmation of the Gospel. Indeed, I judge that they themselves shared these powers, the gift of tongues and other miraculous deeds. This was the worst possible apostasy, and that made their recovery impossible. For Scripture does not say that it is impossible for anyone to recover, except for those who sin against the Holy Spirit. Although people may become guilty of this in different ways, none is so terrible as this, since the truth that was confirmed by the Spirit's mighty deeds in them is rejected. This could not be done without an ascription of his divine power to the devil. However, I would not emphasize those extraordinary gifts to the exclusion of ordinary ones. They belong to **the powers of the coming age.** The extraordinary, miraculous gifts of the Spirit were used to build Christ's kingdom, but this is now continued through ordinary gifts; so these ordinary gifts also belong to **the powers of the coming age.**

From this description of these people we can see who the apostle has in mind. It is clear that these people are not true and sincere believers, in the strict and correct sense of that name. There is no mention of faith or believing. In the following verses they are compared with the ground on which the rain often falls but which bears no useful crop. But this is not so with true believers.

It is clear that these people had been recently converted from Judaism to Christianity. They received special privileges. For they had received extraordinary gifts of the Holy Spirit, such as speaking in tongues or performing miracles. These people had found in themselves and others convincing evidence that God's kingdom and Messiah, which they called **the coming age,** had come on them, and they enjoyed their glories. It must have been some horrible frame of spirit, some malicious enmity against the truth and holiness of Christ and the Gospel, that could turn people like this from the faith and blot out all that light and conviction of truth that they had received. But the least grace is a better security for heaven than the greatest gifts and privileges, wherever they may come from.

6. If they fall away. These are the people the apostle has been describing, those who **fall away.** When Peter fell into sin he was **brought back to repentance,** and then, very speedily. So we may say that those who **fall away** does not refer to any sin that people sometimes fall into through temptation. So it must be an intentional sin. A person may fall away into a way of sin and still retain in his mind light that may be suitable for his recovery. To exclude such people from all hope of recovery is directly against Isaiah 55:7, Ezekiel 18:21, and indeed against the whole sense of the Scripture.

Our apostle makes a distinction between "stumbling" and "falling." The apostle has "falling away" in mind here. It is not falling into this or that actual sin. It is not a falling into temptation. It is not falling by denying some aspect of Christian belief. Rather, this "falling away" consists in total renunciation of all the principles and teachings of Christianity. Such was the sin of those who relinquished the Gospel in order to return to Judaism. To complete this falling away the apostle says that this renunciation must be made publicly.

4. It is impossible. For people who fall away, **it is impossible** for them **who have once been enlightened . . . to be brought back to repentance.**

All future events depend on God, who alone exists in himself. So future things are said to be possible or impossible with respect to God's nature, or his decrees, or his moral rule, order, and law. First, things are impossible with respect to the nature of God. It is impossible that God should lie. So it is impossible that God should forgive sin without satisfaction.

Second, things that are possible in themselves, with respect to God's nature, are made impossible by God's decree and purpose. So it was impossible that Saul and his family should be preserved in the kingdom of Israel. It was not contrary to the nature of God, but God had decreed that it should not be so (1 Samuel 15:28-29). Third, things are possible or impossible with respect to the rule and order of all things that God has appointed. When in things of duty God has neither expressly commanded them, nor appointed means for their performance, then we should think of them as being impossible. This is the impossibility that is meant here. It is a thing that God has neither commanded us attempt, nor appointed the means to achieve it, nor promised his assistance in it. So we should not expect it to be possible through any law, rule, or constitution of God.

The apostle does not instruct us any further about future events except for what concerns our duty. It is not for us either to look, or hope, or pray for, or endeavor the renewal of such people to repentance. God gives laws to us in these things, not to himself. It may be possible with God, for all we know, if there is not a contradiction in it concerning his holy nature. What he does we should gratefully accept; but our duty toward such people is completely finished. And, indeed, they put themselves wholly out of our reach.

6. To be brought back to repentance. What is said to be impossible about these people is that they should **be brought back to repentance. Repentance** in the New Testament means a gracious change of mind about the Gospel, which leads the whole soul to be converted to God.

This is the beginning of our turning to God, without which neither the will nor the affections will be engaged with him, nor is it possible for sinners to find acceptance with him.

To be brought back. It is impossible **to be brought back.** Our being **brought back** is the renovation of God's image in our nature, through which we come to him again. For as we lost God's image through sin and were separated from him by profane things, this being **brought back**

restores our nature and person to God. This is real and internal and happens in regeneration and effectual sanctification: "He saved us through the washing of rebirth and renewal by the Holy Spirit" (Titus 3:5; see also 1 Thessalonians 5:23). But this is not what is intended here. For these apostates never had this and so cannot be said to be **brought back**. For no one can be brought back to what he never possessed in the first place. Being **brought back** is also outward profession and pledge. In this sense it consists of a solemn confession of faith and repentance through Jesus Christ with the seal of baptism. This happened to all those who were converted in the Gospel. But these apostates, although they professed repentance toward God and faith in our Lord Jesus Christ, receiving baptism as the pledge of inner renewal, were in reality not participating in this. So it is impossible to bring them again into this state through a second renewal or a second baptism. Most of these people become openly blasphemous and attack the truth.

7-8. Land that drinks in the rain often falling on it and that produces a crop useful to those for whom it is farmed receives the blessing of God. But land that produces thorns and thistles is worthless and is in danger of being cursed. In the end it will be burned.

Land. The subject of this illustration is **land,** which represents the hearts and minds of everyone who listens to the Gospel. This is how our Savior explained his parable of the Sower.

That drinks in the rain often falling on it. Something must happen to the land to make it fruitful. It needs rain. **Rain** is frequently compared with the teaching of Scripture: "Let my teaching fall like rain and my words descend like dew, like showers on new grass, like abundant rain on tender plants" (Deuteronomy 32:2). This rain falls **often,** just as Jesus himself said: "how often I have longed to gather your children together, as a hen gathers her chicks under her wings" (Matthew 23:37). Where the Lord Christ sends the Gospel to be preached, it is his will that it should be preached "in season and out of season" (2 Timothy 4:2), that it may be like abundant showers of rain on earth.

Produces. This word refers to a woman "bringing forth," "giving birth" (see Luke 1:31) to a child. This is how it always used in the New Testament, except for here and in James 1:15: "Then, after desire has conceived, it gives birth to sin; and sin, when it is full-grown, gives birth to death" (James 1:5). The power of the earth, being cherished by the rain that falls on it, brings forth as from a teeming womb the fruits of those seeds it possesses.

A crop. The word signifies green herbs that are usually produced by careful planting, tilling, and feeding with compost. This product was for people, not for cattle.

Useful. This crop is **useful** as it bears its fruit at the correct time. "Like a tree planted by steams of water, which yields its fruit in season and whose leaf does not wither" (Psalm 1:3). For the fruits of the earth are of no value unless they come at the correct season. So James refers to the farmer who "waits for the land to yield its valuable crop and how patient he is for the autumn and spring rains" (James 5:7).

The crop is useful **to those for whom it is farmed.** In addition to the need for rain, the land needs to be cultivated so that it can be fruitful at the correct season and so be useful to those who farm it.

Receives the blessing of God. God's blessing on the fruitful land comes about as God owns the land, God cares for the land, and because God will ensure that the land is protected from evil. These things are only spoken about the ground, but the unspoken application concerning spiritual things is clear. The land is true believers. The fruit they bear is genuine fruit, fruit of the Spirit, fruit of holiness and righteousness.

But land that produces thorns and thistles is worthless and is in danger of being cursed. In the end it will be burned.

Thorns and thistles. In general, these refer to "the fruitless deeds of darkness" (Ephesians 5:11). They are called **thorns and thistles** because of the curse that came on the ground because of sin: "Cursed is the ground because of you; through painful toil you will eat of it all the days of your life. It will produce thorns and thistles for you" (Genesis 3:17). As a result of this curse, the earth itself, uncultivated, would only produce **thorns and thistles**, or at least they would be prevalent in everything that was produced. So man's heart by nature is wholly overrun with evil, sinful desires, and his life is ruled by sinful actions (Genesis 6:5; Romans 3:10-18). So bearing **thorns and thistles** stems from a corrupt nature under the curse. In contrast, all good actions, all actions of faith and obedience, are the fruit of the Spirit.

Produces. Chrysostom pointed out that this word applies to the barren, cursed ground. The apostle goes on to state three things about the ground.

Worthless. First, its fruit is **worthless.** This word means to "try" something in order to find out its worth. We try gold in the fire to see if it is pure and true. Fire discovers the truth about metals (1 Corinthians 3:13-15). Hence the Lord Christ, in the trial of his church, is compared to a refiner with fire (Malachi 3:2). Faith is tried in this way (1 Peter 1:7). A **worthless** person is one who has been rejected, not approved of as a result of a trial, a reprobate (1 Corinthians 9:27; 2 Corinthians 13:5-6; Titus 1:16). Jeremiah states, "I have made you a tester of metals and my people the ore, that you may observe and test their ways. They are all hardened rebels, going about to slander. They are bronze and iron; they all act corruptly. The bellows blow fiercely to burn away the lead with fire, but the refining goes on in vain; the wicked are not purged out. They are called rejected silver, because the Lord has rejected them" (Jeremiah 6:27-30).

Is in danger of being cursed. Second, the land is **in danger of being cursed.** The farmer does not destroy such a piece of land, but he neglects it so that he can see its barrenness more clearly. It then becomes like a barren wilderness.

In the end it will be burned. Lastly, **it will be burned.** Fire totally destroys every combustible thing it comes into contact with. Hence desolations are called burnings. The burning here indicates the destruction of the land. This illustrates both the temporal destruction of the obstinate Jews and the eternal destruction of all unbelievers. Thus, the apostle declares that God, the great vinedresser and owner of the vineyard, would deal with the impenitent and incredulous Hebrews.

Verses 9-12

In these verses the apostle mollifies the severity of the preceding denunciation and prediction. He also uses this discourse as a transition to the second part of his teaching, which was to encourage true believers.

9. Even though we speak like this, dear friends, we are confident of better things in your case—things that accompany salvation. The special purpose of the apostle, in this and the following verses, is to declare his goodwill toward the Hebrews.

Dear friends. The apostle's love and goodwill is seen in that he calls the Hebrews his **dear friends** ["beloved" in the King James Version—Ed. note]. It is an expression of complete affection and is only used in the Gospels to express the love of God the Father for his Son Jesus Christ. (See Matthew 3:17; 12:18; 27:5; Mark 1:11; 9:7; 12:6; Luke 3:22; 9:35; 20:13.) In the apostles' letters it is often applied to believers, especially by Paul.

We are confident of better things in your case. The apostle expresses his judgment about the Hebrews.

Confident. Chrysostom highlights the force of this word. The apostle does not say, "We think," or "We hope," but he is fully **confident.**

Better things. The apostle is **confident of better things** in their case.

Things that accompany salvation. Literally, "such as have salvation." That is, those who have saving grace in them and eternal salvation infallibly linked to them. Such people are saved by virtue of God's faithfulness in the covenant of grace.

10. God is not unjust; he will not forget your work and the love you have shown him as you have helped his people and continue to help them. In this verse the apostle gives his reasons for what he stated in verse 9. He does this partly to encourage them and partly to reassure them about his sincerity and that he did not give them fair words to entice them.

154

God is not unjust; he will not forget your work. The first thing the apostle reassures them about is their **work.** This is not one specific piece of work but a course in working. This is stated in 1 Thessalonians 1:3: "We continually remember before our God and Father your work produced by faith, your labor prompted by love, and your endurance inspired by hope in our Lord Jesus Christ." This obedience of faith according to the Gospel is called **work** here because it was their main activity; their calling lay in it. They did not attend to it occasionally, or when they had nothing else to do, as is the case with some people. Religion was their business, and Gospel obedience their daily work. It is also called their **work** as they labored in it and took such great pains about it. For faith to be a living faith, it has to be a working faith. We should look on obedience as our work, which never gives place to sloth or negligence.

The love you have shown him. A lazy love, like that described in James 2:15-16, and which most people are satisfied with, is no evidence of a saving faith. Faith and love are often thought of as easy things to do, but they are not thought of in this way by those who put them into practice. As they are the only springs of obedience toward God and usefulness toward other people, so they are greatly opposed from within and from without.

You have shown. The evidence of their love is now stated. **You have shown,** or manifested it. The same word is used by James: "Show me your faith without deeds, and I will show you my faith by what I do" (James 2:18). A person can show something in two ways: first, by doing it; second, by declaring what he has done. Our Savior's command is, "let your light shine before men, that they may see your good deeds and praise your Father in heaven" (Matthew 5:16). Nothing should be done by us so that it may be seen; but what may be seen is to be done so that God is glorified. The Hebrews show their work and love by constantly engaging in it.

Shown him. The goal of their work and love is directed toward God, **him,** literally "toward his name."

His people. Literally, "saints." They exercise their love toward the saints. All true believers are called saints in the New Testament (see Romans 1:7; 1 Corinthians 1:2; Hebrews 2:11). Chrysostom comments, "Hearing these things, I beseech you let us minister to the saints. For every believer, insofar as he is a believer, is a saint. Although he is a secular person" (which he mentions to oppose those who thought that only monks could be saints), "he is a saint." **His people**: "saints" were Christ's disciples.

You have helped his people and continue to help them. "You have ministered, and you do minister." This help (literally, "ministering") is a laborious and industrious ministry. In the church it is twofold: first, a special office; second, common love and charity. The institution of a special office or ministry toward the poor is declared in Acts 6 and is mentioned later as an abiding ordinance in Romans 12:8; 1 Timothy 3:8-13. It is this ministry that is meant here, although not exclusively.

It is God's will that many of his saints are in need of help in this world. The great test of our love centers on our attitude to the saints in their distress.

God is not unjust; he will not forget your work. The apostle has mentioned the first reason for their good spiritual state, their **work** and **love.** The second reason for his conviction is based in the righteousness of God. **God is not unjust,** literally "unrighteous." The righteousness of God sometimes denotes the absolute rectitude and perfect goodness of his nature. All other ways of using this word, as applied to God, are subservient to this. Sometimes the equality of the holy dispensations of his justice, through which he gives to everyone what they deserve, is called the righteousness of God. Often the faithfulness of God in keeping and accomplishing his promises is called the righteousness of God. So the apostle John says, "If we confess our sins, he is faithful and just and will forgive us our sins" (1 John 1:9). The forgiveness of sins is on all accounts an act of mercy. The person who confesses and forsakes his sin will find mercy. Hence it is just with God to forgive the sins of those who do this. This is the righteousness that is principally intended here.

He will not forget your work. This may refer either to their persevering in the work or to the future reward for their work.

It is not an infrequent temptation for believers to think that God disregards them and does not cherish and preserve them. See the complaints of the church about this: "my cause is disregarded by my God" (Isaiah 40:27-28; 49:14). This is denied here. God is not unrighteous, forgetting us or our work, so as not to cherish and preserve it. The same conviction was stated about the Philippians: "being confident of this, that he who began a good work in you will carry it on to completion until the day of Christ Jesus" (Philippians 1:6).

These words, **he will not forget your work**, may also apply to the future and final reward of the faith, love, and deeds of believers. For this also belongs to God's covenant. For neither we nor our works deserve an eternal reward on account of our merit. So the reward is reckoned to us not of grace, but out of debt (Romans 4:4).

11. We want each of you to show this same diligence to the very end, in order to make your hope sure.

We want indicates the manner of the apostle's exhortation. Ministers should have an ardent desire that their hearers become stable. How we wish that all who are called to the care and charge of people's souls would follow the apostle's example here. Do we think that the care, solicitude, watchfulness, tender love and affection, earnest and fervent desires for their good, expressed in prayers, tears, journeys, and dangers, which the apostle testifies to everywhere toward all the churches under his care, were duties prescribed to him alone, or graces necessary only for him?

Each of you. The people exhorted to carry out this duty are **each of you.** He was so concerned for the whole flock that he was solicitous for the good of each individual among them. The love and care of ministers should be extended to all the individuals of their flock.

To show this same diligence. This is how they were to carry out their work, with **this same diligence.** The apostle mentions not just the duty but the carrying out of the duty. "Continue these duties, give the same evidence of your condition, as you did previously." Chrysostom points out the apostle's wisdom in insisting on this **same** diligence. "You have used diligence in this matter; continue to do so."

In order to make your hope sure. The immediate end of this **diligence** is to make their **hope sure.** Hope here means a certain assured expectation of good things promised, through the accomplishment of those promises, accompanied with love and desire for them. Faith links to the promise; hope links to the thing promised. Hope is the fruit and effect of faith as it is the right attitude of the soul toward things believed as good, absent, but certain. So, where our faith brings no hope, it must be feared that it is not genuine; and where our hope exceeds the evidence or assurance of our faith, it is but presumption.

Your hope sure. Hope has its degrees, just as faith has. There is weak faith or a little faith, and a strong or great faith. This **sure** hope is not the essence of hope but a special degree of it as it grows. A weak, imperfect hope will give but a weak and imperfect relief in trouble; but a **sure** hope will bring us relief. **To make your faith sure** means to have a fixed, constant assurance, which stems from faith about the good things promised.

To the very end. These words tell us that our duty must continue **to the very end.** We must **show this same diligence to the very end.** There is never any time or occasion when we are relieved of this duty.

12. We do not want you to become lazy, but to imitate those who through faith and patience inherit what has been promised.

To become lazy. The apostle warns the Hebrews against what would frustrate his exhortation and prevent them from carrying out their duty. We are **lazy** in hearing when we do not learn the truths of the Gospel with diligence and industry, when we do not take them into our minds through the diligent use of the means given for that purpose. We are **lazy** in practice when we do not stir ourselves up to exercise these graces and carry out these duties. We are to "show diligence, and not be lazy."

Imitate those who through faith and patience inherit what has been promised. Positively, we are to follow or **imitate** people who have inherited the promise. Inheriting the **promise** means sharing in God's grace and glory. All the people who followed God in the Old Testament received this, as they were saved by faith, just as we are (see Acts 15:10-11; Hebrews 4:2).

The apostle points out the way these people took and the end they attained. The way they took was **through faith and patience.** This faith was not a general, common faith, but faith in the promise given from the foundation of the world and renewed in Abraham. The purpose of this faith was faith in the Messiah, in Christ himself, as a Savior from sin.

Patience. The next thing said about them is **patience. Patience** is being slow to get angry (James 1:19). It is a gracious frame of mind that is not easily provoked. This grace of **patience** also keeps us quietly waiting on God for the fulfillment of everything that concerns us in our own time. We show patience when we commit our whole cause to God (1 Peter 2:23).

Inherit what has been promised. To encourage the Hebrews to carry out their Christian duties the apostle mentions how others did this. They inherited **what** had **been promised.** He speaks in the present tense, but principally intends those who lived before. We enjoy these promises through "inheritance." We do not merit it, nor buy it, but inherit it. How do we inherit it? By God's gratuitous adoption: "You received the Spirit of sonship. And by him we cry, 'Abba, Father.' The Spirit himself testifies with our spirit that we are God's children. Now if we are children, then we are heirs—heirs of God and co-heirs with Christ" (Romans 8:15-17).

What has been promised. They inherited promises. This is to share in the things promised. These promises are God's grace and glory.

Imitate. They are to be imitators, not as mimics, but as followers, walking in the same steps as the apostles took (Romans 4:12; 1 Peter 2:21). This is to imagine that we hear them saying to us what Abimelech said to his soldiers: "Quick! Do what you have seen me do!" (Judges 9:48).

Verses 13-16

When God made his promise to Abraham, since there was no one greater for him to swear by, he swore by himself, saying, "I will surely bless you and give you many descendants." And so after waiting patiently, Abraham received what was promised.

Men swear by someone greater than themselves, and the oath confirms what is said and puts an end to all argument.

13. To Abraham. The person these promises were made to was **Abraham.** He was originally called "Abram," a "high" or "exalted father." God changed his name to **Abraham,** and the reason for this is clearly stated: "No longer will you be called Abram; your name will be Abraham, for I have made you a father of many nations" (Genesis 17:5). God is now declaring that Abraham should not only be the father of all the nations who would be physically descended from him, but the father of all the nations of the world who would in later generations embrace and imitate his faith.

When God made his promise. God's **promise** made Abraham the person he was. In general, promises are the specific declarations of the grace, goodness, and purpose of God toward people, for their good. "I will make you a great nation and I will bless you; I will make your name great, and you will be a blessing. I will bless those who bless you, and whoever curses you I will curse; and all peoples on earth will be blessed through you" (Genesis 12:2-3).

15. After waiting patiently. Abraham was exposed to trials and temptations about the truth and accomplishment of this promise. If there are not difficulties or delays, it is not possible to know if a person can wait patiently. Abraham did not become weary or exasperated by these delays, but carried on depending on God. The apostle explains the meaning of **waiting patiently** in Romans 4:18-21: "Against all hope, Abraham in hope believed and so became the father of many nations, just as it has been said to him, 'So shall your offspring be.' Without weakening in his faith, he faced the fact that his body was as good as dead—since he was about a hundred years old—and that Sarah's womb was also dead. Yet he did not waver through unbelief regarding the promise of God, but was strengthened in his faith and gave glory to God, being fully persuaded that God had power to do what he had promised." Continuing to believe, and trusting in God's truth and power against all difficulties and oppositions, showed how Abraham was **waiting patiently.**

Received what was promised. The goal was to receive **what was promised.** This promise applies to much more than the birth of his son Isaac. The person who is freely justified in Christ may correctly be said to have received **what was promised.**

16. Men swear by someone greater than themselves. Men swear by people who are superior to them.

Puts an end to all argument. The purpose of an oath among human beings is declared: to put **to an end all argument.** When there is an argument and both sides seem to be equally strong, an oath is necessary for the peace of mankind or else war will break out. About this, the apostle says that an **oath confirms what is said.** An oath **puts an end to all argument.** An oath, which invokes God as the supreme governor of the world, supplies the defects and weaknesses by which human society is ruled. This kind of oath **puts an end to all argument.**

Verses 17-20

In the last part of this chapter the apostle covers two more things. First, an explanation of God's purpose in his promise, as it was confirmed by his oath; and, second, a confirmation of the privilege intended here.

Because God wanted to make the unchanging nature of his purpose very clear to the heirs of what was promised, he confirmed it with an oath. God did this so that, by two unchangeable things in which it is impossible for God to lie, we who have fled to take hold of the hope offered to us may be greatly encouraged. We have this hope as an anchor for the soul, firm and secure. It enters the inner sanctuary behind the curtain, where Jesus, who went before us, has entered on our behalf. He has become a high priest forever, in the order of Melchizedek.

17. God wanted. Everything that follows stems from this. It is all founded in the will of God: **God wanted.** The sovereign will of God is the sole spring of all the grace, mercy, and consolation that believers partake of in this world. This is what is proposed here. This is what **God wanted.** Let those who need grace (and who does not?) expect it from God (James 1:5). Through our own endeavors we seek God's grace, but it is God's will alone that brings this about (2 Timothy 1:9).

The unchanging nature of his purpose. The counsel of God is his **unchanging nature** because of the infinite wisdom that accompanies it. So what is called "his good pleasure, which he purposed in Christ" (Ephesians 1:9) is called "the purpose of his will" (Ephesians 1:11). In particular, the **purpose** of God here is the holy purpose of his will, to give his Son Jesus Christ to be a descendant of Abraham for the salvation of the elect. This is **the unchanging nature of his purpose.**

To make . . . very clear. God was willing to show, manifest, declare, make known, **make . . . very clear . . .** his **unchanging nature.** All God's gracious dealings with us spring from his unchanging purposes. "In him we were also chosen, having been predestined according to the plan of him who works out everything in conformity with the purpose of his will" (Ephesians 1:11).

To the heirs of what was promised. The apostle says to whom God intended to give this evidence of his unchanging nature. It was **to the heirs of what was promised,** that is, believers, all believers both under the old and the new covenant. It may be, indeed, that the Hebrews were in mind here, in the first place. For the promise belonged to them as they were the natural descendants of Abraham (Acts 2:39; 3:25-26; 13:46). But they are not the only people meant. All the children of the faith of Abraham are also heirs (Galatians 4:28-29). So to all believers God confirmed his promise with an oath, though the physical descendants of Abraham were meant in the first place, until they cut themselves off through their unbelief (see Micah 7:20; Luke 1:72-73).

He confirmed it with an oath. The person who confirms anything with an oath is *fidejussor*—"one who gives security to faith." In law, the *fidejussor* is the intervener, the one who comes between two people and gives security. So what is pictured here is that God's nature has been declared. So he rightly demands faith from those who heard this. There were no problems on God's side, but believers had fears and doubts and objections. So God, out of his infinite love, gave them a higher pledge of his faithfulness and **confirmed** what he said **with an oath.** He mediated an oath, he interposed himself between the promise and the faith of believers to solemnly undertake that this would be achieved. And by swearing by himself (6:13), he takes it on his life, his being, his truth, to bring this about.

18. God did this so that, by two unchangeable things in which it is impossible for God to lie, we who have fled to take hold of the hope offered to us may be greatly encouraged. The apostle mentions two more things in this verse. First, God's declaration about his unchanging nature was in every way right; and second, the purpose of this declaration for the **heirs.**

God did this so that, by two unchangeable things. Evidence in nature about God's **unchanging nature** consists in **two unchangeable things.** Security is given through them, both from their nature, and also because there were two of them—two witnesses through which the thing in question is established.

In which it is impossible for God to lie. Moreover, the apostle confirms this witness even more from the nature of the person who gave it: **in which it is impossible for God to lie.** God's immutability in promising and the impossibility of his deceiving, or lying, both come from his nature. This greatly encourages us.

May be greatly encouraged. Encouraged here means to be comforted and consoled, as in most of the New Testament. This consolation comes from the assurance of faith and our help from God's promises. This is what relieves our souls of all fears, doubts, and troubles. It either prevents them or is stronger than them. For comfort is the relief of the mind against sorrow and trouble.

This consolation that God desires to give us is strong, powerful, so we are **greatly encouraged.**

We who have fled. This is a description of those whom God has planned to **greatly encourage.** These people, believers, have fled for refuge. They are alerted to a danger, and so with speed and diligence they seek safety.

Hope offered to us. This **hope** is set before us, proposed to us, **offered**

to us. This is the declaration of the promise or the dispensation of the Gospel.

To take hold of. We **take hold of** what we hold fast to with all our might and power. There will be many attempts to shake off the hand of faith from holding on to God's promises, but it is part of our duty to **take hold of** these promises and firmly keep them in our grip.

Verses 19-20

We have this hope as an anchor for the soul, firm and secure. It enters the inner sanctuary behind the curtain, where Jesus, who went before us, has entered on our behalf. He has become a high priest forever, in the order of Melchizedek.

19. Hope. The commonly held idea about hope, that it is seen as being something that is dubious and uncertain, is quite wrong. Hope springs from faith as it places all its expectation on the good things in the promise. The essence of **hope** is that it trusts in God.

As an anchor for the soul. Faith is compared with an **anchor**. It is **an anchor for the soul;** for the souls of believers, it seems, need anchors.

Firm and secure. This anchor is **firm and secure**. It is **secure** and will not fail. It can be trusted. It is so **firm** that no wind can break or move it. Such is **hope** for the soul. In its nature it is **secure** and it is not a deception of the imagination. "Hope does not disappoint us" (Romans 5:5). **Hope,** built on faith, is infallible and will not deceive. **Hope** is **secure** against all opposition. It is not **secure** in itself, but in the ground in which it is fixed, namely, Christ in the promise.

It enters the inner sanctuary behind the curtain. This is how the spiritual anchor secures the soul. And this is where the illustration breaks down. For an anchor is thrown downward, and it latches itself onto the bottom of the sea, but hope ascends upward and fixes itself in heaven, or on what is there.

Curtain. The **curtain** separated the Most Holy Place from the sanctuary or body of the temple. This is called the "second curtain" in 9:3: "Behind the second curtain was a room called the Most Holy Place." For the body of the temple, where only the priests entered to offer incense, was separated from the people by the first curtain, as the Most Holy Place was from that by the second curtain. The ordinary priest passed through the first curtain every day to offer incense; through the second curtain the high priest passed through just once a year. Christ as priest passed through the heavens in his ascension into the glorious presence of God.

It enters. This hope **enters** or passes through. The heavens are like a

curtain to human senses that limit our reasoning. We cannot discern anything beyond the curtain. But faith, with **hope,** pierces through the curtain—no created thing can keep them at arm's length from God himself.

The inner sanctuary behind the curtain. What is beyond the curtain?
Not an ark and mercy-seat, not tables of stone and cherubim, the work of
human hands; but the things signified by them—God himself on a throne
of grace, and the Lord Jesus Christ, as the high priest of the church at his
right hand; God the Father as the author of the promise of grace, Christ
as the purchaser of all mercy, the counsel of peace being between them
both. Here hope fixes itself, to hold the soul steadfast in all the storms
that may come.

Behind the curtain. As a forerunner, Christ entered into heaven itself,
the place of the glorious presence of God.

**20. Where Jesus, who went before us, has entered on our behalf. He
has become a high priest forever, in the order of Melchizedek.**

The apostle gives new assurance to the efficacy of hope fixed on the
promise, as it enters beyond the curtain, because Christ, our high priest, is
there. Even heaven would be no safe place for us to fix the anchor of our
trust and hope in if Christ were not there.

He has become a high priest. The apostle brings us to the point he has
been heading for all this time, to Christ's priesthood as represented in that
of Melchizedek, which he had asserted in 5:10.

Jesus. The apostle now focuses on the Lord Christ. He says who he is
through his name, **Jesus.** Jesus means Savior, for he was called Jesus
because he was to save his people from their sins (Matthew 1:21). So the
one about whom all these things are affirmed is to be considered as our
Savior, who had the name of a Savior given him by God himself, for the
work which he was to do (1 Thessalonians 1:10). Jesus is still "able to save
completely" (7:25).

Who went before us. Jesus is our forerunner, a title that is only here
given to Jesus. The high priest of old, when he made his annual entry into
the Most Holy Place, was not our forerunner. He entered there himself,
but he did not then allow the people to follow. Here is another example of
Christ's superior high priesthood. When Christ entered the Most Holy
Place, he did not do so just for himself, but he **went before us** so he could
lead the whole church into the same glory.

On our behalf. He entered **on our behalf,** that is, for all believers, for
the whole church, in all times, ages, and places.

Hebrews
Chapter 7

Melchizedek prefigured Christ's priesthood. Melchizedek and his priesthood appears in verses 1-10 of this chapter. Verses 11-24 explain two inferences from this, related to Christ's office. Verses 25-28 show the nature of Christ's priesthood.

The apostle's purpose in this letter, especially in this chapter and the next three chapters, is to open two curtains for us; one curtain is here below, the other in heaven. The apostle shows us what was beyond the curtain on earth, all the ordinances, institutions, ceremonies, and types of the law. This curtain still hangs over the Jews today. The other curtain is the one belonging to the heavenly sanctuary. This he opens for us so we can view the ministry of Christ our high priest. The apostle convinces the Hebrews that their priesthood and worship has ceased, to the unimaginable advantage of the church. So he shows us the main purpose of all the Mosaic types of the Old Testament and God's institution in them.

Verses 1-3

This Melchizedek was king of Salem and priest of God Most High. He met Abraham returning from the defeat of the kings and blessed him, and Abraham gave him a tenth of everything. First, his name means "king of righteousness"; then also, "king of Salem" means "king of peace." Without father or mother, without genealogy, without beginning of days or end of life, like the Son of God he remains a priest forever.

1. This. The person spoken about is described in various ways: first, by his name, **Melchizedek**; second, by his office: he was a **king**; third, by the place of his rule, which was Salem, for he was **king of Salem**; fourth, by another office: a **priest of God Most High;** fifth, by his actions as a priest: he **blessed** Abraham; sixth, by the acknowledgment of his office by Abraham, who **gave him a tenth of everything;** seventh, by the interpretation of his name: **"king of righteousness";** eighth, the place of his reign: **"king of peace";** ninth, by his various characteristics: **without father or mother, without genealogy, without beginning of days or end of life.**

Melchizedek. First, Melchizedek was a mere man and no more than a man. For "every high priest is selected from among men" (5:1). So the Son of God himself could not have been a priest if he had not assumed our nature. If Melchizedek was more than a man he would not have been introduced as **without father or mother,** for only men have them. Second, Melchizedek did not become high priest by right of his birth, which includes a **genealogy,** but was raised up and called directly by God. In this respect Christ is said to be a high priest after his order. Thirdly, Melchizedek had no successor on the earth, nor could he have, as he was a priest because of his extraordinary call.

King of Salem. The first thing said about Melchizedek concerns his office, that he was a **king.** When he is first mentioned he is called "Melchizedek king of Salem" (Genesis 14:18). He is not principally a type of Christ in this respect, as nowhere is it said that Christ is a king after Melchizedek's order; nevertheless, Melchizedek's being a king does make him more eminent.

The place of his rule is stated as **king of Salem.** I judge that Melchizedek lived and reigned in Jerusalem.

Priest. Melchizedek was a **priest,** and the first to be appointed by a special institution. The faith of the church in all ages was directed to believe that all God's institutions of worship referred to Christ. So the institution of the sacrificing priesthood, in the person of so great a person as Melchizedek, acquainted them to some extent with the nature of his work.

Priest of God Most High. This places a limitation on Melchizedek's priesthood. He is only a priest in relation to **God Most High.** This is the first time this title is used of God in Scripture, which is then often used. Sometimes God is called "God over all," or "God above," or "the God of heaven," or "The Most High."

He met Abraham returning from the defeat of the kings. The apostle now describes Melchizedek's actions. Abraham did not only defeat a complete army of kings and take their spoils, he also killed the kings themselves, as Genesis 14:17 records. Hence we are told here that Abraham was **returning from the defeat of the kings.**

Two of Melchizedek's priestly actions are now described: he **blessed** Abraham, and he received tithes from Abraham.

Melchizedek met Abraham and **blessed him.** This solemn benediction is recorded in full in Genesis 14:19-20: "Blessed be Abram by God Most

High, Creator of heaven and earth. And blessed be God Most High, who delivered your enemies into your hands." There are two parts to this blessing. The first part has Abraham as the object, and is a blessing of prayer; and the second part has God as its object, and is a blessing of praise.

The second priestly action performed by Melchizedek is that he received tithes: **Abraham gave him a tenth of everything.** Abraham gave this as a duty, and Melchizedek received it as a symbol of his office. **Of everything** refers to the spoils Abraham had just gained. The receiving of spoils by Melchizedek was a priestly act. The tenth was given firstly to God, and the person who received this tithe was acting as God's officer, in God's name.

First, his name means "king of righteousness"; then also, "king of Salem" means "king of peace." The apostle pursues his argument with Melchizedek's name and its meaning. What does **"king of righteousness"** and **"king of peace"** mean? Most people think that this just means that he was a king who ruled righteously and lived peaceably. This was indeed true. But these names given to him show us how he was a type of Christ. He was a "king of righteousness and peace." The **king of righteousness** is the author, cause, and dispenser of righteousness to others, just as God is said to be "The Lord our Righteousness." So also he is the **king of peace,** in the sense that God is called "the God of peace." This was true of Melchizedek, as he represented Jesus Christ.

The Lord Jesus Christ is the only king of righteousness and peace for the church (see Isaiah 9:6; 32:1-2). Christ is not only a righteous and peaceable king, as were his types, Melchizedek and Solomon, but he is the author and dispenser of righteousness and peace to the church. "'The days are coming,' declares the LORD, 'when I will raise up to David a righteous Branch, a King who will reign wisely and do what is just and right in the land. In his days Judah will be saved and Israel will live in safety. This is the name by which he will be called: The LORD Our Righteousness" (Jeremiah 23:5-6). Christ is righteous and reigns righteously; but this is not all, he is "the LORD Our Righteousness."

Without father or mother. The apostle now describes Melchizedek as being **without father or mother, without genealogy, without beginning of days or end of life.** Melchizedek was **without father or mother** in that the Spirit of God, who so exactly recorded the genealogies of other patriarchs and types of Christ, says Melchizedek does not have one. He is introduced, as it were, like one falling from heaven, suddenly appearing, ruling in Salem, and being a priest to the Most High God.

A mortal has both **beginning of days** and **end of life,** neither of which Melchizedek is said to have had. But obviously he was born and died. All these historical details about him are lacking, and we know no more about him than what Scripture tells us.

Like the Son of God. In these respects Melchizedek was **like the Son of God.** Jesus is here called **the Son of God** to show that although Melchizedek was an excellent person, yet he was infinitely inferior to the person he represented, the Son of God. Melchizedek was not the Son of God, but he had many things that made him like Christ.

He has become a high priest forever. This was the apostle's main point in these verses. He wanted to show that there was in the Scripture, before the institution of the Aaronic priesthood, a representation of the eternal, unchanging priesthood to be introduced to the church, which he demonstrates to be that of Jesus Christ.

Verses 4-5

Just think how great he was: Even the patriarch Abraham gave him a tenth of the plunder! Now the law requires the descendants of Levi who become priests to collect a tenth from the people—that is, their brothers—even though their brothers are descended from Abraham. The Hebrews' duty concerning the state of Melchizedek, which has already been described and insisted on, is here pressed home.

Just think. The special duty the apostle insists on is that they should **think** about the excellency of Melchizedek's office. The apostle calls upon the Hebrews to **think** four times in his letter (3:1; 10:24; 12:3 and here).

How great. Melchizedek's greatness had nothing to do with his personal endowments or his wealth but his office and his nearness to God on account of that. The proof of **how great** Melchizedek was is backed up by the statement that **even the patriarch Abraham gave him a tenth of the plunder!** The Jews esteemed Abraham next to God himself. Hence our apostle says, **even the patriarch Abraham.** A patriarch is a father, that is, a prince or ruler of a family—a ruling father. There were three kinds of patriarchs among the Jews. Abraham was the only one of the first kind of patriarch. He was the first father of all that great family. The second type of patriarch included those who succeeded Abraham, that is, Isaac and Jacob, "who were heirs with him of the same promise" (11:9). The third type of patriarch included the first leaders of the twelve tribes into which the nation was divided; that is, the twelve sons of Jacob (who are called patriarchs in Acts 7:8-9). From this it is clear that Abraham was the pre-eminent patriarch. For anyone to be greater than Abraham, especially in Abraham's time, he must have been given some great privilege that was above the whole nation, as it was descended from Abraham. The apostle proves that this was the case because Abraham gave **a tenth of the plunder** to Melchizedek.

5. Now the law requires the descendants of Levi who become priests to collect a tenth from the people—that is, their brothers—even though their brothers are descended from Abraham. This illustrates the present argument about Melchizedek being superior to Abraham since Abraham gave Melchizedek a tithe.

Now the law requires the descendants of Levi who became priests to collect a tenth from the people. God took the tithe to be his special portion and therefore separated it from the people, who had no part in it. The tithe of the land was said to be the Lord's, and so to withhold it was to "rob" God (Leviticus 27:30; Malachi 3:8).

That is, their brothers—even though their brothers are descended from Abraham. The privilege of the priests taking the tithe is seen in whom they took it from. They were not strangers, or foreigners, but **their brothers**. These brothers enjoyed the same privileges as they did, but this did not exempt them from their duty to pay their tithes.

Verses 6-10

6. This man, however, did not trace his descent from Levi, yet he collected a tenth from Abraham and blessed him who had the promises.

Did not trace his descent. Melchizedek did not trace his descent from among them. This was necessary to show that Christ's priesthood came from eternity.

Yet he collected a tenth from Abraham. The Levitical priests received tithes from Abraham's descendants. This was evidence of their being appointed by God. But Melchizedek received tithes from Abraham himself, which showed his superiority both to the Levitical priests and to Abraham.

Who had the promises. To demonstrate further how great Melchizedek was, who received tithes from Abraham, our apostle explains a special privilege Abraham had. It was he who **had the promises.** This the apostle singles out as the greatest honor Abraham had (see 6:13-16). Through this, Abraham became the father of the faithful, the heir of the world, and the friend of God. This illustrates the greatness of Melchizedek, because Abraham paid tithes to him.

7. And without doubt. Beyond all reasonable contradiction. A truth that cannot and will not be denied.

The lesser person is blessed by the greater. The person who is blessed is inferior to the person who blesses.

8. In the one case, the tenth is collected by men who die; but in the

other case, by him who is declared to be living. This verse compares how the Levitical priests and Melchizedek received tithes.

The tenth is collected. This is the basis of the comparison between Melchizedek and the Levitical priests. They both received tithes.

By men who die. This begins the contrast between Melchizedek and the Levitical priests. For the Levitical priests were men subject to death, mortal men who lived and died according to the laws of nature, as they carried out their duty. But Melchizedek's death is not recorded.

By him who is declared to be living. In contrast with the Levitical priests, Melchizedek is **declared to be living.** This is said about Melchizedek, taking him to be a type, for we know that he would die. The life of the church depends on the everlasting life of Jesus Christ. It is said of Melchizedek, as he was a type of him, **him who is declared to be living.** Christ also lives—forever.

9. One might even say. "To sum up the whole in a word, to put an end to this dispute between the Levitical priesthood and that of Melchizedek, I say that not only Abraham, but even Levi himself was tithed by him."

That Levi, who collects the tenth, paid the tenth through Abraham, namely, when Abraham gave the tithes of everything to Melchizedek. By **Levi** he means not the person of Levi absolutely, the third son of Jacob, but his descendants, or the whole tribe descended from him, insofar as they were linked to the priesthood. For Levi himself never received tithes from anyone, as the priesthood was established in his family long after his death by his great-grandson Aaron. So, **Levi** who received the tithes is the same as the sons of Levi who received the priesthood (verse 5). It is affirmed of **Levi** that he **paid the tithe through Abraham.** When Abraham himself gave tithes to Melchizedek, he did it not in his own name only, but in the name of his whole posterity also. This demonstrates the preeminence of Melchizedek's priesthood over that of the house and family of Levi. All the difficulty of the argument lies in the proof of the assertion, namely, that Levi did indeed pay tithes in Abraham. The apostle demonstrates this by his observation that **Levi . . . paid the tenth through Abraham.**

10. In the body of. The force of this proof seems to depend on a double principle: first, that children, the complete posterity of anyone, are **in the body of** their ancestor before they are born; and, second, that what anyone does, all his descendants are deemed to do in and through him.

Verses 11-14

11. If perfection could have been attained through the Levitical priesthood (for on the basis of it the law was given to the people), why was

there still need for another priest to come—one in the order of Melchizedek, not in the order of Aaron? In this verse, after so long a preparation and introduction by which he cleared his way from objections, the apostle begins his main line of argument about the priesthood of Christ and all its consequences concerning righteousness, salvation, and worshiping God, which depend on this.

Perfection. The apostle's reasoning is built on a case the Hebrews could not deny. This is that **perfection** is the goal of the priesthood of the church.

Could have been attained through the Levitical priesthood. It is assumed that this **perfection** is the goal of the work of the priesthood in the church. This, at one time or another, in one order or another, it must attain, or the whole office is useless. And the apostle denies that this could be **attained through the Levitical priesthood.** This **Levitical priesthood** includes Levi, its originator, and the family of Aaron who were assisted in all priestly activities and duties by the Levites. That **perfection** belonged to this priesthood is denied by the question, **why was there still need for another priest to come?**

Perfection in this verse consists in three things: first, the personal ministry of Christ in the preaching of the Gospel or the declaration of the mystery of the wisdom and grace of God in himself. Second, the mission of the Holy Spirit, to reveal and make fully known the same mystery through the apostles and prophets of the new testament (Ephesians 3:5). Third, the effectual illumination of the minds of those who do believe, enabling them to spiritually discern the mysteries so revealed, each according to the gift and grace he has been given (see Ephesians 3:16-19; 1 Peter 2:9).

The people. The people in the wilderness, the body of the church, to whom the law and priesthood were given directly through Moses' ministry, are referred to here. Following this, all of Abraham's descendants were one people with them. For that people is still the same; as a people never dies until all the individuals who belong to it die, so through this **people** the whole church of all ages under the old testament is intended.

The law was given. The **law was given** to this people, and they also "had the gospel preached" to them (4:2). This happened under the promise made to Abraham, and in the many types of Christ and his offices and sacrifice that were instituted among them. But at the same time, they were so under the power of the law that they did not have the light, freedom, and comfort of the Gospel which we enjoy.

Another priest. Not only a priest who had not yet come, but a priest from a different order or stock. A priest who would not be from the tribe of Levi, nor of the order of Aaron.

Not in the order of Aaron. "And not to be called after the order of

Aaron." A new priest may come and the old legal order might continue. But, the apostle says here, he is not to be of the same order. He will not be in the order of Aaron, but, on the contrary, **in the order of Melchizedek.**

12. For when there is a change of the priesthood, there must also be a change of the law. In this verse the apostle explains what he meant by "the law" in verse 11, which the people received under the Levitical priesthood. It was the whole "law of commandments contained in ordinances," or the whole law of Moses, so far as it was the rule of worship and obedience for the church; for that law governs the priesthood.

There must also be. There is a necessity to change the law. The whole administration of the law, so far as it concerned the expiation of sin by sacrifices and the solemn worship of God in the tabernacle or temple, depended absolutely on, and was confined to, the Aaronic priesthood, so that not one sacrifice could be offered to God, nor could divine worship be observed. That priesthood being abolished and taken away, the law itself of necessity ceases and becomes useless.

There must also be a change of the law. That is, it must be abolished. For the **change** here must be of the same order as the change in the priesthood, which was its abolition. God made this change, and he alone could do this. So "having canceled the written code, with its regulations, that was against us and that stood opposed to us, he took it away, nailing it to the cross" (Colossians 2:14). When Christ did this, the **change** was completed.

13. He of whom these things are said belonged to a different tribe, and no one from that tribe has ever served at the altar.

These things. That is, all that had been said about Melchizedek and his priesthood, and everything that follows from this. Although many of these things were originally spoken about other people and other things, they ultimately refer to Christ alone, whom they represent and make way for.

Belonged to a different tribe. To support his argument about the changing or abolition of the priesthood the apostle points out how the people were put into different tribes. Each tribe had a common interest in the church, and some had special privileges given them by the law. So the priesthood was granted, confirmed, and confined to the tribe of Levi and to the family of Aaron in that family. All other tribes were excluded from this. But to one of the tribes excluded from an interest in the legal priesthood did he belong of whom these things are spoken. This I regard as the main reason for people being put into tribes; namely, that God might provide instruction for the continuation of the legal worship among them. This could not be continued unless the priesthood was reserved for that one tribe to which this privilege belonged.

And no one from that tribe has ever served at the altar. The apostle describes in general this other tribe as the one in which **no one . . . has ever**

served at the altar. In verse 14 he says which tribe that was and why it had to be that tribe.

Served at the altar may stand for the whole priestly office. But I think that the apostle not only includes the priests, who sacrificed at the altar, but all those who attended the services, though they did not burn incense or offer sacrifices.

14. For it is clear that our Lord descended from Judah, and in regard to that tribe Moses said nothing about priests.

There is a double assertion in this verse; first, that **our Lord descended from Judah**; and, second, that **in regard to that tribe Moses said nothing about priests.**

It is clear. It is open or evident, as we say, in itself; a thing easy to be proved, which no one can deny. **It is clear** by Christ's genealogy; for, by God's providence, his parents were publicly enrolled from that tribe, and from the family of David, by order of Augustus Caesar (Luke 2:4-5).

Descended. Literally, "sprang from" or "rose from." "The sun of righteousness will rise with healing in its wings" (Malachi 4:2; see also Luke 1:78). Christ rose illustriously from the tribe of Judah.

In regard to that tribe Moses said nothing about priests. The apostle shows that the priesthood in no way belonged to the tribe of Judah, and he appeals to the lawgiver, or rather, to the law itself. For by **Moses** is meant not just the person himself, but his ministry in giving the law. It is the law about worship that is under consideration.

Verses 15-17

15-17. The purpose of this discourse is to confirm that the Aaronic priesthood would be changed and consequently the whole law of ordinances that depended on this. The time for this change had now come. For without the removal of the old there is no place for the new.

And what we have said is even more clear if another priest like Melchizedek appears, one who has become a priest not on the basis of a regulation as to his ancestry but on the basis of the power of an indestructible life. For it is declared: "You are a priest forever, in the order of Melchizedek."

15. Even more clear. This topic is introduced emphatically.

One who has become. This priest was not succeeding any order of priesthood that had been previously established.

Like Melchizedek. The nature of his priesthood is declared: it is to be like Melchizedek's. God had ordered everything in the Scripture about Melchizedek that he might be "like the Son of God" (verse 3), but here

Christ is to be **like Melchizedek.** From this it is clear that there will be another **priest** who will come from another stock, and a priest who will be **like Melchizedek.**

16. This verse states how this priest, who was not a descendant of Aaron, would come into that office. **Become a priest.** The Lord Christ did not just on his own authority and power take this office on himself; he was appointed to it by the Father.

Not on the basis of a regulation as to his ancestry. How he was appointed priest is first described in a negative way. He was not made a priest through the law, that is, **on the basis of a regulation.** His human **ancestry**, and its institution, is opposed to the dispensation of the Spirit under the Gospel.

How then is Christ made a priest **on the basis of the power of an indestructible life?** This **indestructible life** is the life of Christ himself. Christ was made a priest according to this **power** because in this way alone he was equipped to carry out that office in which God was to redeem his church with Christ's own blood (see Acts 20:28). Christ had this **power** from his divine nature, his **indestructible life.**

17. Declared. This witness is given by David, or rather by the Holy Spirit speaking through David. **You are a priest,** although you are not from Aaron's stock, **in the order of Melchizedek.** Christ's priesthood, in the mind of God was the eternal idea of the priesthood of Melchizedek. Christ is said to be a **priest forever** because he was endued with endless life, because he ever lives to make intercession for us, and because he saves believers with an everlasting salvation.

Verses 18-19

The former regulation is set aside because it was weak and useless (for the law made nothing perfect), and a better hope is introduced, by which we draw near to God.

18. Regulation. This **regulation** or "commandment" refers to more than just the institution of the legal priesthood. It refers to the whole system of Mosaic institutions.

Former. That is, before the Gospel as now preached and dispensed.

Set aside. The law is abrogated, abolished, disannulled.

Because it was weak and useless. This is the reason for the abrogation of the **regulation.**

19. (For the law made nothing perfect.) That is, none of the things we are about to consider was made **perfect.** It did not make the church-state perfect, it did not make the worship of God perfect, it did not make a perfect covenant between God and human beings. It was a shadow, an obscure representation of all these things, but it **made nothing perfect.**

Introduced. The introduction of one thing after another. This was the priesthood and sacrifice of Christ, which were brought in after the law, to do what the law could not do (10:1-10).

So, the sense of these words is, "The introduction of the better hope, after and in place of the law, when it was discovered to be weak and insufficient to carry out is purpose, made all things perfect, or brought the church into the state of consummation that it was designed for."

Better. It is a **better hope** as we are complete in Christ (Colossians 2:10), and because "by one sacrifice he has made perfect forever those who are being made holy" (10:14).

Hope. This refers to Christ's coming and the carrying out of his work.

By which we draw near to God. This explains what our **better hope** is.

Draw near. This word comes from the priestly office and denotes the approach of the priests to God as they worship him. Under the Levitical priesthood, the priests in their sacrifices drew near to God. The same is now done for all believers through the priestly ministry of Jesus Christ. Now, all of them **draw near to God.** In all their worship, especially in their prayers and supplications, they have, through Christ, access to God (Ephesians 2:18).

Verses 20-22

And it was not without an oath! Others became priests without any oath, but he became a priest with an oath when God said to him: "The Lord has sworn and will not change his mind: 'You are a priest forever.'" Because of this oath, Jesus has become the guarantee of a better covenant.

The apostle has been explaining that the Lord Christ would be a priest; that he would be "another" priest, a priest of another order, namely, that of Melchizedek, and that he would be a priest forever. Now he explains that this took place with **an oath.** There are three things in these verses. First, a proposition of a new medium for the confirmation of the principal argument, verse 20; second, an illustration and proof of this assertion, verse 21; third, an inference from this, verse 22.

20. And it was not without an oath! Others became priests without an oath. People became priests in two ways, with or without an oath. The dignity of the priesthood depended on and was declared by the way God was pleased to initiate men into that office.

21. But he became a priest with an oath when God said to him: "The

Lord has sworn and will not change his mind: 'You are a priest forever.'" The apostle asserts that "others became priests," that is, the priests under the law, "without an oath." No oath is mentioned in the record about their call and consecration. **But he became a priest with an oath.** The apostle declares that Christ became a priest after the order of Melchizedek. He was made a priest **with an oath.** This **oath** was constituent of his office. His call and consecration came from this **oath.**

"**The Lord has sworn and will not change his mind.**" The person giving the oath is God the Father, who speaks to the Son in Psalm 110:1, "The LORD says to my Lord." God's oath is nothing less than the solemn, eternal, and unchanging decree of his will. While this oath was not the sole constituent cause of Christ's priesthood, it was necessary before he could start this work.

Will not change his mind. When God changes any law or rule it is said that he "repents" or "changes his mind." God says that this will never happen in this matter.

You are a priest forever. The oath is that Christ should be **a priest forever.** Christ was not only made a priest with an oath, which the others were not, but a priest **forever.** This confirms that his office was unchanging and that he himself, not any successor, will hold and discharge this office.

22. Because of this oath, Jesus has become the guarantee of a better covenant. This **covenant** or testament would be **better** than the previous one, which is to be annulled. After God had made one covenant with his people, he would not remove it, abolish it, unless its replacement was a better one. This **better covenant** would have a surety, **become the guarantee.** Christ undertook, on our behalf, what was needed, and so the promise was fulfilled. Christ being our surety places the highest obligation on us to obey the covenant. No one is a believer who does not understand the power of this obligation.

Verses 23-25

Now there have been many of those priests, since death prevented them from continuing in office; but because Jesus lives forever, he has a permanent priesthood. Therefore he is able to save completely those who come to God through him, because he always lives to intercede for them.

The apostle now moves on to his last argument from the priesthood of Christ, as represented by Melchizedek. He continues to show that Christ's priesthood, and his own person, was superior to that of the Levitical priesthood. He shows first the state of the Levitical priests because of their mortality; second, the condition of Christ's priesthood because of his immortality; and third, the results that stem from Christ's priesthood being forever.

23. Since death prevented them from continuing in office. These priests were mortal men, subject to death, and they died.

24. But because Jesus lives forever, he has a permanent priesthood. The only reason for the Levitical priests being many is that they died and so had to be replaced. So the perpetuity of Christ's priesthood is demonstrated in that he lives forever. This is the faith the Jews had about the Messiah: "We have heard from the Law that the Christ will remain forever" (John 12:34).

Permanent priesthood. This is a priesthood that is subject to no change or alteration, and that cannot pass away.

25. Therefore he is able to save completely those who come to God through him, because he always lives to intercede for them.

The main aim of the apostle's discourse was not merely to open mysterious truths, or to demonstrate the glory and preeminence of the Gospel church-state over that of the same church under the institutions of Moses. His principal purpose was to demonstrate the spiritual and eternal advantages of all true believers through these things. The sum of what he intends is proposed in this verse and expanded upon until the end of the next chapter. What believers should seek from and what they may expect from this blessed, glorious priesthood is now declared by the apostle.

He is able. What is inferred about this priest is that he has power and ability. **He is able** (see 2:18).

He is able to save completely. Save completely may refer to the perfection of the work or to its duration. In the first sense it means it will not bring about part of our salvation and leave what remains to ourselves and to others. Rather he is our Rock, and his work is perfect. Whatever belongs to our entire, complete salvation, he is able to effect it.

Those who come to God. To **come to God** has a double meaning in Scripture, sometimes expressing faith and sometimes expressing worship. To **come to God** is to believe. Faith or believing is a coming to God. So when Christ calls us to faith in him, he is calling us to him (Matthew 11:28). Unbelief is refusing to come to him. Faith in God **through him** is coming to the Father through him (John 14:6); so to come to God through Christ is through him to believe in God (1 Peter 1:21).

Our access to God in his worship is also our coming to him. So it is most frequently expressed in the Old Testament—"Draw near to God." And the expression is taken from the approach that was made to the tabernacle in and with all holy services. Those who worship God **come to God.** Worshipers are "comers," not those who come to the worship, but those who through that worship **come to God.** In our worship of God we draw near to him and come to God (Ephesians 2:18; Hebrews 10:22).

The latter sense is principally intended here, since the apostle's theme concerns the state of the church under the new testament and its advantage over the old through its relation to Christ's priesthood.

Through him. That is, **through him** as a high priest, as is explained in 10:19-22.

Because he always lives to intercede for them. This shows the state of Christ as high priest: he **always lives,** lives forever. Christ is always living. The Lord Christ, in his divine person, lives in heaven in that he is alive in himself as he has the eternal life of God in his divine nature (John 5:26). The Lord Christ also lives a mediatory life in heaven, a life for us. He describes himself in this way in Revelation 1:18: "I am the Living One; I was dead, and behold I am alive forever and ever!"

This verse also shows what Christ does as high priest—he intercedes for us. **He always lives to intercede for them** expresses all that the Lord Christ, as the high priest of the church, does for us now with God, and upon which the certainty of our salvation depends.

Verses 26-28

26. Such a high priest meets our needs—one who is holy, blameless, pure, set apart from sinners, exalted above the heavens. In this verse, the apostle gives a reason for all of his preceding discourse. There is something supposed in this assertion—namely, that if we intend to come to God, we are in need of a high priest to encourage us and enable us to do this. So the basis of the apostle's argument is that sinners, which we all are, can have no access to God except through a high priest. This verse states the personal qualifications of Christ as high priest, as well as his outward condition.

Such a high priest meets our needs. Unholy sinners stand in need of a holy priest and a holy sacrifice. What we do not have in ourselves we must have in him, or we will not be accepted by the holy God, who has such pure eyes that he cannot look on sin. **Such a high priest** is the Lord Christ.

One who is holy. As he was **holy,** he does not have sin present with him as we have (Romans 7:18, 21), neither is he entangled in sin (12:1).

Blameless. A **blameless** person is one who does no evil, not just one who can suffer no evil. To be **blameless** is to be free from evil. "He committed no sin, and no deceit was found in his mouth" (1 Peter 2:22).

Pure. This means unpolluted, undefiled; that is, "in every way happy and blessed, not touched with the defilement of any adversity."

Set apart from sinners. We ask: In what way was Christ **set apart from sinners?** He was not set apart from them in his nature, for God sent his own Son "in the likeness of sinful men" (Romans 8:3). He was not set apart from sinners during his ministry on earth. He did not live apart from everyone in a desert. He spoke with tax collectors and prostitutes, and the hypocritical Pharisees rebuked him for this. Being **set apart from sinners** declares what Christ is, his state and condition. He is holy and undefiled. He was separate from sinners in the sense that he was separate from sin, in its nature, causes, and effects. He had to be like this for our benefit. He became the middle person between God and sinners and had to be separate from those sinners in the thing he stood in their place for.

These are the four characteristics of the human nature of our high priest: **holy, blameless, pure, set apart from sinners.**

His present state is expressed as being **exalted above the heavens,** literally "becoming higher than the heavens." Or, as we say, "made higher." God is called the Most High God, "God above." Glory is ascribed to him "in the highest" (Luke 2:14). And the Lord Christ in his exaltation is said to sit down "at the right hand of the Majesty" (1:3)—"in heaven."

The heavens has two meanings. Heaven is referred to as a place. Christ passed "through the heavens" (4:14) when he went into God's presence. **The heavens** may also refer to a condition, or the glorious state on the right hand of the Majesty on high where Christ is exalted. And in this sense, Christ is **exalted** above the angels and the sacred inhabitants of those heavenly places. This great manifestation of Christ's glory is often mentioned (Ephesians 1:21-22; Philippians 2:10-11; Hebrews 1:4; 2:7-8).

I think that both these meanings may be included in the expression **the heavens.** Christ was **exalted** from earth to reside in this place where he is above all the inhabitants of heaven in honor, dignity, and power.

27-28. Unlike the other high priests, he does not need to offer sacrifices day after day, first for his own sins, and then for the sins of the people. He sacrificed for their sins once for all when he offered himself. For the law appoints as high priests men who are weak; but the oath, which came after the law, appointed the Son, who has been made perfect forever.

27. This verse excludes all imperfections from Christ, which other high priests are subject to. Three differences are intimated between our high priest and them. First, the frequency of their offerings. These needed to be offered **day after day,** whereas Christ's offering was **once.** Second, they offered animals, but Christ **offered himself.** Third, they offered up sacrifices for their own sins, but Christ had none of his own sins to offer for. All these things ascribed to the Levitical priests are weaknesses and imperfections in their office. This is the main point of the apostle's argument, which destroyed the whole fabric of Mosaic worship, namely, that the law made nothing perfect.

Himself. The priests had nothing of their own to offer but had to offer calves and sheep and goats. But the Lord Christ had something of his own to offer, which was originally his own and not borrowed or taken from other creatures. This was **himself**—a sacrifice able to make atonement for all the sins of mankind.

28. The law. This is the ceremonial law, as we call it, the law given at Horeb concerning the religious rites and the manner of solemn worship of God in the tabernacle. It was not the moral law, not directly the Ten Commandments, but the law for divine service and worship that is meant.

The oath. This was the Word, the will, the promise of God, declared in and by his oath.

Men. The law made **men** to be high priests; that is, those who were mere men and no more. In contrast with this, **the oath . . . appointed a Son** as high priest.

Who are weak. The law made men **who are weak** priests. Men are subject to moral and natural infirmities. They had their own sins, for which they had to constantly offer sacrifices, and their weakness always led to their own death.

Made perfect forever. The high priest Christ was free from any such human weaknesses, had no sin, and so did not need to offer sacrifices for his sins. He was free from any infirmities and so he could be a sacrifice.

Hebrews
Chapter 8

There are two main parts to this chapter. First, a further explanation of the excellency of Christ's priesthood, or of Christ himself in that office, above those of Aaron's order (verses 1-5). Second, a further confirmation of this through the consideration of the two covenants, the old and the new. For to the former the whole administration of the Levitical priests was confined, but, of the latter, Christ, as our priest, was the mediator and guarantee. Therefore the apostle demonstrates the superiority of this new covenant over the old, which gives glory to its mediator (verses 6-13).

Verses 1-5

1. The point of what we are saying is this: We do have such a high priest, who sat down at the right hand of the throne of the Majesty in heaven.

The point of what we are saying is this. "This is what my arguments amount to, the sum of what I have pleaded."

Such. He does not say only, "we have a high priest"; nor does he say, "we have another high priest, not according to the ordinances of the law," but we have **such** a high priest who has the excellencies the apostle is about to describe.

Sat down. The priests never **sat down** in the holy place.

At the right hand of the throne of the Majesty in heaven. A throne was the sign of royal power, which here manifests God's glory and power, as he had authority and reigned as sovereign over all. **The right hand of the throne of the Majesty** is the same as "the right hand of God."

2. And who serves in the sanctuary, the true tabernacle set up by the

Lord, not by man. The second preeminence of our Lord Christ as our high priest is in this verse.

Who serves. Literally, a "minister of the holy things." To serve or minister can be either with God or before God, as a priest for others; or for God, in the name of God toward others, like magistrates and ministers of the Gospel. The Lord Christ is specifically spoken of here as a priest; it is the name of his priestly office, in which he acts toward God. Christ is now not a minister because he carries out God's purposes toward us, but as he acts toward God and before God on our behalf, according to the duty of a priest. He went into heaven to appear in the presence of God for us, and to discharge his office before God on our behalf. Because of this he also communicates all good things from God to us, as the whole administration of things sacred between God and the church is committed to him.

The true tabernacle. True means here what is substantial and abiding as opposed to what is transitory and figurative. The old tabernacle was in no sense false, for it was appointed by God's ordinance. But it was figurative and typical, denoting the true and substantial tabernacle of God. I think that **the true tabernacle** refers to the human nature of the Lord Christ. He is the only way to approach God in holy worship, as the tabernacle was of old. Christ himself called his own body his temple when referring to the temple of Jerusalem, which was put to the same use as the tabernacle (John 2:19-22). The old tabernacle was a type. It was a token, pledge, and means for God's presence to be with his people here on earth, and for him to be near them. So he said he dwelt among them. This can only really and substantially happen through Christ. He alone, therefore, is this **true tabernacle.**

Set up by the Lord. Set up, or pitched, or fixed, is the correct word to use for erecting the tabernacle. Stakes and pillars fastened with cords was the way the tabernacle was set up (Isaiah 54:2). What is meant here is the preparation of the human nature or body of Christ. "A body you prepared for me" (10:5). This body was taken down, and folded up for a time, and then erected again, without any part of it being lost. This is the same as the body of Christ in his death and resurrection.

The Lord. The author of this work is **the Lord.** This is the name New Testament writers gave to the name Jehovah.

Not by man. Whereas the tabernacle, at God's command, was erected by men, this **true tabernacle** was the work of God alone.

3. Every high priest is appointed to offer both gifts and sacrifices, and so it was necessary for this one also to have something to offer.

Necessary for this one also to have something to offer. Whatever else a high priest did, he had to offer **gifts and sacrifices.** That was the sole purpose of his office. This necessity was absolute. For without this no office of priesthood could be carried out, and consequently no atonement made, nor could we be brought to God. What Christ had to offer was himself.

4. If he were on earth, he would not be a priest, for there are already men who offer the gifts prescribed by the law. This verse contains a hypothetical proposition—**if he were on earth, he would not be a priest**; and a reason to support the proposition—**for there are already men who offer the gifts prescribed by the law.**

If he were on earth. That is, if he were not exalted to heaven to carry out his work there. **If he were on earth** also refers to the condition of his priesthood. If he were still on this earth he would be offering the same sacrifices as the Levitical priests.

5. They serve at a sanctuary that is a copy and shadow of what is in heaven. This is why Moses was warned when he was about to build the tabernacle: "See to it that you make everything according to the pattern shown you on the mountain." Note the following in this verse: first, the people spoken about—**they**; second, what is ascribed to them—**they serve**; third, the limitation of that service—that its immediate object is to be **a copy and shadow,** whilst the ultimate things intended are **in heaven;** fourth, the proof of the whole assertion, from Moses' words—the way the instruction was given to him (**Moses was warned**), and the warning itself (**"See to it that you make everything according to the pattern shown you on the mountain"**).

They. This refers to the priests spoken about in verse 4. Their work is to **serve.** This word applies to both the inner and spiritual, as well as to the outward, instituted holy worship of God (see Matthew 4:10; Acts 7:7; Romans 1:9). It therefore refers to all that the high priests did, or had to do, in the worship of God in the tabernacle or temple.

A copy and shadow. This indicates the limitation of their sacred service. The word **copy,** literally "example," comes again in the New Testament only in Jude 7, where Sodom and Gomorrah "serve as an example" of God's dealing with sinners on the last day.

Shadow refers to the fact that "the law is only a shadow of the good things that are coming" (10:1). **Shadow** is also used to mean the opposite to a body or substance. "These are a shadow of the things that were to come; the reality, however, is found in Christ" (Colossians 2:17).

Warned. This word means a divine warning. Joseph was "warned in a dream" (Matthew 2:22) to avoid the danger Jesus was placed in. This was a divine warning. Noah was "warned about things not yet seen" (11:7). The word is also used of immediate, private revelations (Luke 2:26; Acts 10:22). So, in this verse, two things are indicated by this word. First, Moses had an immediate word, or command from God; second, he was to use great caution to make sure no mistake was made.

"See to it that you make everything according to the pattern shown

you on the mountain." This manifestation to Moses was the foundation of the faith of the church of Israel in all generations. Their faith in God was not confined to the outward things they enjoyed, but rested in Christ in them, and represented through them. Their prototype of him was the line of life, wisdom, beauty, and usefulness that ran through them all.

Verses 6-13

6. But the ministry Jesus has received is as superior to theirs as the covenant of which he is mediator is superior to the old one, and is founded on better promises.

This verse starts the second part of the chapter, about the difference between the old and the new covenants, and the superiority of the latter over the former, and therefore the superiority of Christ over the high priests. The whole church-state of the Jews, with all its ordinances and worship and consequent privileges, depended wholly on the covenant God made with them at Sinai. But the introduction of this new priesthood, which the apostle is explaining, abolished that covenant and ended all sacred ministrations that belonged to it. This could not be offered to them without supplying another covenant, which had to excel the former in privileges and advantages.

The apostle shows two things from the prophet Jeremiah: first, that in addition to the covenant made with their fathers in Sinai, God had promised to make another covenant with the church at his appointed time. Second, that this other promised covenant would be different in nature from the former, superior to it, having more spiritual advantages for those who took part in it. From this the apostle infers the abrogation of the first covenant. In the rest of this chapter the apostle states the nature and differences between these two covenants.

Verse 6 is a transition from one subject to another; namely, from the superiority of Christ's priesthood over that of the law, and the superiority of the new covenant over the old. This verse starts with the assertion of the superiority of Christ's ministry and ends with evidence for this assertion, in that his new covenant is **superior to the old one, and is founded on better promises.**

But the ministry Jesus has. A **ministry** is ascribed to the Lord Christ. The priests of old had a ministry; they ministered at the altar. And the Lord Christ was "a minister" also (verse 2). The Lord Christ undertook the work of ministry. He was not called a minister concerning one particular act of ministry, such as ministering to the necessity of the saints, but rather he had the office of ministry committed to him. Included in this was subordination to God. His office is supreme in the church and is accompanied with sovereign power and authority. But he holds his office in subordination to God and is faithful to him who appointed him.

Received. Christ obtained his ministry through the eternal purpose of God and by the actual call of God.

Superior. Literally, "More excellent." This word is only used in this sense here and in 1:4. The original word denotes only a difference from other things; but when used comparatively, as here, it signifies a difference with a preference, or a comparative excellency. The ministry of the Levitical priests was good and useful in its time, but that of our Lord Jesus Christ was so different from it as to be better than it and **superior** to it.

Covenant. Christ is mediator of a **covenant.** Two things are meant here. First, there was a covenant made between God and human beings. It was made in that God made it and prepared its terms in a sovereign act of wisdom and grace. Second, there was need for a mediator, so that this covenant might achieve its purpose, to the glory of God and the obedience of mankind.

Better promises. The ministry Jesus received is founded on **better promises** than those of the old covenant.

7. For if there had been nothing wrong with that first covenant, no place would have been sought for another.

There is a necessity for a new and better covenant, accompanied with better promises and more excellent ordinances of worship than the former. From this it follows that the first covenant had to be disannulled and abolished, which is the apostle's main thesis. All the privileges and all the benefits of the Aaronic priesthood and sacrifices belong to the covenant they are attached to. The Hebrews neither could nor did question this. All they pleaded for was the covenant God made with their fathers at Sinai. So that priesthood, those sacrifices, with all the tabernacle and temple worship, corresponded to that covenant. So long as that covenant continued, they were to continue; and if that covenant ceased, they would also cease. There, things were agreed between the apostle and them.

So the apostle continues, "But another covenant is mentioned, one that will be made with the whole church, which will be introduced long after the one made at Sinai." They were unable to deny this. But to put this beyond question, the apostle proves it through a specific testimony from the prophet Jeremiah. In that testimony it is declared that this new covenant, which was promised to be introduced "in the latter days," should be better than the former, as is clear from the promises on which it is based. In this verse the apostle only mentions in general terms the promise God would make about another covenant with the church.

From this supposition the apostle demonstrates that the first covenant is imperfect and can be removed. The force of his inference depends on a common idea that when a covenant is made and established there is no reason for another covenant. If the first covenant had made the church perfect and passed on all the grace and mercy God meant humankind to have, then its wise and holy author would have no reason to establish another covenant. "For if a law had been given that could impart life, then righteousness would certainly have come by the law" (Galatians 3:21). The first covenant was imperfect and therefore had to be removed.

That first covenant. This is the covenant made by their fathers at Sinai, with all the ordinances of worship linked to it.

If there had been nothing wrong. Literally, "faultless." When compared with the perfect, sanctified, and saved church, this covenant was insufficient and imperfect. Note that the discussion is not about whether the first covenant was in itself holy, just, good, and in every way perfect as far as its own goals were concerned. If nothing more was required of the old covenant and it could have completely sanctified the church, it would have been perfect. But it was not, as it had never been designed for this purpose. The apostle argues the same thing in 7:11, 19. In this respect "the law was weak" (Romans 8:3; see also Acts 13:38-39; Galatians 3:21). The first covenant was so constituted that it could not perfectly convey God's grace to the church, nor was it ever meant to do this, as the Jews, both then and now, foolishly imagine it to have done.

No place would have been sought for another. His argument is clearly this: "The promise of the new covenant proves the insufficiency of the old covenant, at least in what the new covenant promises. Or else what is the purpose of the promise and the promised covenant?"

8. But God found fault with the people and said: "The time is coming, declares the Lord, when I will make a new covenant with the house of Israel and with the house of Judah."

God found fault. The new covenant was introduced as **God found fault with the people.** God complains that the people broke his covenant. God gives this promise of a new covenant along with a complaint against the people, so that it would be known that this new covenant was the result of his free and sovereign grace. There was nothing in the people to procure it or to qualify them for it.

"The time is coming." The timing of this promise is stated. The imminent approach of the day is intended here, as is its certainty.

New covenant. The subject matter of this promise is the **covenant.** This **covenant** was a collection and confirmation of all the promises of grace that had been given to the church since the world began. **I will make** emphasizes that it was God alone who could provide a guarantee for this covenant. It underlines God's infinite wisdom, goodness, grace, power, and faithfulness.

Israel . . . Judah. Those who are first and most favored with outward privileges are often the least advanced in the grace and mercy of them. This was the case with **the house of Israel and the house of Judah.** They had all the benefits of the dispensation of the covenant, and while they were as numerous as the grains of sand on the seashore, only a remnant of them was saved.

9. "It will not be like the covenant I made with their forefathers when I took them by the hand to lead them out of Egypt, because they did not remain faithful to my covenant, and I turned away from them, declares the Lord."

The greatest mercies that God ever gave to the church were enclosed in the new covenant. Previously, God had made a covenant with his people. It was a good and holy covenant, but proved ineffective when many people refused to obtain God's grace through it. So God promised to make a new covenant with them since they had forfeited the advantage of the old one. But if it was like the old covenant, might not the new covenant also prove to be ineffective? To meet this objection, and the fear that it might bring, God, who not only provides for the safety of his church but also for their comfort and assurance, declares that this new covenant **"will not be like the covenant I made with their forefathers."**

Their forefathers. Their **forefathers** were the people these people were always boasting about, namely, Abraham, Isaac, Jacob, and the twelve patriarchs.

"When I took them by the hand." This emphasizes their helpless condition in Egypt, as well as God's infinite condescension toward these people and his power in being able to help them and actually deliver them.

"I turned away from them." The worst judgment that can happen to any people is that they should be separated from God's special care after they have broken his covenant.

10-12. "This is the covenant I will make with the house of Israel after that time, declares the Lord. I will put my laws in their minds and write them on their hearts. I will be their God, and they will be my people. No longer will a man teach his neighbor, or a man his brother, saying, 'Know the Lord,' because they will all know me, from the least of them to the greatest. For I will forgive their wickedness and will remember their sins no more."

The apostle's general argument must be borne in mind all the time that thought is given to the testimonies he brings forward to substantiate his case. He is showing that the Lord Christ is the mediator and guarantee of a better covenant than the one undertaken by the high priests under the law. From this it follows that Christ's priesthood is superior to theirs. So the apostle shows that God not only promised to make such a covenant but also explains its nature and characteristics as stated in the words of the prophet Jeremiah. By comparing this new covenant with the old covenant, the superiority of the new covenant is established. These three verses describe the covenant the Lord Christ is mediator and guarantee of.

With the house of Israel. This states whom this new covenant will be made with: **the house of Israel.** In verse 8 they are called "the house of Israel" and "the house of Judah." During the days of Rehoboam the descendants of Israel were split into Israel and Judah. Before this they were just called "Israel." Verse 8 mentions them separately to show that none of Abraham's descendants were excluded from the grace of the covenant. In this verse they are spoken about by their ancient name **Israel,** by which the whole of the Israel of God, or the church of the elect, is intended.

In their minds. The apostle speaks about **minds** and **hearts.** When the apostle speaks about the corruption and depravity of our nature, he writes, "they are darkened in their understanding and separated from the life of God because of the ignorance that is in them due to the hardening of their hearts" (Ephesians 4:18). In Scripture the mind and the heart are the center of natural corruption. The **mind** is the most secret, inner part or power of the soul. The prophet refers to it as "the inward part" because it is the only safe place for God's laws. When they are put in there we will not lose them, and neither men nor devils can take them from us.

On their hearts. The second part of the promise of this new covenant involves **their hearts.** There is meant to be a comparison here with the law that was given on Mount Sinai, that is, with the first covenant. For then the law (that is, "the ten words") was written on tablets of stone. The original tablets of stone were broken by Moses when the people broke the covenant, but God would not change that dispensation, or write his laws in any other way, but commanded new tablets of stone to be made and wrote on them. But the people continued to break the laws and disobey God. God promised to prevent this from happening under the new covenant by writing these laws **on their hearts,** which he had previously written on tablets of stone. God will effectually work that obedience in us which the law requires, for "it is God who works in you to will and to act according to his good pleasure" (Philippians 2:13).

The heart, as distinguished from the mind, is made up of the will and the affections, which are compared with the stone tablets on which the letter of the law was engraved. For as by that writing and engraving the tablets received the impression of the letters and words that contained the law, so they were nothing but law as they were used. So, by the grace of the new covenant there is a durable impression of God's law on the wills and affections of men, through which they are able to carry it out since they have a living principle of it living within them. This work has two parts, namely, the removal from the heart of what is contrary to God's law and the implanting of the principles of obedience to God's law. So, in Scripture this double action is described. Sometimes it is called a "taking away of the heart of stone," or "circumcising of the heart," and sometimes the "giving of a heart of flesh," the "writing of the law in our hearts," which is the renewal of our natures to God's image in righteousness and holiness of truth. So in this promise all of our sanctification, its start and its progress, in its work on our whole souls and all their faculties, is comprised.

"**I will be their God, and they will be my people.**" This is a separate promise in itself, which summarizes all the blessings and privileges of the covenant.

11. "**No longer will a man teach his neighbor, or a man his brother, saying, 'Know the Lord,' because they will all know me, from the least of them to the greatest.**" The second general promise, declaring the nature of the new covenant, comes in this verse. It is expressed in a negative and a positive way. Negatively, it opposes what was used and necessary under the old covenant: "**No longer will a man teach his neighbor, or a man his brother, saying, 'Know the Lord.'**" Positively, it states what should take its place and be enjoyed under this new covenant: "**because they will all know me, from the least of them to the greatest.**"

"**They will all know me.**" What is promised under the new covenant is knowledge of God. "**They will all know me.**" No duty is more often commanded than this is and no grace more frequently promised. "You ate no bread and drank no wine or other fermented drink. I did this so that you might know that I am the LORD your God" (Deuteronomy 29:6); "I will give them a heart to know me, that I am the LORD. They will be my people, and I will be their God, for they will return to me with all their heart" (Jeremiah 24:7); "I will drive you out of the city and hand you over to foreigners and inflict punishment on you. You will fall by the sword, and I will execute judgment on you at the borders of Israel. Then you will know that I am the LORD" (Ezekiel 11:10); "I will show the holiness of my great name, which has been profaned among the nations, the name you have profaned among them. Then the nations will know that I am the LORD, declares the Sovereign LORD, when I show myself holy through you before their eyes. . . . I will give you a new heart and put a new spirit in you; I will remove from you your heart of stone and give you a heart of flesh. And I will put my Spirit in you and move you to follow my decrees and be careful to keep my laws" (Ezekiel 36:23, 26-27). This is the foundation of all other duties of obedience and of all communion with God in them. Exercising all graces, such as faith, love, and hope, is founded in this.

12. "**For I will forgive their wickedness and will remember their sins no more.**"

This is the great fundamental promise and grace of the new covenant. The house of Israel and the house of Judah, representing everyone else under the old covenant, had broken God's covenant through their disobedience. Nothing is said about any other qualification for the new covenant.

This first thing that is necessary is the free pardon of sin. Without this it is impossible to take part in any other mercy, for while people continue under the guilt of sin, they are also under the curse. So the reason given here, and the only reason, why God will give them the other blessings is, **"I will forgive their wickedness."**

"I will forgive . . . and will remember . . . no more." Pardon for sin is meant by both these expressions. **"I will forgive"** is literally "I will be merciful." In Christ alone is God "merciful" to our sins.

The law was God's appointed means to bring sin into judicial remembrance and trial. So the dissolution of the obligation of the law to punish, which is an act of God, the supreme judge of all, belongs to the pardon of sin. This is stated in different ways in Scripture: here it is said that God **will remember their sins no more.**

Verse 13

By calling this covenant "new," he has made the first one obsolete; and what is obsolete and aging will soon disappear.

In this verse the apostle makes a special inference from one of Jeremiah's words to strengthen his main argument. The Hebrews were convinced that no matter what sort of new covenant was promised, the first one should continue in force, which meant that the church was obliged to carry out all its institutions of worship. This was the heart of the disagreement between the apostle and the Hebrews. The apostle knew that the conviction the Hebrews held would destroy the faith of the Gospel and ruin their own souls. So he presses home his arguments about the ending of the first covenant. In this verse he drives home a new argument to demonstrate the necessity and certainty of the abolition of the old covenant.

"New." God himself calls this covenant **"new."**

Obsolete and aging. The old covenant is described in a double expression: **obsolete and aging.** The words are generally supposed to be synonymous and are used for emphasis only. **Obsolete** is literally "being made old." Strictly speaking it refers to things and not people. But **aging,** literally, "growing aged," refers to people and not things.

Soon disappear. All the glorious institutions of the law were at best but as stars in the firmament of the church and therefore were all to disappear at the rising of the Sun of Righteousness.

Hebrews
Chapter 9

The main purpose of the apostle in these discourses is to demonstrate that the old covenant made with the church at Sinai, with all its ordinances of worship and privileges, has now been taken away, or ceased to be of any force in the church. This would involve a complete change for the present church-state of the Hebrews, on which they relied. It is easy to imagine how difficult this would be for them to forgo. For they both viewed it as God's own appointment, as it was, and expected all their happiness to come from careful obedience to it. So that they might more readily embrace the truth, the apostle not only declares that the covenant had ended *de facto*, but gives all kinds of reasons why it was necessary for it to end, as well as mentioning the unimaginable advantages that accrue to the church as a result.

To achieve his purpose, the apostle unfolds before them the greatest mysteries of the wisdom and counsel of God that had ever been revealed to the church, before he spoke to us through the Son. He takes off the veil from the face of Moses, declaring the nature and end of the old covenant and the use, meaning, and efficacy of all the institutions and ordinances of worship that belonged to this. They were all prescribed for the diligent observation of the church of the old testament; and their adherence to them was the great test of their obedience to God while that church-state continued (Malachi 4:4). But the best among them were much in the dark about their correct use and meaning. For the veil was on the face of Moses in such a way that the Israelites were kept from gazing at it while the radiance was fading away (2 Corinthians 3:13). This veil the apostle now doctrinally removes. The only reason why the Hebrews did not get up to now behold "the glory of God in the face of Christ" (2 Corinthians 4:6), nor do to this day, is because there was and is a veil blinding their minds, just as there was a veil of darkness on Moses' face. "Whenever anyone turns to the Lord, the veil is taken away" (2 Corinthians 3:16).

The apostle then moves on to declare the great mystery of the redemption of the church through Christ, the office he held, and the work he performed in it.

This chapter has two main parts. First, it outlines the fabric of the tabernacle, its furniture, and the services performed there (verses 1-10). Second, it states the nature of the tabernacle and the sacrifice of the Lord Christ, with their purpose and efficacy (verses 11-28).

Verses 1-10

1. Now the first covenant had regulations for worship and also an earthly sanctuary. The subject here is **the first covenant.** It had **regulations for worship.** These ordinances or statutes were for **worship,** literally, "service," or as we say "divine service."

An earthly sanctuary. So that these ordinances of divine worship might be correctly carried out under the first covenant, God appointed a place where they should take place: **an earthly sanctuary**—literally, "a worldly holy place." This tabernacle was a visible pledge of God's presence among his people, as he owned, blessed, and protected them. It was also the focus of all divine worship and a continual representation of the incarnation of the Son of God.

2. A tabernacle was set up. In its first room were the lampstand, the table and the consecrated bread; this was called the Holy Place. The theme here is the **tabernacle.** This was a type of Christ's incarnation, by which the "fullness of the Deity lives in bodily form" (Colossians 2:9). "The Word became flesh and made his dwelling among us," "pitched his tent among" or "with us," "tabernacled with us" (John 1:14). This tabernacle was **set up,** as the materials were provided by the people, the materials were worked on by Bezaleel, put in position under Moses' directions, and adorned for use (see Exodus 25—40).

Lampstand. In the first part of the tabernacle furniture was provided and had to be used. There was the **lampstand,** or candlestick. Its meticulous construction is described in Exodus 25:31-40: "Make a lampstand of pure gold and hammer it out, base and shaft; its flowerlike cups, buds and blossoms shall be of one piece with it. . . . The buds and branches shall all be of one piece with the lampstand, hammered out of pure gold" (Exodus 25:31, 36). It was placed on the south side of the tabernacle, close to the curtains that divided off the Most Holy Place.

The lampstand, with its seven branches and its perpetual light, burning pure oil, giving light to all holy ministries, represented the fullness of the spiritual light which is in Christ Jesus, and which through him is communicated to the whole church. "In him was life, and that life was the light of men" (John 1:4). God gave him the Spirit without limit. "For the one whom God has sent speaks the words of God, for God gives the Spirit without limit" (John 3:34). And the Holy Spirit rested on him in all the varieties of his gifts and works, especially those of spiritual light, wisdom, and understanding (Isaiah 11:2-3). This seven-branched lampstand is called "the seven spirits before his throne" (Revelation 1:4). For the Spirit in and through the Lord Christ gives full and perfect light and gifts to illuminate the whole church, just as the light of the tabernacle depended on the seven-branched lampstand.

The table and the consecrated bread. Next to the lampstand **the table** with its **consecrated bread** was placed. In the middle, at the entrance of the Most Holy Place, was the altar of incense (see Exodus 40:20-27). The table was made to be beautiful (Numbers 4:7-8). On this **table** were placed the "holy loaves" or **consecrated bread.** "Take fine flour and bake twelve loaves of bread, using two-tenths of an ephah for each loaf. Set them in two rows, six in each row, on the table of pure gold before the LORD. Along each row put some pure incense as a memorial portion to represent the bread and to be an offering made to the Lord by fire. This bread is to be set out before the Lord regularly, Sabbath after Sabbath, on behalf of the Israelites, as a lasting covenant. It belongs to Aaron and his sons, who are to eat it in a holy pace, because it is a most holy part of their regular share of the offerings made to the LORD by fire" (Leviticus 24:5-9). God said that this bread had to be before him continually: "Put the bread of the Presence on this table to be before me at all times" (Exodus 25:30). The Lord Christ is the only bread of life for the church, the only spiritual food for our souls (see John 6:32-35). Therefore, he alone was represented by this bread that was continually in the sanctuary.

3-5. Behind the second curtain was a room called the Most Holy Place, which had the golden altar of incense and the gold-covered ark of the covenant. This ark contained the gold jar of manna, Aaron's staff that had budded, and the stone tablets of the covenant. Above the ark were the cherubim of the Glory, overshadowing the atonement cover. But we cannot discuss these things in detail now.

The apostle now describes the second part of the tabernacle and its furniture. As he says in verse 5, his purpose is not to give an exact description of these things but to show their use and significance.

The second curtain. The first thing the apostle mentions in this part of the tabernacle is **the second curtain.** People who entered the tabernacle had to travel the whole length of the first part of it before they came to this. There was no other way to enter. By calling it **the second curtain** the apostle means that there must have been a "first curtain." But the first curtain did not separate rooms as **the second curtain** did; it hung at the entrance of the tent. **The second curtain,** literally "veil," prevented the priests from seeing into the Most Holy Place. It is this **curtain** that "was torn in two from top to bottom" (Matthew 27:51) just after Christ's crucifixion.

A room called the Most Holy Place. The apostle now describes the part of the tabernacle called **the Most Holy Place.** "The holy of holies," **the Most Holy Place,** was given this name by God (Exodus 26:33-34).

The golden altar of incense. This has been translated as "the house of spices," as it was the place where spices that went into incense were burned. The altar of incense was overlaid with beaten gold and so is called **the golden altar of incense.**

In general, incense signifies prayer. "May my prayer be set before you like incense" (Psalm 141:2). There are four ways in which incense is like prayer. First, incense was beaten and pounded before it was used. So acceptable prayer proceeds from "a broken and contrite heart" (Psalm 51:17). Second, incense was useless until fire was put under it, which was taken from the altar. Prayer has no virtue unless it is set alight by the fire from above, God's Holy Spirit, which we have from our altar, Christ Jesus. Third, it rises toward heaven; and the point of prayer is that it should ascend to God's throne. Fourth, incense gives off a sweet aroma. This was one of its purposes in temple services, where there was so much burning of flesh and blood. So prayer yields a sweet savor to God.

The gold-covered ark of the covenant. Sometimes this is called "the ark of the testimony," or "the ark of God," but most frequently the **ark of the covenant.** It was given this name because of what it contained. It contained the Ten Commandments, "the two tablets of Testimony" (Exodus 31:18).

The gold jar of manna. When the manna first fell, everyone was told to gather an omer, to eat himself (Exodus 16:16). "Moses said to Aaron, 'Take a jar and put an omer of manna in it. Then place it before the LORD to be kept for the generations to come.' As the LORD commanded Moses, Aaron put the manna in front of the Testimony, that it might be kept. The Israelites ate manna for forty years, until they came to a land that was settled; they ate manna until they reached the border of Canaan" (Exodus 16:33-35).

The sacred preservation of this manna in the Most Holy Place was because it was a type of Christ. Christ declared this himself: "I am the bread of life. Your forefathers ate the manna in the desert, yet they died. But here is the bread that comes down from heaven, which a man may eat and not die. I am the living bread that came down from heaven. If anyone eats of this bread, he will live forever. This bread is my flesh, which I will give for the life of the world" (John 6:48-51).

Aaron's staff that had budded. This **staff** had originally been with

Moses when he fed the sheep that belonged to his father-in-law Jethro, and which he had in his hand when God called to him out of the bush. God ordained that it should be the token of his power in performing miracles, having confirmed Moses' faith concerning it (Exodus 4:17). In this way it became sacred, and when Aaron was called to become high priest, it was given to him. When it budded, on the occasion of the trial about priest-hood, it was put "in front of the Testimony, to be kept as a sign to the rebellious" (Numbers 17:10). This same staff Moses took from the ark to strike a rock and perform a miracle (Numbers 20:8-11).

Moses' staff belonged to the holy furniture of the tabernacle because the spiritual Rock that followed them was to be struck with the rod of the law, that it might bring forth the waters of life for the church.

The stone tablets of the covenant, the Ten Commandments, were put in the ark on God's instructions (Exodus 16:34).

5. Above the ark were the cherubim of the Glory, overshadowing the atonement cover. But we cannot discuss these things in detail now.

Cherubim. The making, design, and use of these **cherubim** come in Exodus 25. There were two of them, one at each end of the ark. Their faces were turned inwards, toward each other, so that their wings touched one another.

Glory. Here, **Glory** means the majestic presence of God himself. The cherubim represented the glorious presence of God himself as he lived among his people.

Overshadowing. "The cherubim are to have their wings spread upward, overshadowing the cover with them" (Exodus 25:20).

The atonement cover. Its construction is recorded in Exodus 25:17: "Make an atonement cover of pure gold—two and a half cubits long and a cubit and a half wide." Our apostle literally calls this atonement cover a "mercy-seat." This is applied to the Lord Christ whom "God presented . . . as a sacrifice of atonement" (Romans 3:25).

But we cannot discuss these things in detail now. The apostle says this because he did not want to be distracted from his main aim, which was to concentrate on the ministry of the high priest in all of this.

6-7. When everything had been arranged like this, the priests entered regularly into the outer room to carry on their ministry. But only the high priest entered the inner room, and that only once a year, and never without blood, which he offered for himself and for the sins the people had committed in ignorance.

6. To carry on their ministry. The priests were involved in two kinds of ministry each day. First, they attended to the lampstand, supplying it with holy oil and cleaning it; second, they were involved in serving at the golden altar, the altar of incense.

7. The use and service of the second part of the tabernacle, the Most

Holy Place, which the apostle uses for his present argument, are stated here. He first describes the person who alone may perform the service that belonged to this part of the sanctuary: the high priest. Second, he states that the high priest **entered** the inner room. Third, he says that the high priest only went into **the inner room once a year,** whereas the priests went into the other part of the tabernacle every day. Fourth, he states how the high priest entered the inner room: **never without blood,** that is, always with blood. Fifth, he states how this blood was used: it was **offered for himself and for the sins the people had committed.**

Only the high priest. No other person was allowed to do this work (Leviticus 16:2, 32). As all the people were kept out of the sanctuary and waited at the door of the tabernacle while the priests entered daily into it; so all the priests were kept outside the sanctuary while the high priest entered the Most Holy Place (Leviticus 16:17).

Entered. The high priest carried out this word by entering into the Most Holy Place. For it was a type both of the entry of Christ into heaven and of us entering through him to the throne of grace (verse 24; 10:19-20).

Never without blood. The apostle states the nature of the high priest's work: it was **never without blood.** He states this to show how impossible it was to enter the Most Holy Place in any other way. From this he proceeds to his following argument about the necessity of the death and shedding of blood of the mediator and high priest of the new testament.

After the high priest had filled the Most Holy Place with a cloud of incense, he went back to the altar of burnt-offerings outside the tabernacle, where the sacrifice had just been killed. He took in his hand the fresh blood, which, as it were, was living (10:20) and went back into the Most Holy Place, where he sprinkled the blood seven times with his finger toward the ark of the covenant (Leviticus 16:11-14). The expression **never without blood** emphasizes how impossible it was to go into God's presence without the blood of the sacrifice of Christ. The only propitiation for sins is made by the blood of Christ. It is through faith alone that we partake in this (Romans 3:25-26).

8. The Holy Spirit was showing by this that the way into the Most Holy Place had not yet been disclosed as long as the first tabernacle was standing.

The Holy Spirit is the author of this instruction.

Had not yet been disclosed. The word **disclosed,** literally "manifested," is specially chosen by the apostle to fulfill his purpose. He does not say that there was no way then into the Most Holy Place, that none had been made, none provided, none made use of, but that it had **not yet been disclosed**—no open manifestation about it had yet been made. There was an entrance under the old testament into God's presence to find grace and glory, namely, the virtue of the oblation of Christ; but this **had not yet been disclosed.**

This did not actually exist, but only was virtually so. The Lord Christ had not yet actually offered himself to God or made atonement for sin. But by virtue of the eternal agreement between the Father and him about what he would accomplish in the fullness of time, the benefit of what he would do was applied to those who did believe. They were saved by faith, as we are. Hence he is called "the Lamb that was slain from the creation of the world" (Revelation 13:8), that is, in and from the giving of the first promise.

Still standing. The tabernacle, that is, its laws and services, continued being used in the church, by God's appointment, until Christ's death. Then he pronounced over it and over everything that belonged to it, "It is finished." Then the curtain was torn and the way into the Most Holy Place was open. Then peace with God was publicly confirmed through the blood of the cross (Ephesians 2:14-16).

9-10. This is an illustration for the present time, indicating that the gifts and sacrifices being offered were not able to clear the conscience of the worshiper. They are only a matter of food and drink and various ceremonial washings—external regulations applying until the time of the new order.

9. Not able to clear the conscience. Literally, "not being able to perfect the conscience." Outwardly, the sacrifices dedicated, sanctified, consecrated, as he confirms in verse 13, but only in a certain respect. They could not do this for the conscience of the sinner before God; see 10:2. These sacrifices could not help a guilty conscience. They were not able to do this. If they could have done so, the sinner would have had complete peace with God and would not have needed to offer these sacrifices anymore.

10. The apostle shows here the weakness of the services of the tabernacle, and their inability to achieve what they set out to do. The things mentioned here cover a great part of the Levitical institutions, which may be extended to apply to them all.

Verses 11-28

11. When Christ came as high priest of the good things that are already here, he went through the greater and more perfect tabernacle that is not man-made, that is to say, not a part of this creation. The apostle focuses on the high priest and his special work in the Most Holy Place as he compares type and anti-type. In verses 11-12 the apostle states what he then goes on to demonstrate, up to 10:20. In verse 11 he states who the high priest of the new covenant is, and what tabernacle he carries on his work in. In verse 12 he states what the special services are which he carries out, in comparison with the legal high priest, and that are superior to them.

When Christ came. The apostle mentions Christ by his name. "He who was promised of old that he should come, on whose coming the faith of the church was built, by whom and at whose coming they expected the last revelation of God's will, and consequently a change in their present administrations, the promised Messiah had come." The church was founded of old on the name Jehovah, which denoted God's unchanging nature and his faithfulness to carry out his promises (Exodus 6:2-3). So by calling him by this name, as was most appropriate when speaking about his coming, it reminded the Hebrews about the ancient faith of their church concerning him, and what in general they expected when he came.

Came. This word is not used anywhere else to express Christ's coming. It indicates the accomplishment of God's promise in sending and manifesting Christ in the flesh. "He has now come, as was promised from the foundation of the world." No single act is meant by this word **came** here, as his coming usually refers to his incarnation only. The sense of this word is comprehensive of all the work God had sent him to do.

12. He did not enter by means of the blood of goats and calves; but he entered the Most Holy Place once for all by his own blood, having obtained eternal redemption. This verse speaks of the great mystery of the priestly work of Christ, especially the sacrifice he offered to make atonement for sin. The apostle shows, first, how this happened: negatively, not **by means of the blood of goats and calves** and positively, **by his own blood.** Second, he states when this happened, **once;** and, third, the effect of his blood was that he **obtained eternal salvation.**

By his own blood. This shows Christ's unimaginable love in offering himself and his own blood for us (see Galatians 2:20; Ephesians 5:25-27; 1 John 3:16; Revelation 1:5). As there was no other way to purge our sins (see 10:5-7), from his infinite love and grace he humbly went this way, so God could be glorified and his church sanctified and saved. It is right for us always to consider what love, gratitude, and obedience we owe Christ on account of this.

The efficacy of Christ's sacrifice is also seen here, that through him our faith and hope may be in God. He who offered this sacrifice was "the only-begotten of the Father," the eternal Son of God. What he offered was **his own blood.** For "the church of God . . . he bought with his own blood" (Acts 20:28). How perfect the atonement must be that was made in this way! How glorious the redemption that was procured like this!

Redemption. All redemption assumes a state of slavery. The aim of redemption is to deliver people from their bondage. This is done through power or through a payment of a price. So his deliverance of the Israelites from Egypt, performed by acts of power, is called their redemption. And Moses, because of his ministry in this respect, is called "deliverer" (Acts 7:35).

The Greek word for *ransom* comes from the word translated **redemption**. So the redemption that is through Christ is everywhere said to be a "price," a "ransom" (see Matthew 20:28; Mark 10:45; 1 Corinthians 6:20; 1 Timothy 2:6; 1 Peter 1:18-19). It is delivering people out of slavery by paying a valuable ransom. The price or ransom in this redemption is the person of Christ himself. "Christ . . . gave himself for me" (Galatians 2:20); he "gave himself as a ransom for all men" (1 Timothy 2:6); "he offered himself unblemished to God" (9:14); "Christ . . . gave himself up for us" (Ephesians 5:2). Christ made the ransom of infinite value, suitable to redeem the whole church. Its special nature was that it was by **blood**—"the church of God, which he bought with his own blood" (Acts 20:28; see also Ephesians 1:7; 1 Peter 1:18-19). Christ's blood was a ransom, the price of redemption. For it was through blood, and in no other way, that atonement was made (Leviticus 17:11). So we are "justified freely by his grace through the redemption which came by Christ Jesus. God presented him as a sacrifice of atonement" (Romans 3:24-25).

13-14. The blood of goats and bulls and the ashes of a heifer sprinkled on those who are ceremonially unclean sanctify them so that they are outwardly clean. How much more, then, will the blood of Christ, who through the eternal Spirit offered himself unblemished to God, cleanse our consciences from acts that lead to death, so that we may serve the living God! To appreciate the force of the apostle's argument here we observe, first, that what he had previously demonstrated he takes for granted here. And this was that all the Levitical services and ordinances were in themselves carnal, and had carnal goals, and only obscurely represented spiritual and eternal things. But the tabernacle, office, and sacrifice of Christ were spiritual and effected eternal things. Second, the carnal things were types, appointed by God, of spiritual and eternal things.

There are two things in this verse that form the basis of an argument that the apostle later uses. First, a proposition about the sacrifices and services of the law, and, second, the efficacy assigned to them.

Goats and bulls. All the different types of clean animals whose blood was given to make atonement are meant here.

Blood. It is the **blood of goats and bulls** that is stated as the first way to expiate sin. For it was by their blood, as offered at the altar, that atonement was made (Leviticus 17:11). In this way, as it was sprinkled, purification was made.

The ashes of a heifer. This second thing has the same purpose as the blood of goats and bulls. Its institution comes in Numbers 19. It is a clear type of Christ, both of his suffering and of the constant efficacy of the cleansing power of his blood in the church.

Sprinkled. How **the ashes of a heifer** are **sprinkled** is set out in Numbers 19:17-18. The ashes were kept by themselves. When they were needed, they were mixed with clean spring water. The virtue stemmed from the ashes, as they were the ashes of the heifer slain and burnt as a sin-offering. The water was used as the means of their application. Any clean person could dip a bunch of hyssop (see Psalm 51:7) into it and sprinkle anything or any person who was defiled. Christ's blood is called "sprinkled blood" (12:24) because it brings about our sanctification, as applied through faith to our souls and consciences.

14. How much more, then, will the blood of Christ, who through the eternal Spirit offered himself unblemished to God, cleanse our consciences from acts that lead to death, so that we may serve the living God!

How much more. This is the apostle's usual way of drawing any inference from a comparison between Christ and the high priest, or the Gospel and the law (see 2:2-3; 3:3; 10:28-29; 12:25).

The blood of Christ. All Christ's sufferings are ascribed to his **blood.** "He became obedient to death—even death on a cross" (Philippians 2:8), where his blood was shed. God gave the people the blood to make atonement on the altar because "the life of a creature is in the blood" (Leviticus 17:11). So was the life of Christ in his blood, and so he died when his blood was shed. And through his death, since he was the Son of God, we are redeemed. In this way he made his soul an offering for sin. "The LORD makes his life a guilt-offering" (Isaiah 53:10). So this expression, **the blood of Christ,** with reference to our redemption, or to the expiation of sin, encompasses everything that he did and suffered for this purpose. For the shedding of his blood was the way in which he offered himself, in and by it, to God.

Through the eternal Spirit. The action of his own eternal Spirit brought about a cleansed conscience, while the action of the Holy Spirit in Christ was the method through which this took place. Without the first, Christ's offering would not have cleansed **our consciences from acts that lead to death.** No sacrifice of any mere creature could have produced this effect. So Christ offered himself to God, through or by his own eternal Spirit, the divine nature acting in the person of the Son.

Consciences. The apostle does not say "cleanse your souls, or your minds," but your **consciences.** This is in contrast with the purification under the law, which sanctified **them so that they are outwardly clean** (verse 13), a sanctification of the flesh. But the defilements meant here are spiritual, internal, relating to the **conscience;** and therefore such is the purification.

The apostle specifically mentions that Christ can **cleanse our consciences from acts that lead to death,** because it is the conscience that is concerned about peace with God. Sin affects all the faculties of the soul, and it defiles the conscience in a special way, so that "consciences are corrupted" (Titus 1:15). The conscience alone brings a sense of guilt, which leads to fear and a dread about approaching God's presence. It was Adam's conscience that reduced Adam to hiding himself from God as his eyes were opened through a sense of the guilt of sin. Just as a person is unclean through contact with a dead body and so may not approach God in worship until purified, so a guilty sinner, whose conscience is affected with a sense of the guilt of sin, does not dare to approach God's presence until sin is removed from the conscience, until "worshipers . . . no longer" feel "guilty for their sins" (10:2). So the cleansing of **consciences from acts that lead to death** removes the guilt of sin through the blood of Christ. Conscience is used to represent our whole spirits, souls, and bodies that are all to be cleansed and sanctified (1 Thessalonians 5:23). To **cleanse our consciences** is to cleanse our whole being.

15. For this reason Christ is the mediator of a new covenant, that those who are called may receive the promised eternal inheritance— now that he has died as a ransom to set them free from the sins committed under the first covenant.

In this verse it is asserted that **Christ is the mediator of a new covenant,** that the special reason for this is that he is **a ransom to set them free from the sins committed under the first covenant,** and that the way this will be achieved is through his death, and the purpose for this is so **that those who are called may receive the promised eternal inheritance.**

Promised. The promise meant here is the one given to Abraham, for the **eternal inheritance** was a promise: "For if the inheritance depends on the law, then it no longer depends on a promise; but God in his grace gave it to Abraham through a promise" (Galatians 3:18). What was **promised** was that through the descendants of Abraham all the nations would be blessed by God.

Those who are called. This inheritance is meant for **those who are called,** those who actually receive the promise. It was God's plan in this whole dispensation that everyone who is called should receive the promise. These people are those "called according to his purpose" (Romans 8:28), those who obtain the inheritance "having been predestined according to the plan of him who works out everything in conformity with the purpose of his will" (Ephesians 1:11). God demonstrates his mighty power here, that his purpose may be established in giving the inheritance to all **who are called:** "And those he predestined, he also

201

called; those he called, he also justified; those he justified, he also glorified" (Romans 8:30).

He has died. Christ became **the mediator** by means of his death. What verse 14 described as the blood of Christ, which he offered as a priest, is here ascribed to his death as a mediator.

16-17. In the case of a will, it is necessary to prove the death of the one who made it, because a will is in force only when somebody has died; it never takes effect while the one who made it is living. These verses show the necessity of Christ's death if he was to be mediator of the new covenant, using the illustration of a will. In a will a person states what he wants done with his possessions after his death. **A will is in force only when somebody has died.** It is in the will and power of the person making the will (literally, "covenant") to assign what possessions should be bequeathed to whom. So, with the Lord Christ, he has determined how the elect should actually possess their legacies, namely, "by faith in" Jesus (Acts 26:18).

18-22. This is why even the first covenant was not put into effect without blood. When Moses had proclaimed every commandment of the law to all the people, he took the blood of calves, together with water, scarlet wool and branches of hyssop, and sprinkled the scroll and all the people. He said, "This is the blood of the covenant, which God has commanded you to keep." In the same way, he sprinkled with the blood both the tabernacle and everything used in its ceremonies. In fact, the law requires that nearly everything be cleansed with blood, and without the shedding of blood there is no forgiveness. In these verses the apostle does not just want to demonstrate that the first covenant was dedicated with blood, which he could have said in very few words, but he declares what was the use of blood in sacrifices on all occasions under the law. In this way he shows the use and efficacy of Christ's blood and the whole purpose of the new covenant. He shows that blood was used under the old covenant to purify and to pardon, which are both included in the expiation of sin. These things are applied to the blood and sacrifice of Christ in the following verses.

18. Put into effect. The word used here is one that signified the solemn separation of anything for sacred use. So these verses mean, "That first covenant, which God made with the people at Mount Sinai, when he became their God, the God of Israel, and they became his people, was dedicated for sacred use through blood, in that it was sprinkled on the scroll and the people, after some of the same blood had been offered in sacrifice at the altar." From this it follows that this was also necessary for the dedication and confirmation of the new covenant.

19. When Moses had proclaimed every commandment of the law. This does not refer to Moses' first words to the people in the confirmation of the covenant—"When Moses went and told the people all the LORD'S words and laws" (Exodus 24:3). It refers to his reading to the people— "Then he took the Book of the Covenant and read it to the people" (Exodus 24:7). Moses read it to the people, and the apostle adds that he read **every commandment of the law.** Moses read the "law with its commandments and regulations" (Ephesians 2:15). That old covenant consisted, in the main, of commandments to obey, without the promise of help in carrying them out. The new covenant has a different nature: it is a covenant of promises.

He took the blood of calves, together with water, scarlet wool and branches of hyssop. Moses' dedication or consecration of the old covenant is now described. Moses took the blood of the animals that had been offered for burnt-offerings and peace-offerings (Exodus 24:5-6, 8). He took all their blood in bowls and divided them equally into two. One half he sprinkled on the altar, and the other half he sprinkled on the people. What was sprinkled on the altar was God's part, and the other was put on the people. The main strength of the apostle's argument lies here: "Blood was used in the dedication of the first covenant. This was the blood of the animals offered in sacrifice to God. So both death, and death by shedding blood, was required to confirm a covenant. So also, therefore, the new covenant must be confirmed, but with blood and a sacrifice far more precious than they were."

This distribution of blood, half on the altar, half on the people, one to make atonement, the other to purify or sanctify, taught the double efficacy of Christ's blood in making atonement for sin for our justification and the purifying of our natures in sanctification.

The blood was put in bowls, mixed with water to keep it fluid, and then a bunch or bundle of hyssop tied with scarlet wool was dipped into the bowls and the blood was sprinkled.

Sprinkled the scroll and all the people. The scroll and **all the people** were what was sprinkled. The same blood was on the scroll where the covenant was recorded and on the people who entered into this covenant.

If God gave them such light under the old testament, so that they should know, believe, and profess that **without the shedding of blood there is no forgiveness,** how great is the darkness of men under the new covenant who look or seek for any other way for the pardon of sin except through the blood of Christ.

23. It was necessary, then, for the copies of the heavenly things to be purified with these sacrifices, but the heavenly things themselves with better sacrifices than these.

In verses 23-28 the apostle uses his whole discussion about the services and sacrifices of the tabernacle—with their use and efficacy on the one hand, and Christ's sacrifice and its nature, use, and efficacy on the other hand—to present his argument. He does this to show the virtue of Christ's priesthood and sacrifice, as he was the mediator of the new covenant. He does this by comparing them with each other. He concludes by comparing the law and the Gospel and their effects on men's souls.

With better sacrifices than these. This means the one sacrifice of Christ.

24. For Christ did not enter a man-made sanctuary that was only a copy of the true one; he entered heaven itself, now to appear for us in God's presence. The contrast between the high priests of the law and their sacrifices, with their efficacy, and the Lord Christ with his sacrifice and its efficacy, is further carried on in this verse.

In God's presence. That is, in the immediate presence of God, in contrast with the typical symbols of this in the tabernacle, before which the high priest presented himself. Christ has entered into God's presence. The high priest appeared in front of the ark and cherubim: Christ enters into the real presence of God. This indicates the certainty he had in his undertaking and his complete freedom from the guilt of sin. Had Christ not made an end of it, had he not absolutely been freed from it, he could not have appeared in this way with confidence and boldness in God's presence.

25. Nor did he enter heaven to offer himself again and again, the way the high priest enters the Most Holy Place every year with blood that is not his own. The one offering of Christ is here proposed not absolutely, but in comparison with the high priest of the law, whose entry into the Most Holy Place did not end his offering of sacrifices, but was repeated annually.

26. Then Christ would have had to suffer many times since the creation of the world. But now he has appeared once for all at the end of the ages to do away with sin by the sacrifice of himself.

Suffer. The suffering and offering of Christ are inseparable. The high priest of old often offered sacrifices, yet never once suffered himself. For he was not the sacrifice itself. It was the lamb that was slain that suffered. Christ is both—he could not offer without suffering, no more than the high priest could offer without the animal that was slain suffering. This is the heart of the apostle's argument. For he demonstrates that Christ did not, nor could offer himself often but **once**.

The end of the ages. This is the time when our Lord Jesus Christ appeared in the flesh and offered himself to God.

27-28. Just as man is destined to die once, and after that to face judgment, so Christ was sacrificed once to take away the sins of many people; and he will appear a second time, not to bear sin, but to bring salvation to those who are waiting for him.

Appear a second time. Christ's appearance, for the **second time**, his return from heaven, completes the salvation of the church and is the great fundamental principle of our faith and hope. Faith in the second coming of Christ is sufficient support for the souls of believers in their difficulties and trials. All true believers wait, with expectation, for the coming of Christ, and this is one of the distinguishing characteristics of sincere believers. At Christ's second appearance all sin will be dealt with.

Hebrews
Chapter 10

There are two parts to this chapter. The first, verses 1-18, is about the necessity and efficacy of Christ's sacrifice. The second, verses 19-39, applies this teaching to our faith, obedience, and perseverance. The first part of the chapter divides into two parts. Verses 1-4 show the insufficiency of legal sacrifices to expiate sin. Verses 5-18 declare how Christ's sacrifice achieved this. This declaration is divided into two parts. In verses 5-10, the substitution of Christ's sacrifice in place of all legal sacrifices, without which the church could not be saved, is explained. In verses 11-18, Christ's priesthood and sacrifice are compared with those of the law.

In verses 1-4 three things are considered: first, there is an assertion about the inadequacy of the legal sacrifices to expiate sin, and why this is so (verse 1); second, the truth of that assertion is confirmed by considering how often these sacrifices were repeated, which clearly shows how inadequate they were (verses 2-3); and, third, a general statement, derived from the nature of these sacrifices, is stated (verse 4).

Verses 1-4

1. The law is only a shadow of the good things that are coming—not the realities themselves. For this reason it can never, by the same sacrifices repeated endlessly year after year, make perfect those who draw near to worship.

The law. The apostle states two things about this **law.** Positively, and by way of concession, it was **a shadow of the good things that are coming.** Negatively, the law is not the reality itself.

2-3. If it could, would they not have stopped being offered? For the worshipers would have been cleansed once for all, and would no longer

HEBREWS

have felt guilty for their sins. But those sacrifices are an annual
reminder of sins. In these verses the apostle's argument is taken from the
impotency and insufficiency of the law, which he had just asserted in verse
1. The words should be read as if they were a question. **Would they not
have stopped being offered?** That is, they would have ceased, or else God
would not have appointed that they should be repeated. The apostle
observes that Christ's sacrifice was offered once, once for all, because by
one offering, and that offered once, the sacrifice was carried out perfectly.

**4. Because it is impossible for the blood of bulls and goats to take
away sins.**

It is impossible because it was divinely instituted that **the blood of
bulls and goats** could not **take away sins.** The blood of bulls and goats, as
offered in sacrifice and carried into the Most Holy Place, was designed by
God to represent the way of taking away sin, but could not, by itself,
achieve this. Therefore it was **impossible** that it should do so.

Verses 5-10

Therefore, when Christ came into the world, he said: "Sacrifice and
offering you did not desire, but a body you prepared for me; with burnt
offerings and sin offerings you were not pleased. Then I said, 'Here I
am—it is written about me in the scroll—I have come to do your will,
O God.'" First he said, "Sacrifices and offerings, burnt offerings and sin
offerings you did not desire, nor were you pleased with them"
(although the law required them to be made). Then he said, "Here I
am, I have come to do your will." He sets aside the first to establish the
second. And by that will, we have been made holy through the sacrifice
of the body of Jesus Christ once for all.

These verses declare God's provision to make up for the defect in legal
sacrifices as concerns the expiation of sin, peace of conscience with himself, and the sanctification of the souls of worshipers. For they have our
Lord Jesus Christ's undertaking that he will fulfill, perform, and suffer all
things required by God's will, wisdom, holiness, and righteousness.

The quotation in verses 5-7 is from Psalm 40:6-8. **"Sacrifice and offering you do not desire."** No sacrifices of the law, not all of them together,
were a means for the expiation of sin, suited to the glory of God or the
needs of the souls of men. The constant use of sacrifices to signify those
things that they could not effect in worshipers was a great part of the slavery that the church was held in under the old testament.

9. "I have come to do your will." Christ came to do God's will. The will
of God is taken in two ways: first, for his eternal purpose and design, called

"the purpose of his will" (Ephesians 1:11); and most often his will itself, that is, God's will being done. Second, the will of God means the declaration of his will and pleasure about what he wants us to do in obeying him. It is the will of God in the former sense in this verse. This is evident from verse 10, which says, "by that will, we have been made holy"; that is, our sins were expiated according to God's will. But the second sense is not totally excluded, for the Lord Christ came to fulfill God's will, in that we may be enabled to fulfill his command. Yes, and Christ himself had a command from God to lay down his life for the accomplishment of this work.

10. Once for all. This is how Christ's offering of himself was made. It was **once for all,** or, as we say, "once only." It never happened before that time, nor will it ever happen in the future; "there is no longer any sacrifice for sin" (10:18). Through Christ's sacrifice the church was perfectly sanctified, so there is no need for the sacrifice to be repeated. It also paved the way for Christ's present state—that is, glory, absolute, and perfection—which is not consistent with the repetition of the same sacrifice of himself. For, as the apostle shows in, verses 12-13, after this sacrifice had been offered, he had nothing more to do but to enter into its glory. The apostle stresses this teaching, which is the foundation of the faith of the church. He often mentions it and from it argues for the superiority of Christ's sacrifice above that of the sacrifices of the law. This foundation is destroyed by those who fancy that a renewed offering of the body of Christ happens every day in the Mass. Nothing could be more directly opposed to what the apostle asserts here.

Verses 11-14

Day after day every priest stands and performs his religious duties; again and again he offers the same sacrifices, which can never take away sins. But when this priest had offered for all time one sacrifice for sins, he sat down at the right hand of God. Since that time he waits for his enemies to be made his footstool, because by one sacrifice he has made perfect forever those who are being made holy.

The apostle states four things here, by way of recapitulation, about what he had already declared. First comes the state of the legal priests and sacrifices and their repetition, which demonstrates their utter inability to take away sin, verse 11. Second is the complete contrast between the old covenant offerings and the one offering of Christ, and that once offered, verse 12. Third, this results in Christ showing the absolute perfection of his offering, verse 12, and his continuing state after this, verse 13. Fourth, the absolute effect of his sacrifice is stated, which was the sanctification of the church, verse 14.

12. He sat down. Note in verse 11 that "every priest stands and performs his religious duty." But the immediate result of Christ's offering was that **he sat down at the right hand of God.** This glorious exaltation of Christ is in great contrast with the high priest who stood throughout his service in the tabernacle. Also the high priest only went into the Most Holy Place for a short time, whereas Christ sits at God's throne, which lasts "forever and ever" (1:8). This is Christ's unalterable state and condition. Christ **sat down,** never to offer sacrifice anymore. And this is the best pledge of these two things, which are the two pillars and principal foundations of the faith of the church. First, that God was completely pleased, satisfied, and highly glorified in and through Christ's offering; for had this not been so, Christ's human nature would not have been immediately exalted to the highest glory possible (see Ephesians 5:1-2; Philippians 2:7-9). Second, that Christ had through his offering perfectly expiated the sin of the world, so that there is no need ever again to offer any sacrifice for this.

Verses 15-18

The Holy Spirit also testifies to us about this. First he says: "This is the covenant I will make with them after that time, says the Lord. I will put my laws in their hearts, and I will write them on their minds." Then he adds: "Their sins and lawless acts I will remember no more." And where these have been forgiven, there is no longer any sacrifice for sin.

The Holy Spirit also testifies to us about this. The author of this testimony is **the Holy Spirit.** This is ascribed to him, as is all that is written in the Scripture, not only because holy men of old wrote as they were prompted by him, so that the Holy Spirit is the author of the whole Scripture, but also because of his presence and authority in it and with it continually. Hence, whatever is spoken in the Scripture is, and should be for us, the immediate word of the Holy Spirit.

These verses bring to an end the doctrinal part of this letter, a part of Scripture filled with heavenly and glorious mysteries, the light of the church of the Gentiles, the glory of the people Israel, the foundation of evangelical faith.

Verses 19-39

19-23. Therefore, brothers, since we have confidence to enter the Most Holy Place by the blood of Jesus, by a new and living way opened for us

through the curtain, that is, his body, and since we have a great priest over the house of God, let us draw near to God with a sincere heart in full assurance of faith, having our hearts sprinkled to cleanse us from a guilty conscience and having our bodies washed with pure water. Let us hold unswervingly to the hope we profess, for he who promised is faithful.

These verses begin the last part of this letter, which is wholly hortatory. For while there are some doctrinal points made, the stated purpose of all the rest of this letter is to propose to and press on the Hebrews the various duties the truths he has explained insist on. In all his exhortations he blends in the reasons for them, namely, the privilege they have in entering into these duties. Everything stems from the priesthood and sacrifice of Christ, which affects it all and benefits those who receive God's grace in this way.

Three things come in these verses. First, the reason for the duty they are exhorted to carry out is given, with its foundation being the special privilege of the Gospel (verses 19-21). Second, the way to use this privilege unto the end is stated (verse 22). Third, the special duty to persevere is commanded (verse 23).

22. Let us draw near. This phrase encompasses the whole performance of divine, solemn worship, as it was constantly expressed. For God had fixed the signs of his presence in a certain place, namely, the tabernacle and altar. Nobody could worship God without approaching, drawing near to that place, the means of their worship, and the pledges of God's presence there. In this way they were to bring their gifts, their offerings, their sacrifices; everything with which they worshiped in it was an approximation to God. Now all these things—tabernacle, temple, and altar—were types of Christ and the gracious presence of God in him. They were appointed for this sole purpose, to teach the church to look for a way to God in and through Christ alone.

So the apostle tells the Hebrews that, as they had an approach to God under the old testament, they were then "those who came and drew near to them." But this was defective for three reasons. First, it was through carnal means, "the blood of bulls and goats." Second, this was not an approach to God himself, but only some outward pledge of his presence. Third, in their approach to God they were excluded from entering into the holiest place. This approach to God was now removed, and what was appointed in its place had none of these defects. For, first, the approach to God is now not through carnal things, but in a holy, spiritual manner, as is then described. Second, the approach to God is not now through any outward pledges of his divine presence, but immediately to God himself, even the Father. Third, the approach to God is now into the most holy place itself, the special residence of God and of our high priest, Christ Jesus. So this drawing near includes all the holy worship of the church, both public and private, all the ways of our access to God through Christ. And the exhortation given for this duty is the first inference the apostle makes about the benefits we receive from Christ's priesthood and sacrifice.

A sincere heart. The main qualification of the people exhorted to draw near to God is to have **a sincere heart,** literally, a "true" heart. In a special way, God requires inner truth. "Surely you desire truth in the inner parts; you teach me wisdom in the inmost place" (Psalm 51:6). This is particularly the case in worship. "God is spirit, and his worshipers must worship in spirit and in truth" (John 4:24). In the mind, truth opposes falsehood; in the affections, truth opposes hypocrisy. In the first case all false worship is rejected, all means of worshiping God in ways he did not intend. But the truth of the heart, which is meant here, is the sincerity of heart that is opposed to all hypocrisy. From this it follows that the heart is what God is most interested in when we approach him, and that universal, internal sincerity of heart is required of everyone who comes close to God in holy worship.

23. Let us hold unswervingly to the hope we profess. This is the second exhortation that the apostle draws out from the truths he has just declared. This is the substance or purpose of the whole hortatory part of the letter. To obtain this the apostle has written all of the doctrinal part of the letter. The apostle spends the rest of the letter pressing home this exhortation. For on compliance with this rests the eternal condition of our souls. This the apostle does, partly by declaring the means whereby we may be helped to carry out this duty; partly by denouncing the eternal ruin and sure destruction that will follow if we neglect to do this; partly by encouragements from our previous experiences and the strength of our faith; and partly by showing us in numerous examples how we may overcome the difficulties we meet.

Unswervingly. That is, not bent one way or another by impressions made from anything, but to stay firm, fixed, stable, not wavering—literally, to be "unyielding." This contrasts with being divided between two opinions, God or Baal, Judaism or Christianity, truth or error. This is to waver doctrinally. Holding to our hope **unswervingly** is also in contrast with a feeble, irresolute mind about continuing in the profession of faith against difficulties and opposition. Holding **unswervingly** onto our hope is also in contrast with giving in on any points of doctrine or worship that would be inconsistent with the faith we have professed. In this sense the apostle would give no place, "no, not for an hour," to those who taught circumcision. To **hold unswervingly to the hope we profess** further contrasts with final apostasy from the truth, which this wavering leads to, as the apostle goes on to demonstrate.

24. And let us consider how we may spur one another on toward love and good deeds.

Love and good deeds are the fruit of saving faith. So the apostle now exhorts the Hebrews to **spur** each other on in these things. These duties are put in the correct order by the apostle. For **love** is the spring and foundation of all acceptable **good deeds.**

25. Let us not give up meeting together, as some are in the habit of doing, but let us encourage one another—and all the more as you see the Day approaching.

Meeting together. Literally, "coming together ourselves." For it is not the church-state absolutely, but the actual assemblies of believers, walking together in that state, which the apostle intends. These assemblies were of two kinds: first, the regular ones, on the Lord's day, or first day of the week (Acts 20:7; 1 Corinthians 16:2); second, occasional ones, as the duties of the church required (1 Corinthians 5:4).

26-27. If we deliberately keep on sinning after we have received the knowledge of the truth, no sacrifice for sins is left, but only a fearful expectation of judgment and of raging fire that will consume the enemies of God. In these verses the apostle gives a vehement enforcement of his preceding exhortation, showing what dreadful consequences flow from totally neglecting his command. He does this by, first, stating the nature of the sin involved; second, by showing that it is impossible to be delivered from it; and, third, by saying what punishment will inevitably follow.

If we deliberately keep on sinning. The apostle places himself with them, as he often does when rebuking them.

Deliberately. That is, obstinately, maliciously, from choice, without compulsion or fear; and this is all that the word will bear.

It is clear from these opening words of this verse what sin is intended, which is then denounced. It is the sin of renouncing the truth of the Gospel and its promises after we have been convinced of its truth and experienced its power. This is done **deliberately,** and not when taken by surprise or falling through a sudden temptation, as when Peter denied Christ. This sinning **deliberately** does not refer to those times of spiritual darkness that may press down on our minds, even though they are evil and dangerous.

To sin **deliberately** happens when people through choice and from an evil heart of unbelief depart from the living God. They publicly declare that God was not in Christ's sacrifice. (See comments on verse 29.)

27. But only a fearful expectation of judgment and of raging fire that will consume the enemies of God. When a person under the law was guilty of a sin that carried the death penalty, and which no sacrifice could expiate, such as adultery, murder, and blasphemy, he could only look forward to the fearful prospect of the carrying out of his sentence. And it is clear that in this context the apostle argues from the less to the greater: "If it was so, that this was the case for the person who sinned against Moses' law, how much more must it be so for those who sin against the Gospel, whose sin is incomparably greater, and whose punishment is more severe?"

Judgment. This is not something that is dubious and that may or may not happen. It is not an irrationally severe punishment that is threatened, but it is a just and righteous sentence, a punishment that fits the sin and crime. **Judgment** is sometimes taken for punishment itself (Psalm 9:16; James 2:13; 1 Peter 4:17; 2 Peter 2:3). But most often it refers to the sentence of judicial condemnation and trial, passed on to the offender who is to be then punished. In this way it expresses the general judgment that will fall on mankind on the last day (Matthew 10:15; 11:22, 24; 12:36; Mark 6:11; 2 Peter 2:9, 3:7; 1 John 4:17).

Raging fire. The punishment and destruction of those sinners is achieved through **raging fire.** God himself is in Scripture said to be "a consuming fire" (Deuteronomy 4:24, 9:3; Isaiah 33:14; Hebrews 12:29). This indicates God's essential holiness and righteousness.

The judgment of God concerning the punishment of sin, as an effect of his will in a way consonant with the holiness of his nature, is called "fire" (1 Corinthians 3:13). But that is not the fire meant here. Here, the **fire** is devouring, consuming, destroying, matching the severity of God's justice, as in Deuteronomy 32:22; Psalm 11:6; Isaiah 9:5; 30:33; 66:15; Amos 7:4; Matthew 18:8; 2 Thessalonians 1:8. So, this **raging fire** speaks of God's holy nature, his righteous actions, and the dreadful severity of the punishment itself.

28-29. Anyone who rejected the law of Moses died without mercy on the testimony of two or three witnesses. How much more severely do you think a man deserves to be punished who has trampled the Son of God under foot, who has treated as an unholy thing the blood of the covenant that sanctified him, and who has insulted the Spirit of grace?

28. On the testimony of two or three witnesses. This law is laid down in Deuteronomy 17:6, 19:13, and Numbers 35:30. God's judgment could only be carried out if **two or three witnesses** were available to testify.

The Son of God. Whoever rejects, refuses, forsakes the Gospel, rejects and forsakes the person of Christ.

Trampled. It might be thought that the Son of God is only involved here in a small degree. "No," says the apostle, "for he who is guilty of this sin tramples on the Son of God, that is, treads him underfoot." This word expresses the highest kind of scorn, contempt, and malice among men. To "tread under foot" is to despise and insult, as is plain from the metaphor. This contempt is directed toward both the person of Christ and his authority.

30-31. For we know him who said, "It is mine to avenge; I will

repay," and again, "The Lord will judge his people." It is a dreadful thing to fall into the hands of the living God.

Fall into the hands of. To **fall into the hands of** someone is a common expression and refers to anyone falling into and under the power of his enemies. When a person falls into the hands of his enemies there is no law or love between him and them, and he can expect nothing but death. This is what it is to **fall into the hands of the living God.** There is nothing in the law, there is nothing in the Gospel that can be appealed to to stop the punishment.

A dreadful thing. People are prone not to think about this. But God's judgment exists and will be **dreadful,** terrible, and eternally destructive of everything that is not good.

32-34. Remember those earlier days after you had received the light, when you stood your ground in great contest in the face of suffering. Sometimes you were publicly exposed to insult and persecution; at other times you stood side by side with those who were so treated. You sympathized with those in prison and joyfully accepted the confiscation of your property, because you knew that you yourselves had better and lasting possessions.

These verses exhort the Hebrews to avoid the evil they are warned against. Hence the apostle returns to his previous themes about perseverance so that they can overcome all their difficulties. He begins by telling them to do something that will help them in their situation: **Remember those earlier days,** verse 32. He then describes their suffering in those **earlier days,** verses 32-33. He reminds them how they acted in these situations and how they were enabled to do this, verse 34.

34. You sympathized. Literally, "you suffered together." They were not unconcerned about other people's suffering just because they were free from suffering themselves. Compassion consists of, first, a real grief and troubled mind about the imprisonment of others, as if we were ourselves in prison with them; second, great prayer support for their deliverance (Acts 12); third, ministering to the physical needs, as many did to Paul (Acts 24:23); fourth, not being ashamed of their chains or sufferings (2 Timothy 1:16-17); and, fifth, being prepared to undertake dangerous action (Romans 16:4). The apostle does not mean a heartless, fruitless, ineffective pity, but rather, a real practical concern for the welfare of those imprisoned.

35-36. So do not throw away your confidence; it will be richly rewarded. You need to persevere so that when you have done the will of God, you will receive what he has promised.

36. You need to persevere. The apostle does not accuse them of lacking perseverance, but reminds them about the necessity of continually exercising patience. Perseverance is the grace of suffering Christians (James 1:4-5) and the correct reaction to all tribulations (Romans 5:4-5).

37-39. For in just a very little while, "He who is coming will come and will not delay. But my righteous one will live by faith. And if he shrinks back, I will not be pleased with him." But we are not of those who shrink back and are destroyed, but of those who believe and are saved.

Note three things in these verses: first, a proposal about the object of faith, which is the coming of Christ, verse 37; second, the necessity for faith in this matter, and a warning about the definite ruin of those who **shrink back,** verse 38; and, third, the apostle's judgment about their faith, verse 39.

"My righteous one will live by faith." Three times in his letters the apostle uses this prophetic assertion from Habakkuk 2:3-4 (Romans 1:17; Galatians 3:11). The person referred to here is said to be **"my righteous one,"** a person really made just, or justified by faith. What is principally meant here is that characteristic of a righteous person that is the opposite of pride and unbelief, which makes people shrink back from God. The **righteous one** is humble, meek, sincere, submissive to God's will, waiting to do his wishes.

Sincere faith will carry people through all difficulties, hazards, and troubles, to the certain enjoyment of eternal blessedness.

Hebrews
Chapter 11

Faith alone, from the beginning of the world, in all ages, under all dispensations of divine grace, and all alterations in the church-state and worship, has been the only principle in the church of living to God, of obtaining the promises, of inheriting eternal life, and continues to be unto the consummation of all things. The record here of what faith has done is only evidence about what it will do. Faith can do all things that belong to the life of God; and without it nothing can be done. Spiritual life is by faith (Galatians 2:20), as are victory (1 John 5:4), perseverance (1 Peter 1:5), and salvation (Ephesians 2:8; 1 Peter 1:9); and so they were from the beginning.

Verses 1-16

1. The first verse describes the nature of faith and shows how suitably to do the great work assigned to it, namely, the preservation of believers in the profession of the Gospel with constancy.

Now faith is being sure of what we hope for and certain of what we do not see.

Faith. Faith is the subject spoken about here, by which the just live. This is divine, supernatural, justifying, and saving faith. It is the faith of God's elect, the faith that is not of ourselves but God's work, with which all true believers are endowed from above. It is therefore justifying faith that the apostle speaks about here; but he does not speak of it as justifying, but as being effectually useful in all our life with God, especially for our perseverance.

Being sure of what we hope for. What we hope for, "things hoped for," in general are good things which are promised in the future and expected on certain grounds. What **we hope for** here, therefore, is all the things that are divinely promised to those who believe, all things of present grace and future glory.

Certain of what we do not see. There are things that are objects of faith that are unseen and yet not what we hope for. The creation of the world is an example of this. But generally **what we hope for** and **what we do not see** are the same, and faith gives evidence about their truth.

Being sure. This is what faith gives; it gives those things hoped for, and as they are hoped for, a real substance in the minds and souls of believers. This is the meaning of these words. Oecumenius says, "Faith is the essence of these things, and their subsistence, causing them to be, and to be present, because it believes them."

2. This is what the ancients were commended for.

The ancients. Who these **ancients** were becomes clear from the following verses. All true believers from the foundation of the world, or the giving of the first promise, until the end of the dispensation of the old testament, are intended.

Commended. They received this witness in the Scripture, although it was very different in the world.

This. This testimony was founded on their "faith." They were commended in, by, or through their believing. Many other great things, such as heroic deeds, are ascribed to them, but they are only commended because of their faith.

3. By faith we understand that the universe was formed at God's command, so that what is seen was not made out of what was visible.

Faith. Where it says **by faith we understand that the universe was formed at God's command,** faith includes its object, namely, the divine revelation that is made about this in God's Word. For there is no other way for faith to teach us except through its assent to divine revelation. Once the revelation is made, faith is the only way we understand it and assent to it. **By faith we understand;** that is, by faith we assent to its divine revelation. For by faith we are assured about the creation of the world out of nothing, which is contrary to natural reason, as "nothing comes out of nothing."

Was formed. By faith we understand that the world **was formed.** Nowhere does this word mean the original production of anything, but the ordering, disposing, fitting, perfecting, or adorning of what is produced.

At God's command. The effective cause of this forming of the universe is **God's command.** For by **God's command the universe was formed.** He spoke and it was made; he commanded and it stood fast.

So that what is seen was not made out of what was visible. These words declare how the world was made. **What is seen** is more than **the universe.** For **what is seen** includes "all things in heaven and earth, visible and invisible" (Colossians 1:16). But the apostle confines the subject to the things that our senses and reason can understand.

Made. These things were **not made out of what was visible.** They were **made** but **not made out of what was visible,** which seems to be a denial of any preexisting material. They were made by the invisible power of God. "For since the creation of the world God's invisible qualities—his eternal power and divine nature—have been clearly seen, being understood from what has been made" (Romans 1:20). These visible things were made by those that are invisible, the eternal power and wisdom of God.

4. From the proposition of the nature of faith in general, the apostle now gives examples of its power and efficacy in particular people.

By faith Abel offered God a better sacrifice than Cain did. By faith he was commended as a righteous man, when God spoke well of his offerings. And by faith he still speaks, even though he is dead.

Abel. The example given is **Abel,** the second son of Adam and first son of the promise. Abel was the first person to be killed for Christ, and this at the hands of his brother. This has made him well-known in all generations, which, as Chrysostom thinks, is intended by the last clause, **he still speaks, even though he is dead.**

Offered God. Abel offered his sacrifice to **God** (Genesis 4:3). This was the best way of paying homage to the Divine Being. Whoever sacrifice is offered to is God. Therefore, when the Gentiles sacrificed to the devil, as they did (1 Corinthians 10:20, "the sacrifices of pagans are offered to demons"), they owned him as "the god of this age" (2 Corinthians 4:4).

By faith. Abel offered his sacrifice **by faith.** He was not doing something that he had invented, but his sacrifice was in response to God's command and promise. He did it in **faith,** in that he exercised faith in God as he sacrificed.

A better sacrifice. The difference between Cain and Abel was Abel's faith. As their faith differed, so did their actions and the objects they used to sacrifice with. Cain considered God only as a creator and preserver, whom he offered the fruits of the earth. He had not thought about sin or how to be delivered from it. Abel's faith was fixed on God, not only as a creator, but as redeemer also, as the one who, in his infinite wisdom and grace, had appointed the way of redemption through sacrifice and atonement. So Abel's sacrifice was accompanied with a sense of sin and guilt, with its lost condition by the fall, and a trust in the way of redemption and recovery that God had provided. This is borne out by his type of sacrifice, which was by death and blood: death, which he deserved because of his sin; blood, which was the way atonement came.

Commended. That is, God **commended** Abel. This was so famous in the church that he seemed to be known by the name "righteous Abel," which is how our Savior referred to him (Matthew 23:35). The apostle testifies that Abel was indeed righteous with the words, he was **commended as a righteous man.**

His offerings. How God spoke well of Abel's **offerings** is not stated. Most people think God brought fire from heaven to set his sacrifice on fire on the altar. What is certain is that in some way, through some token, Abel's faith was strengthened, and Cain became angry, knowing that God had accepted his brother's sacrifice.

Here is a prototype of the believing and malignant churches in all ages—of those who are born after the Spirit and those born after the flesh. "At that time the son born in the ordinary way persecuted the son born by the power of the Spirit" (Galatians 5:29). This was the first public display of the enmity between the descendants of the woman and the descendants of the serpent. "Cain, who belonged to the evil one [the descendant of the serpent] . . . murdered his brother" (1 John 3:12).

And by faith he still speaks. The second result of Abel's faith happened after his death. **And by faith he still speaks, even though he is dead. By faith,** that is, through the means of that faith that was the ground of his acceptance with God, **he still speaks.** The apostle interprets the meaning of this in 12:24, where he specifically ascribes these words to Abel's blood.

5. By faith Enoch was taken from this life, so that he did not experience death; he could not be found, because God had taken him away. For before he was taken, he was commended as one who pleased God.

His second example is **Enoch.** Enoch has a double witness given to him in Scripture; once in the Old Testament, and once in the New Testament. In the Old Testament his faith and holiness are mentioned (Genesis 5), while in the New Testament his prophecy is remembered: "Enoch, the seventh from Adam, prophesied about these men: 'See, the Lord is coming with thousands upon thousands of his holy ones to judge everyone, and to convict all the ungodly of all the ungodly acts they have done in the ungodly way, and of all the harsh words ungodly sinners have spoken against him'" (Jude 14-15). Enoch preached about the warnings of the law, the future judgment on ungodly sinners, especially those who scoffed and persecuted.

Taken from this life. Literally, "removed." He was "translated" out of one state and condition into another. There are only two states for good men such as Enoch. The first is the state of faith and obedience here in this world. Enoch lived in this state for "300 years." "He walked with God" (Genesis 5:22-24), leading a life of faith as he obeyed God. The second state, in the next world, is the blessed state of enjoying God. No other state for good people is once intimated in the Scripture or is consistent with God's covenant. So Enoch, being translated from the first state, immediately was installed into the second. The Scripture leaves no room for any conjecture about the whereabouts of the particular place, or the kind of place it is, and only rash and foolish people make such conjectures.

He did not experience death. For "God took him away" (Genesis 5:24). Enoch was removed from one state to the other, without the intervention of death.

6. And without faith it is impossible to please God, because anyone who comes to him must believe that he exists and that he rewards those who earnestly seek him.

Faith is not specifically mentioned in Genesis in connection with Enoch, just that he walked with God and pleased God. This verse shows that he pleased God through his faith and consequently "was taken from this life." The apostle now states that **without faith it is impossible to please God.** It follows that Enoch "pleased God" and was translated because he had faith.

To please God. Literally, "to have been well-pleasing." What is impossible without faith is **to please God.** This verb is only used in the passive in these two verses and in 13:16 in the whole of the New Testament. The adjective, often translated "pleasing," is constantly applied to people or things that are accepted with God: "anyone who serves God in this way is pleasing to God" (Romans 14:18; see also Romans 12:1-2; 2 Corinthians 5:9; Ephesians 5:10; Philippians 4:18; Colossians 3:20). Three things are included here. First, for a person to be accepted by God, God needs to be well pleased with him; second, the person's actions need to please God, as did Abel's gifts and Enoch's obedience—see 13:16; third, such people are righteous, just or justified, as Abel and Enoch were, as all true believers were in the Scripture. Faith alone pleases God. Otherwise there could be many acts that pleased God. But God is only pleased by those who are accepted and justified by God. So our coming to God and our believing in God must be interpreted in the light of pleasing God.

God **rewards those who earnestly seek him,** not those who just seek him. To "seek" the Lord is used in general for any inquiry after him (Acts 17:27). But this word, which literally means "to seek out," indicates that the person is diligently seeking God. So a faith that is not diligent is no faith.

7. By faith Noah, when warned about things not yet seen, in holy fear built an ark to save his family. By his faith he condemned the world and became heir of the righteousness that comes by faith.

Chrysostom particularly commends this third example the apostle gives because it not only shows the efficacy of faith in Noah, but because it also shows the effect of unbelief in the world. This was a most relevant example for the Hebrews who were being tested about whom they would follow and abide with.

Warned about things not yet seen. This warning is recorded in

221

Genesis 6:13-16. In the first part, Noah is told that God will destroy the world (Genesis 6:13), and in the second part he is told what he has to do: build an ark (Genesis 6:14-16). This had a double effect on Noah. First, it made him fearful, and second, he obeyed God as he built the ark according to God's directions. Both parts of this divine warning were **about things not yet seen.** The apostle said in verse 1 that "what we do not see" is the correct object of our faith. But the things meant by this were not invisible in themselves; they were seen well enough when they existed. Therefore, the apostle says these things were not **yet** seen, that is, the flood, and Noah's being saved by the ark. These were **not yet seen** when Noah warned about them, nor were they "seen" a hundred years later. The cause of the flood, the wickedness of the world, and the destruction of the world, through God's power, was invisible. So it was a pure act of faith for Noah to believe what he had no evidence for, except through divine revelation, especially since the thing itself seemed so incredible.

In holy fear. Noah was moved with fear and at this point was exercising faith. For although Noah may be said to be warned by God inasmuch as he became accepted with God by faith, and then received this divine warning, yet the emphasis here is the effect this faith had on Noah. "By faith Noah . . . was moved by fear." This is the effect that believing God's word had on Noah. Thus **holy fear** was a reverential fear about God's warnings and is meant here, not an anxious fear about the evil threatened. In the warning Noah received, he considered the greatness, the holiness, and the power of God. Seeing God through faith in this way, he was filled with a reverential fear of him (see Psalm 119:120; Habakkuk 3:16; Malachi 2:5).

He condemned the world. Noah did not condemn the world as its judge, but as an advocate and a witness, through a plea and testimony. He **condemned the world** by his teaching, through his obedience, by his example, and through the faith he exercised.

Heir of righteousness. The way Noah obtained his righteousness is that he was made the **heir** of it. The way we partake of this righteousness is through gratuitous adoption. This is through faith (John 1:12). So in justification, forgiveness of sin and the inheritance go together (Acts 26:18). And this inheritance is through the promise, not through the law or deeds (Romans 4:14; Galatians 3:18-19). So Noah was **heir of righteousness that comes by faith** in free adoption, through faith, and he came to have an interest in and right to the righteousness that is offered in the promise, through which it is given us as an inheritance.

8. By faith Abraham, when called to go to a place he would later receive as his inheritance, obeyed and went, even though he did not know where he was going.

The apostle has now passed over the first period of the scriptural record, namely, from the beginning of the world to the flood. He has considered the examples of those who "pleased God" and were accepted with him in their obedience. Two things he shows from them that relate to his argument: first, that they all pleased God and were righteous by faith; second, that their faith enabled them to stand in God's favor and to carry out their duties despite the opposition they met. Here the apostle shows the Hebrews that if they did not persevere in their Christian profession, it was because of their unbelief, as true faith would certainly carry them through.

Now the apostle moves on to the next period of time, from the flood to the giving of the law. This shows that in every era of the church the way to please God was the same. The apostle urges them to follow the example of Abraham (verses 8-19).

In Abraham a foundation of a new state of the church after the flood was laid, more excellent than that which preceded it. He was the first person after the flood who is said to have pleased God. He was the progenitor of the Hebrews; from him they derived all their privileges; in his person they were initiated into the covenant, with a right to the promises. He was also through promise "the father of all that believe." So it was most relevant for the Hebrews then, and for us now, to consider his example of faith and obedience.

Inheritance. The country Abraham was called to go to **he would later receive as his inheritance.** God, as the great possessor of heaven and earth, as the sovereign Lord of all things, transferred the right and title to that land and invested it in Abraham. It is frequently repeated that God gave them this or that land.

He did not know where he was going. What the land was, who lived there, or the way to travel to it, Abraham was not told. It might appear that God had told him from the start that it was the land of Canaan. For when Abraham first left Canaan he set out "to go to Canaan" (Genesis 11:31), but it is stated **he did not know where he was going.** He did not understand anything about the circumstances of the route he took, or about the land he was called to, or where it was. So it can be said of him, **he did not know where he was going.** Abraham wholly committed himself to the power, faithfulness, goodness, and direction of God without having the least encouragement about the place he was going to.

9. By faith he made his home in the promised land like a stranger in a foreign country; he lived in tents, as did Isaac and Jacob, who were heirs with him of the same promise.

He made his home . . . like a stranger. Literally, "he sojourned." The word means to live as a stranger. It is used in Luke 24:18: "Are you only a visitor to Jerusalem?"—a visitor for a short time, not a resident. Nowhere else is this word used in the New Testament. So this word indicates that

Abraham lived as a **stranger,** for he had no inheritance, with no permanent building to live in.

In the promised land. Literally, "a land of promise." That is, the land that God had recently promised to give him, and where all the other promises would be fulfilled.

As did Isaac and Jacob. As Abraham was **like a stranger in a foreign country,** in the land of Canaan, without any inheritance or possession, living in tents, so it was for **Isaac and Jacob.** Jacob was the last person in his family who lived like a stranger in Canaan; all those after him lived in Egypt and did not go into Canaan until they took possession of it themselves.

Heirs with him of the same promise. For not only did they inherit the promise made to Abraham, but God specifically made the promise to them both: to Isaac (Genesis 26:3-4), and to Jacob (Genesis 28:13-15). So they were **heirs with him of the same promise** (see Psalm 105:9-11).

10. For he was looking forward to the city with foundations, whose architect and builder is God. This verse explains why Abraham was so content to be a pilgrim in the world without any possessions or inheritance.

The city. The **city** that Abraham looked for is that heavenly city, that heavenly mansion, which God has provided and prepared for all true believers. After this life they will be with him there, as verse 16 states. It is also sometimes called a house, or a tabernacle or a mansion (Luke 16:9; John 14:2; 2 Corinthians 5:1), as it is a place for them to live in, rest in, and be refreshed in forever. Here the whole reward and glory of heaven is linked to enjoying God's presence. With this expectation in front of him, Abraham was refreshed in the middle of his tough pilgrimage.

With foundations. Heaven is a settled, quiet habitation; a suitable dwelling for those who have had a life of trouble in this world. The city is first described as one that has **foundations.** This is in contrast with the tents or tabernacles in which Abraham lived, which had no foundation and were only supported by stakes and cords.

The city is then described as one **whose architect and builder is God.** Most commentators take **architect** and **builder** to indicate the same thing. Strictly speaking the **architect,** literally "artificer," designs the building, while the **builder,** literally "maker," is in charge of the people who carry out the building work. God alone is the only builder of the heavenly city and does so with no help whatsoever from anyone else.

11. By faith Abraham, even though he was past age—and Sarah herself was barren—was enabled to become a father because he considered him faithful who had made the promise. The apostle gives examples of Abraham's faith concerning the promise made to him, namely, that through his descendants all the nations of the earth will be blessed. This centered around the birth of Isaac, through whom the promise would be fulfilled, and through Abraham's faith would be offered up as the son of the promise to God as a sacrifice.

In the first of these examples, or what concerned the birth of Isaac, the son of the promise, Abraham was not alone, as Sarah his wife was both naturally and spiritually as much involved as he was. So, in the middle of writing about Abraham's faith, the apostle introduces Sarah.

And Sarah herself. As Abraham was the father of the faithful, or the church, so Sarah was the mother of it. She was the free woman from which the church sprang (Galatians 4:22-23). And all believing women are her daughters (1 Peter 3:6; see also Genesis 17:16). Her work and obedience are held up to the church as an example, and so her faith may be as well (1 Peter 3:5-6). Sarah was equally involved with Abraham in the divine revelation. The blessing of the promised Seed was confined and appropriated to Sarah no less than to Abraham: "I will bless her . . . I will bless her so that she will be the mother of nations; kings of peoples will come from her" (Genesis 17:16; see also Genesis 17:19; 18:10). Sarah's faith was necessary in all this, and it is recorded here.

12. And so from this one man, and he as good as dead, came descendants as numerous as the stars in the sky and as countless as the sand on the seashore. Note that the first testimony given about the justification of Abraham by faith was because he believed in the promise that his seed would be like the stars of heaven, which cannot be numbered. For it is immediately added, "Abram believed the LORD, and he credited it to him as righteousness" (Genesis 15:5-6). For although this promise was about temporal things, it also belonged to the way of redemption through Christ, the promised Seed.

As good as dead. Literally, "and that too having died." Translations from Tyndale say **as good as dead.** Abraham's natural body was useless for procreation, as if he had been dead.

13. All these people were still living by faith when they died. They did not receive the things promised; they only saw them and welcomed them from a distance. And they admitted that they were aliens and strangers on earth.

Were still living by faith when they died. The apostle commends the faith of these people as they persevered in faith to the end. Their faith did not fail them, either before or during their last moments. They were exercising faith when they died. To do this, firm belief in the existence of life after death is needed, for without this all faith and hope must perish in death. This faith also requires that they entrusted their departing souls into God's care and power.

They only saw them . . . from a distance. These words refer to time and not to measured distance. It was a long space of time before those promises were fulfilled. This was gradually shortened until it became a very "little while" (Haggai 2:6-7), and then the promised one would come "suddenly" (Malachi 3:1). But, at present, it was a long way off. This kept the church expectant and desiring the arrival of this day, and in this consisted its main work of faith.

Welcomed them. Literally, "greeted them." This word means to salute and refers to greetings that are accompanied by delight and veneration. It usually involves a handshake and an embrace. So, this embracing of the promises is the heart clinging to them with love and delight.

They were aliens and strangers on earth. Believers said that this world was not their home, their country, or their city of residence. They were just passing through the world. This was the case with Abraham (Genesis 23:4), Jacob (Genesis 47:8-9), and David (1 Chronicles 29:15; Psalm 39:12). And, declares Peter, it is the case with all believers: "Dear friends, I urge you, as aliens and strangers in the world . . ." (1 Peter 2:11).

14. People who say such things show that they are looking for a country of their own.

Show. "Declare plainly." They make it evident to all. When they knew in their minds they spoke with their mouths.

15. If they had been thinking of the country they had left, they would have had opportunity to return. If these patriarchs did desire a country, it might be because, having lost their own country and their relatives, and now wandering through life, they wished to return home again and live quietly and settle down. If this were the case, it would overthrow the apostle's present argument. In this verse the apostle demonstrates that this was not the case.

If they had been thinking of the country they had left. It is natural for all people to remember and desire their own country. But this desire to return to their original home was put to death in these holy people through faith as they obeyed God. From this it is seen that when the hearts and minds of believers are fixed on spiritual and heavenly things, it takes away from them an inordinate longing for things that would otherwise be so desirable.

16. Instead, they were longing for a better country—a heavenly one. Therefore God is not ashamed to be called their God, for he has prepared a city for them. The apostle explains how they were being "aliens and strangers." They were not just making a complaint about their present way of living, Nor were they longing for a better earthly country. They were seeking another country, a different kind of country on which they had fixed their faith.

A better country. What they desired was **a better country,** not the country they were in, or the country they had come from, but another one, a **better** one. This means **a heavenly one.** This is "the city with foundations, whose architect and builder is God" (11:10). This is heaven itself, or living with God and enjoying him forever. The apostle is ascribing to the holy patriarchs a faith in the immortality and glory after this life.

Verses 17-19

By faith Abraham, when God tested him, offered Isaac as a sacrifice. He who had received the promises was about to sacrifice his one and only son, even though God had said to him, "It is through Isaac that your offspring will be reckoned." Abraham reasoned that God could raise the dead, and figuratively speaking, he did receive Isaac back from death.

We may consider in these words:

1. The person whose faith is chosen, who is Abraham.

2. The occasion of this exercise of his faith, **when God tested him.**

3. The act and result of his faith, the offering of Isaac.

4. The details of his exercise of faith here: first, from Isaac, who was **his one and only son;** second, from thinking about Abraham himself **who had received the promises;** and, third, from the promises themselves, which concerned Isaac being Abraham's **offspring.**

5. The reconciliation that faith made in his mind between the promises and the present duty that he was called to: **Abraham reasoned.**

6. The result of his faith, **figuratively speaking, he did receive Isaac back from the dead.**

Abraham . . . offered Isaac as a sacrifice. The command was to "offer him as a burnt-offering," which first had to be killed and then consumed by fire. So the apostle affirms that **Abraham . . . offered Isaac as a sacrifice,** whereas we know how he was delivered. But this means that Abraham fully obeyed God's command here. He did it in his will, heart, and affections, although it was never eventually carried out. The will is accepted for the deed. The correct meaning is that Abraham fully obeyed God's command.

His one and only son. In what sense is Isaac said to be Abraham's **one and only son** since Abraham had one son before Isaac and many sons after Isaac? Isaac was the **only son** in whom the promise of Abraham's offspring would be fulfilled. **"It is through Isaac that your offspring will be reckoned."**

Sometimes, through God's providence, there may appear to be inconsistency between God's commands and his promises. Nothing but faith bowing the soul to divine sovereignty can reconcile this (Genesis 23:8-12).

He did receive Isaac back from the dead. Abraham fully obeyed God, for he had parted completely with Isaac. It was as if Isaac had already been killed, that he was no more since he was dead. From this position Abraham **did receive Isaac back from death.** Isaac was made to be God's alone, as devoted; and God gave him back again to Abraham.

Verses 20-23

20. By faith Isaac blessed Jacob and Esau in regard to their future. Isaac was a holy person who was undoubtedly a son of the promise who led a life of faith, and the promise was specifically renewed to him: "I will make your descendants as numerous as the stars in the sky and will give them all these lands, and through your offspring all nations on earth will be blessed" (Genesis 26:4). The example of Isaac's faith that the apostle chooses to highlight is his blessing his sons when he was very old, which was a striking act of faith, as it passed on to them the promise.

Isaac blessed Jacob and Esau. Patriarchal blessings were partly prayers and partly prophetic predictions. They consisted of the promise made in them and nothing else. They did not pray for, they could not foretell, anything other than what God had promised. They were authoritative applications of God's promises to the people to whom they belonged, for the confirmation of their faith (see Genesis 27).

21. By faith Jacob, when he was dying, blessed each of Joseph's sons, and worshiped as he leaned on the top of his staff.

Two things are mentioned in this verse. First, that **Jacob . . . blessed each of Joseph's sons;** and, second, that he **worshiped as he leaned on the top of his staff.** But they did not occur in this order. The second is recorded before the first: "Israel worshiped as he leaned on the top of his staff" (Genesis 47:31). "Some time later" (Genesis 48:1) Joseph brought his children to Jacob (Israel).

From Genesis 47:29 to the end of that book, an account is given of Jacob's death and what he did **when he was dying.** How long he took to die is uncertain, but it was probably not many days. The first thing he did was to send for his son Joseph, to put him in charge of his burial in the land of Canaan, which was an act of faith about God's promise concerning his descendants (Genesis 47:29-31). When he had done this, it says, "he leaned on the top of his staff" (Genesis 47:31); that is, he bowed and worshiped God. This is only mentioned once in the whole story, but this indicates what Jacob did on similar occasions, especially in all his words and deeds as he died. When he had said something or done something, he was to retire to God, acknowledging his mercy and asking for more grace. This indeed is the way the holy act as they die.

22. By faith Joseph, when his end was near, spoke about the exodus of the Israelites from Egypt and gave instructions about his bones. Two examples of Joseph's faith are mentioned: first, that he **spoke about the exodus of the Israelites from Egypt**; second, that he **gave instructions about his bones.**

The exodus of the Israelites from Egypt is not intended absolutely as just leaving that place, but in such a way that fulfilled the promise made to their fathers. For it is stated in the record, "Then Joseph said to his brothers, 'I am about to die. But God will surely come to your aid and take you up out of this land to the land he promised on oath to Abraham, Isaac and Jacob'" (Genesis 50:24). The fulfillment of this promise was the focus of Joseph's faith.

There is a particular example of Joseph's faith in that he **gave instructions about his bones.** This was unique to Joseph. When the apostle says that Joseph **gave instructions,** he was putting his brothers under oath and putting their children under the same oath to carry out his orders (Exodus 13:19).

The apostle just says he **gave instructions about his bones,** but does not say what these instructions were. But the story recorded in Genesis says that when God visited them and rescued them from Egypt, they should take Joseph's bones with them to Canaan (Genesis 50:25). To do this, "they embalmed him" and placed him "in a coffin in Egypt" (Genesis 50:26). Probably the Egyptians left the funeral arrangements to his brothers, and his coffin remained in their custody and in that of their children until they left Egypt. Then Moses took charge of the bones (Exodus 13:19), and they were safely transported to Canaan and buried at Shechem in the plot of land that Jacob had bought (Joshua 24:32).

That is the story, but we ask, why did Joseph give these **instructions about his bones?** All the other bones stayed in Egypt and were not taken off to Canaan. There were some things that were unique to Joseph that made him, through faith, act in this way concerning the disposal of his bones. He did it to encourage the faith and expectation of his brothers and their descendants concerning their future deliverance from Egypt.

23. By faith Moses' parents hid him for three months after he was born, because they saw he was no ordinary child, and they were not afraid of the king's edict. In searching the sacred records for eminent examples of the power and efficacy of faith, the apostle arrived at that of Moses. And because this is the greatest example, next to that of Abraham, he emphasizes many of the results and acts of Moses' faith. And if we consider correctly his person and his circumstances, the work he was called to do, the trials, difficulties, and temptations he had to contend with, his concern for God's glory and for the whole church, we will see how this wonderfully represents the redemption and deliverance of the church by Christ.

With Moses' victory over all opposition we must acknowledge that there is not a better example of the power of faith. For this reason the apostle takes one step back and declares the faith of Moses' parents in preserving Moses' life as a baby. When God planned that a person should carry out some great work he often indicated this in some way at their birth. This was the case with Samson, Samuel, and John the Baptist and others. And so it was with the birth and preservation of Moses, as is declared in this verse.

By faith Moses' parents. The faith of the **parents** of Moses is celebrated here. Their faith was so strong that **they were not afraid of the king's edict.**

Verses 24-26

By faith Moses, when he had grown up, refused to be known as the son of Pharaoh's daughter. He chose to be mistreated along with the people of God rather than to enjoy the pleasures of sin for a short time. He regarded disgrace for the sake of Christ as of greater value than the treasures of Egypt, because he was looking ahead to his reward.

24. By faith Moses. Nobody in the world was more marked out by Providence in his birth, education, and actions than Moses. Yet Moses lived and worked by faith.

Self-denial is not just saying no to outward actions but is a mortification of the desires and affections of the mind that wants to place a value on things in life, especially the things of this world that oppose spiritual things. Moses crucified his heart to his outward enjoyments, thinking of them as rubbish in comparison with Christ. **He chose to be mistreated along with the people of God rather than to enjoy the pleasures of sin for a short time** (verse 25). Moses had to choose between **the people of God** in their afflicted state and enjoying **the pleasures of sin.** Moses' determination is seen in the words **he chose. He chose to be mistreated. . . .**

Mistreated. This word occurs only here in the whole of the New Testament. Literally, it means, "to be mistreated with," and signifies "to be pressed, distressed with evil things that destroy nature."

26. Disgrace for the sake of Christ. This must be the same as being "mistreated along with the people of God." **Christ,** as used here, is never used for any type of Christ, but only for Christ himself. If Moses went through disgrace as the type of Christ, knowing that he was doing this, then he believed in Christ. From the first promise about the manifestation of the Son of God in the flesh, Christ was the life, soul, and everything for everyone in the church, in all ages. From him everything came and centered in, for "Jesus Christ is the same yesterday and today and for ever"

(Hebrews 13:8). He is "the Lamb that was slain from the creation of the world" (Revelation 13:8).

The treasures of Egypt. Treasures are the riches in gold, silver, precious stones, and other very valuable things that are stored and hidden. But when treasures of a nation are mentioned they include all the advantages that may be derived from these treasures. In both respects Egypt, while it flourished, was second to none. Moses was well aware of **the treasures of Egypt,** but he preferred **disgrace for the sake of Christ.**

His reward. God gave this **reward** to Moses, just as he had given him faith and obedience. Moses did not deserve it or earn it, but it was given to him as sovereign bounty.

Verses 27-38

27. By faith he left Egypt, not fearing the king's anger; he persevered because he saw him who is invisible.

Three things are ascribed to Moses' faith here.
1. What he did: **he left Egypt.**
2. How he did this: **not fearing the king's anger.**
3. The basis on which he did it: **he persevered.**

He left Egypt. Moses left Egypt by faith. Moses left Egypt twice; first after he killed an Egyptian (Exodus 2:14-15); and second, when he delivered the people out of Egypt (Exodus 10:29). The apostle is referring to Moses' second departure from Egypt here. While this leaving of Egypt may be a general expression of Moses taking the people into the desert, the apostle has a special reason for recording it: "Pharaoh said to Moses, 'Get out of my sight! Make sure you do not appear before me again! The day you see my face you will die.' 'Just as you say,' Moses replied, 'I will never appear before you again'" (Exodus 10:28-29). Never has there been a greater expression of faith and spiritual courage than this. It is stated that Moses threatened Pharaoh, that all his servants would come and bow down before him; and so "Moses, hot with anger, left Pharaoh" (Exodus 11:8). Moses was indignant about Pharaoh's obstinate rebellion against God. He had in front of him a bloody tyrant, armed with all the power of Egypt, threatening him with death if he persisted in the work God had given him. But, far from being terrified, or failing in his duty in any way, he professed his resolve to carry on and called down destruction on the tyrant himself. This is how Moses left Egypt. He did not fear **the king's anger.**

28. By faith he kept the Passover and the sprinkling of blood, so that the destroyer of the firstborn would not touch the firstborn of Israel.

This story is recorded in Exodus 12. There are two things to note in this verse. First, the commendation of Moses' faith, which is seen in the observation of the double divine ordinance of worship. One became of perpetual use in the church, namely, **the Passover**. The other was temporary, suited only to that time, namely, **the sprinkling of blood**; or it may be thought of as a temporary addition to the other. Second, the result of his faith in observing these ordinances, of which they were a sign: **that the destroyer of the firstborn would not touch the firstborn of Israel.**

He kept the Passover. The Passover. The Greeks call it *"pascha,"* which they derive from the word meaning "to suffer," because the lamb suffered when it was slain. But the Greeks are very foolish in this, for the word is a Hebrew one meaning "to pass over." The word was chosen to intimate the manner of the distinction that God made by the destroying angel between the Egyptian houses and the Israelite houses, when he passed over one untouched and entered into another, which might have been next-door, with death.

Moses demonstrated his faith in various ways as he kept or observed the Passover. First, he showed respect to its original institution, which came through divine revelation. God revealed the ordinance to him, with all its rites and ceremonies (Exodus 12:1-4, etc.).

Second, Moses showed respect through faith about its sacramental nature, in which the promise was included. For this is the nature of sacraments, that in and by a visible pledge they contain a promise and show the thing promised to those who believe. This is expressed in Exodus 12:11, where, speaking of the lamb to be killed and eaten, with all its rites and ceremonies, God adds, "it is the LORD's Passover." Here the application of the name of the thing signified for the sacramental sign is consecrated to be used in the church. So it was taken for granted by our Savior in the institution of the sacrament of his Supper, when he says of the bread and wine that they are his holy body and blood, applying the names of the things signified to those that were appointed signs of them by divine institution. This contained the promise of the people's deliverance that was exemplified through their faith in all the rites.

The sprinkling of blood. This temporary ordinance had the same purpose as the first celebration of the Passover. Its institution is recorded in Exodus 12:7. The blood of the lamb after it had been killed was kept in a bowl, into which a bunch of hyssop was dipped, which was then used to strike the sides and tops of the doorframes of their houses. This would be a token so that God would pass over the houses that were so sprinkled and marked with blood, and so none of them would be destroyed (Exodus 12:12-13).

The destroyer. The agent used in this word was **the destroyer.** "Some of them . . . were killed by the destroying angel" (1 Corinthians 10:10).

The destroyer was an angel whom God used to execute his judgments, as he did once later, in the destruction of Sennacherib's army; and as he did once before, in the city of Sodom. There is therefore no reason to think, as some of the Jews do, that it was an evil angel whom they call Ashmodaeus in the Book of Tobit, and by the name of "the angel of death," or, "him that had the power of death, that is, the devil." Psalm 78:49 has a reference to "destroying angels."

29. **By faith the people passed through the Red Sea as on dry land; but when the Egyptians tried to do so, they were drowned.** Having laid the foundation of the deliverance of the church on the exercise of faith through observing the holy institution of divine worship, prescribed to be the signs and token of this, the apostle moves on to give an example of one of the most remarkable moments of divine providence that happened to them during their deliverance. A greater instance about the work of divine providence, of the power of faith on the one hand and of unbelief with obdurate presumption on the other, is not recorded in the whole Book of God.

The Egyptians tried. The Egyptian army of men, horses, and chariots tried to do what they saw the children of Israel do in front of them, namely, pass through the Red Sea while the waters were parted. This was the worst height these obdurate pagans could rise to. They had seen all of God's mighty works that God had performed on behalf of his people among them, and yet, now, as they saw the wonderful work of God in opening the sea, they attempted to follow them.

When the oppressors of the church are closest to their own ruin they often rage most and are most obstinate in their bloody persecutions. It is the same to this day among the anti-Christian enemies of the church. Notwithstanding all their pride and fury, they seem to be entering into the Red Sea.

They were drowned. They were drowned and swallowed up (see Exodus 15). This destruction of the Egyptians, with Israel's deliverance being secured, was a type and pledge of the victory that the church will have over its anti-Christian adversaries (Revelation 15:2-4).

30. **By faith the walls of Jericho fell, after the people had marched around them for seven days.** In this verse the apostle adds another instance of the faith of the whole congregation. For although Joshua's faith is doubtless in mind, yet the faith of the whole people is expressed. The apostle gives a summary of the taking and destruction of Jericho that is recorded in Joshua 6 along along with what is mentioned previously about the spies in Joshua 2.

The walls of Jericho. The city was not a large one, as the whole Israelite army was able to march around it seven times in one day. But most probably it was fortified and had high and strong walls which had terrified the spies Moses had sent (Numbers 13:28). The Israelites showed their faith because they had entered Canaan at God's command and now showed how willingly they were following God's instructions, marching around the town, blowing trumpets, without attempting to capture it. So the apostle rightly commends them for their faith, which they held to despite so many difficulties.

31. By faith the prostitute Rahab, because she welcomed the spies, was not killed with those who were disobedient. Up to now all the examples of faith have been of men, with just one woman mentioned—Sarah—because of her husband. In this verse the apostle gives the example of faith from a woman. The story of Rahab, her faith and deeds, are recorded in Joshua 6.

Rahab. This Rahab was by birth a Gentile, an alien from the stock and covenant of Abraham. So, as her conversion to God was an act of free grace and mercy in a special manner, so it was a type and pledge of calling a church from among the Gentiles. She was not just a Gentile—Rahab was an Amorite, that race that was given over in general to being utterly destroyed. Rahab was, therefore, an example of God's sovereignty in dispensing with his laws as it seems good to him, for out of his own mere pleasure he exempted her from the denounced doom of her race.

The prostitute. Rahab was known as **the prostitute Rahab.** This is a blessed example both of the sovereignty of God's grace and of its power; of its freedom and sovereignty, in the calling and conversion of a person given up through her own choice to the vilest of sins. Nobody, no sin, should lead to despair when the cure of God's sovereign, almighty grace is engaged (1 Corinthians 6:9-11).

She welcomed the spies. Rahab showed her faith by her deeds. **She welcomed the spies.** In these few words the apostle compresses the whole story of her receiving the spies, concealing them, giving them intelligence, and arranging for their safe escape, which is all recorded in Joshua 2. Rahab's work is remembered in James 2:25: "was not even Rahab the prostitute considered righteous for what she did when she gave lodging to the spies and sent them off in a different direction?"

The apostle ends his particular examples of people's faith here and moves on to a more general summary, confirming the truth about the power and efficacy of faith, which he had undertaken to demonstrate.

32. And what more shall I say? I do not have time to tell about Gideon, Barak, Samson, Jephthah, David, Samuel and the prophets. In this verse and up to the end of verse 38, the apostle sums up the remaining testimonies that he might have singled out and used, intimating that there were even more like them that he does not mention. He changes the method he had used up to now. No longer does he single out his witnesses and show how each one is an example of faith. Now he proposes two things to confirm in general: first, faith effects all kinds of things when we are called to them; second, faith can enable us to suffer the most terrible things that we can be exposed to. With examples of the latter the apostle closes his discourse, because they were especially relevant to support his purpose, namely, to encourage the Hebrews in their suffering for the Gospel. The apostle gives them through these examples the assurance that faith would carry them victoriously through them all.

The apostle mentions the people first and then goes on to say what things they did. He does not say what happened to each of them, but leaves that to be read in the sacred story. From verse 35 he moves on to his second topic about the great things that faith will enable believers to undergo and suffer. There he mentions first the things that were suffered but not the people who suffered them. I suppose this is because their names were not recorded in the Scripture, although the things themselves were well known in the church.

We observe two things about his first section (verses 32-34). First, in naming them, Gideon, Barak, Samson, Jephthah, David, and Samuel, he does not do so in the same order in which they lived; for Barak was before Gideon, and Jephthah before Samson, and Samuel before David. Second, the apostle does not mention the things they did in the same order as their list of names. The first thing mentioned does not match up with the first person mentioned.

33. Who through faith conquered kingdoms, administered justice, and gained what was promised; who shut the mouths of lions. After his list of the people who believed, the apostle now states the things they did through faith. The apostle does this to encourage us to make use of the same grace on every occasion. In this verse he mentions four things.

Conquered kingdoms. The first thing some of these people did was to conquer kingdoms. This is generally and rightly assigned to Joshua and David. Joshua subdued all the kingdoms of Canaan; and David all those around it, such as Moab, Ammon, Edom, Syria, and the Philistines.

But it might be asked how this conquering of kingdoms can be thought of as a fruit or effect of faith. Most people who have **conquered kingdoms** have not only been unbelievers, but for the most part wicked and bloody tyrants. People who did this **through faith** were those who did so at God's command.

Administered justice. Literally, "wrought righteousness." To work righteousness in a political sense is to be righteous in rule and government, to administer justice and judgment to everyone under their rule. The particular people mentioned are all rulers or judges and did what is here ascribed to them. David, who is intended here, gives such an account in Psalm 101:1-8. Samuel is also intended here, and his actions of righteousness of this kind are recorded in 1 Samuel 7:15-17: "Samuel continued to judge over Israel all the days of his life. From year to year he went on a circuit from Bethel to Gilgal to Mizpah, judging Israel in all those places. But he always went back to Ramah, where his home was, and there he also judged Israel."

Gained what was promised. The promises intended here, which were obtained by faith, were made in specific ways: to Joshua, that he should conquer Canaan; to Gideon, that he should defeat the Midianites; and to David, that he should be king of all Israel.

Who shut the mouths of lions. This could refer to Samson, who, when a young lion was about to attack him, tore the lion apart with his bare hands (Judges 14:5-6). In a similar way, David shut the mouth of a lion when he killed one (1 Samuel 17:34-35). But if the word is taken in its correct meaning, to put a bridge or stop to the mouth of a lion so that it cannot hurt anyone though it remains alive and free, this can only be applied to Daniel. "My God sent his angel, and he shut the mouths of the lions" (Daniel 6:22). And Daniel did this through faith, for although this was performed through the ministry of angels, it was still done "because he had trusted in God" (Daniel 6:23).

34-35a. Quenched the fury of the flames, and escaped the edge of the sword; whose weakness was turned to strength; and who became powerful in battle and routed foreign armies. Women received back their dead, raised to life again. Six more instances of the power of faith are added.

Quenched the fury of the flames. This describes Daniel's three companions, Shadrach, Meshach, and Abednego, who were thrown "into the blazing furnace" (Daniel 3:23). They so **quenched the fury of the flames** that "the fire had not harmed their bodies, nor was a hair of their heads singed; their robes were not scorched and there was no smell of fire on them" (Daniel 3:27). The faith of these men was considerable in that they were not assured that they would be miraculously delivered, and all they could do was to commit themselves to God's sovereignty (Daniel 3:16-18).

Escaped the edge of the sword. Literally, "mouths," and hence "edges," but note the plural, which refers to the two-edged swords. Their way of escape was to flee from the danger. David often did this when Saul sought him, as did Elijah when Jezebel threatened his life (1 Kings 19:3).

Whose weakness was turned to strength. Weakness here means any kind of moral or bodily infirmity. In each of these senses it is used in the Scripture, to be without or to lack strength of any kind. Frequently it is applied to bodily ailments (Luke 13:11-12; John 5:5; 11:4; Acts 28:9).

Who became powerful in battle. This may be applied to many people, such as Joshua, Barak, Gideon, and Jephthah. David says of himself, "He trains my hands for battle; my arms can bend a bow of bronze. . . . You armed me with strength for battle" (Psalm 18:34, 39).

Routed foreign armies. This signifies Barak, Jonathan against the Philistines, the victories of Asa and Jehoshaphat. In all of these faith was strongly exercised, as is seen from each story.

Women received back their dead, raised to life again. These **women** are the widow of Zarephath, whose son Elijah raised from death (1 Kings 17:22-24), and the Shunammite, whose son was raised by Elisha (2 Kings 4:36). And it is said of them that they received their children from the dead; for in both places the prophets, having raised them from the dead, gave them into their mothers' arms, who received them with joy and thankfulness. Their faith is not expressed, but the faith of the prophets who obtained this miraculous work through faith is. However, at least one of them, namely, the Shunammite, seems to have exercised much faith in the whole matter.

Through these ten examples the apostle demonstrates what great things had been done through faith, to assure the Hebrews, and us with them, that there is nothing too hard or difficult for faith to effect when it is applied according to the mind of God.

35b-37. Others were tortured and refused to be released, so that they might gain a better resurrection. Some faced jeers and flogging, while still others were chained and put in prison. They were stoned; they were sawed in two; they were put to death by the sword. They went about in sheepskins and goatskins, destitute, persecuted, and mistreated. The apostle now gives a different set of examples, which are more readily suited to the condition of the Hebrews. For hearing about the previous ten glorious examples they might think that they had nothing to do with them. For their condition was poor, persecuted, exposed to all evils and to death itself for the profession of the Gospel. They wanted to know: what will faith do when people are exposed to persecution and martyrdom? The apostle now applies himself to this condition. He did not want to hide from these believers what they might have to go through. He also wanted the Hebrews to know that all the evils listed befell people because of their faith.

35b. Others were tortured and refused to be released, so that they might gain a better resurrection. The reason for their steadfastness under torture lay in their hope of gaining **a better resurrection.** One of the brothers in Maccabees 7:9 affirmed specifically that he endured those torments and death itself, since he believed that God would raise him up at the last day.

This the apostle calls the **better resurrection,** not just compared with the deliverance that they refused, a resurrection that was better than that deliverance, but because he intends that better resurrection that leads to eternal life.

36. Some faced jeers and flogging, while still others were chained and

put in prison. In the next example the apostle draws on those who also suffered but were not killed, but were nevertheless greatly tested about their faith. There are four things mentioned here: first, **jeers;** second, **flogging;** third, **chained;** and, fourth, **put in prison.** They contain all the outward ways of the sufferings of the church, when God restrains the rage of the world, so that it does not go so far as killing people.

Jeers. This word was constantly used for the mockings that were thrown onto our Lord Jesus Christ himself (Matthew 20:19; 27:29, 31, 41; Mark 10:34; 15;31; Luke 14:29; 18:32; 22:63; 23:11, 36).

Flogging was a servile punishment used on vagabonds and the vilest of men.

37. They were stoned; they were sawed in two; they were put to death by the sword. They went about in sheepskins and goatskins, destitute, persecuted and mistreated. Two kinds of people and two kinds of persecution are here. First, such as came about as a result of the worst anger of the world, which ended in death. Second, such as escaped death, but were exposed to all sorts of miseries. The same faith works in both examples.

Those of the first sort were killed in three ways. First, **they were stoned.** This happened to Stephen.

Some were **sawed in two,** but their names and other details are not recorded.

They were put to death by the sword. The sword intended is either that of injustice in the form of the law or of violence and mere force. Many have been beheaded for the testimony of Jesus (Revelation 20:4), just as John the Baptist was (Luke 9:9). Countless thousands have been killed both under pagan and anti-Christian tyranny with the sword.

They went about in sheepskins and goatskins. This means that their condition was poor, mean, and contemptible.

Destitute. This means to be poor and in need. I think what is especially meant is to be in need of friends.

Persecuted. Here the word seems to have the special respect to the great pressure that people in the condition are brought into by the great dangers that are continually brought on them.

Mistreated. We translate this word "tormented."

38. The world was not worthy of them. They wandered in deserts and mountains, and in caves and holes in the ground. There are two things in this verse. First, the character of the people who suffered: **the world was not worthy of them.** Second, the rest of their sufferings which he goes on to describe: **they wandered in deserts . . .**

The world was not worthy of them. The world thinks that they are not worthy of it, or to live in it, or to enjoy any name or place among them. Here the testimony is to the contrary: **the world was not worthy of them.**

They **wandered** around with nowhere to go and nowhere to rest. **Deserts and mountains** were uninhabited wastes. **Holes in the ground** may refer to hollow places where wild beasts sheltered.

This was the state of these servants of the living God. They were driven out of all inhabited places. They found no rest in **deserts and mountains,** but **wandered** up and down, taking **caves and holes in the ground** for their shelter.

Verses 39-40

These are all commended for their faith, yet none of them received what had been promised. God had planned something better for us so that only together with us would they be made perfect. As the apostle ends his observations about all these instances of faith of believers under the old testament, he states four things.

1. About whom he is speaking, and that is, "All of these."

2. What he ascribes to them: they were **commended for their faith.**

3. What he still denies them, which is receiving the promise: **none of them received what was promised.**

4. The reason for this, which is God's sovereign disposal of the states, times, and privileges of the church: **God had planned...**

These are all commended. These people are all those who have been cited since the beginning of the world or since the first promise about the Savior and Redeemer of the church.

Commended for their faith. Literally, "having obtained witness through their faith." They were God's martyrs, and he gave witness to their faith.

Yet none of them received what had been promised. This promise refers to Christ's coming in the flesh and his accomplishing his work of our redemption. This promise was made to the elders from the beginning of the world. It was not actually fulfilled until "the fullness of time." This was the state of believers under the old testament. They had the promise of the manifestation of Christ, the Son of God in the flesh, for the redemption of the church. This promise they received, saw afar off as to its actual accomplishment, were convinced about its truth, and embraced it (verse 13). The actual fulfillment of it they desired, longed for, and expected (Luke 10:24), inquiring diligently into the grace of God contained in it (1 Peter 1:10-11). Hereby they enjoyed its benefits, just as we do (Acts

15:11). However, they did not receive its actual accomplishment in the coming of Christ. The reason for this the apostle states in the next verse.

40. God had planned something better for us so that only together with us would they be made perfect. The apostle compares the state of those under the old testament with that of the believers under the Gospel, giving the preeminence to the latter and stating his reason for doing this. He states this in the following ways.

1. The reason for the difference between the two states of the church, and this was God's disposal of things in this order: **God had planned.**

2. The difference itself, namely, **something better** that was provided for us.

3. A declaration of that **better** thing: **that only together with us would they be made perfect.**

Only together with us would they be made perfect. With us amounts to "with the things that are actually exhibited to us, the things provided for us, and our sharing them." All the advantages of grace and mercy that they received and enjoyed, were by virtue of those better things that were actually exhibited to us, applied through faith, and not in virtue of anything committed to them and enjoyed by them. All the outward glorious worship of the old testament had no perfection in it. And so it had no glory when compared with that glory that the Gospel ushered in (2 Corinthians 3:10).

Hebrews
Chapter 12

This chapter contains an application for the Hebrews of the doctrine stated in chapter 11. Teaching and application were the apostle's method, and preachers should follow him in this.

There are three parts to this chapter.

1. A pressing of the exhortation in hand from the testimonies previously insisted on, with new motives, encouragements, and directions (verses 1-11).

2. A direction to carry out special duties, necessary in order to comply with the general exhortation, and subservient to its complete observance (verses 12-17).

3. A new cogent argument for the same purpose, taken from a comparison between the two states of the law and the Gospel, with their origin, nature, and effects (verses 18-29).

There are four things in the first part.

1. The deduction it makes from the previous examples (verse 1).

2. Its confirmation from considering Christ himself and his sufferings (verses 2-3).

3. The same is insisted on from their known duty (verse 4).

4. What they had to go through and persevere in, and the benefits they would derive from this (verses 5-11).

Verses 1-11

1. Therefore, since we are surrounded by such a great cloud of witnesses, let us throw off everything that hinders and the sin that so easily entangles, and let us run with perseverance the race marked out for us. Some things about the kind of speech these words use may be noted. First, it is all fig-

urative, consisting of various metaphors. The main one is the comparison of our patient abiding in the profession of the Gospel with running or competing in a race for a prize. Second, the allusions are plain and familiar. They throw great light on our understanding. Third, this being the case, the exposition of words should not come from taking them precisely but from seeing what is clearly meant by them.

In the words themselves there are four things to note.

1. An inference from what has preceded: **Therefore.** "Seeing it is thus with us in respect to those who went before us, whose faith is recorded for our use and example."

2. An exhortation to patient perseverance in the profession of the Gospel, despite all the difficulties: **let us run with perseverance the race marked out for us.**

3. A motive and encouragement for this, taken from our present state with respect to those who went before us in the profession of the faith and whose example we are obliged to follow: **since we are surrounded by such a great cloud of witnesses.**

4. A declaration of something that must be done to comply with this exhortation: **Let us throw off everything that hinders and the sin that so easily entangles.**

Witnesses. At the contest in public games alluded to here, there were multitudes, clouds of spectators, who looked on to encourage those who competed with applause and to testify to their success. So it is with our patient perseverance. All the old testament saints, as it were, stand looking at us in our striving, encouraging us in our duty, ready to testify to our success with their applause. They are positioned around us for this purpose, and so **we are surrounded** by them.

Let us throw off. The Greek word is used once in the New Testament to refer to natural things: "The witnesses laid their clothes at the feet of a young man named Saul" (Acts 7:58). The people about to stone Stephen laid down, or took off, their clothes, which sheds light on how we are to understand this metaphor. In other places it is used of vicious habits, or causes of them, which we are to part from and cast away, since they hinder us (see Ephesians 4:22, 25; Colossians 3:8; James 1:21; 1 Peter 2:1). The word concerns our duty to all vicious habits, especially those that hinder our Christian life. Unless these things are disposed of, laid aside, thrown off, we cannot run successfully the race we are called to.

2. Let us fix our eyes on Jesus, the author and perfecter of our faith, who for the joy set before him endured the cross, scorning its shame, and sat down at the right hand of the throne of God. The apostle gives the best encouragement possible. Until now he had suggested that they look to people who had professed the Christian faith in the past, but now the focus is on him who is **the author and perfecter of our faith.** Thus the apostle urges them to persevere in the faith and obedience of the Gospel.

Let us fix our eyes on Jesus. Literally, "looking away." We are to look to Jesus in a special way, a way that is different from the way we looked at the cloud of witnesses. The verb is in the present tense, so a continual act is intended. In all that we do, in our profession and obedience, we are constantly to look to Christ.

"Looking," in Scripture, when it refers to God or Christ, denotes an act of faith or trust, with hope and expectation. It is not just an act of understanding or considering what we are looking at; it is an act of the whole soul in faith and trust (see Psalm 34:4-6; Isaiah 45:22). Such is the look of believers on the pierced Christ (Zechariah 12:10). (See Hebrews 9:28; 11:10; also Micah 7:7, "I watch in hope for the LORD, I wait for God my Savior; my God will hear me.")

So the Lord Jesus is not set before us here merely as an example for us but as him in whom we place our faith, trust, and confidence, with all our expectation of success in our Christian course. Without this faith and trust in him, we will derive no benefit from his example.

The author and perfecter of our faith. Our faith from first to last is from Jesus Christ.

Scorning its shame. In his death the Lord Jesus was exposed to ignominy, contempt, shame, and scorn. This he literally "despised"; that is, he did not sink under its weight. He did not faint because of it. He kept his eyes trained on the glorious effect of his sufferings.

3. Consider him who endured such opposition from sinful men, so that you will not grow weary and lose heart.

So that you will not grow weary. Growing weary is "to labor in such a way that you become weary," and "to be sick," which is accompanied with weariness. "Faith will make the sick person well" (James 5:15). "You have persevered and have endured hardships for my name, and have not grown weary" (Revelation 2:3). To abide and persevere in suffering and work for the name of Christ is not to faint or be wearied. So, to **grow weary** in this case is to be so discouraged with the greatness or amount of the difficulties that you draw back and partially or totally withdraw from the profession of the Gospel. The apostle warns against a profession that is lacking in life, vigor, and cheerfulness.

So that you will not . . . lose heart. Literally, "faint." This fainting consists in a remission of the due acting of faith by all graces and in all duties. It is faith that stirs up and engages spiritual courage, resolution, patience, perseverance, prayer, all preserving graces and duties. If it fails here and we are left to fight our difficulties in our own natural strength, we will quickly grow weary. This is where all spiritual decline starts, namely, in not exercising faith in all these graces and duties.

4. In your struggle against sin, you have not yet resisted to the point of shedding your blood. Having set before us the great example of Jesus, the apostle moves on to more general arguments to support his exhortation to persevere. The verse considers their present state and what they may possibly be called to do. The argument compares their present state with what they may yet reasonably expect to have to endure.

You have not yet resisted to the point of shedding your blood. He tells them what they might expect, and that is **blood.** All kinds of violent deaths, by the sword, by tortures, by fire, are included here.

In your struggle against sin. Here is the cause of their suffering, or rather, the party they are struggling against as they suffer. It was **sin.** The apostle is using his illustration about the contest for victory in the public games. There, everyone had an opponent against whom he had to fight. So believers, as they run, have an opponent, **sin.** It was not their persecutors directly, but sin in them that they had to battle against. Sin, against which we fight, is either in others or in ourselves. These others are either devils or people. We have a contest with sin in devils, "Our struggle is not against flesh and blood, but against the rulers, against the authorities, against the powers of this dark world and against the spiritual forces of evil in the heavenly realms" (Ephesians 6:12). Such people, wicked angels, continually sin as they attempt to destroy the church. They especially stir up persecution against the church. "The devil will put some of you in prison" (Revelation 2:10). Against sin in them we are to contend. It is the same with people who persecute the church. They give many reasons for their actions, but it is sin acting in malice, hating truth, blind zeal, envy, and bloody cruelty that governs what they do. Against all the effects and fruits of sin in them believers also contend.

They also have a battle against sin in themselves. "Abstain from sinful desires, which war against your soul" (1 Peter 2:11). These "sinful desires" try to overthrow our faith and obedience.

5. And you have forgotten that word of encouragement that addresses you as sons: "My son, do not make light of the Lord's discipline, and do not lose heart when he rebukes you." The apostle starts a new argument here to press home his exhortation to persevere under suffering. This line of argument is taken from the nature and purpose, on God's part, for all the sufferings that he sends or calls us to endure. He carries on this theme until verse 13.

"Do not make light of the Lord's discipline." We tend to fall into one of two extremes about suffering: either we despise it, or, we faint under it. **Do not make light of** is only used here in the Scripture. It means, "to set lightly by, to have little esteem of, not to value anything according to its worth and use." The evil warned against is lack of due regard for divine admonitions and instructions in all our troubles and afflictions. All divine reproofs, in which God shows that we are his adopted children, are intended for our benefit and as an effective way to preserve us in our trials.

6. "Because the Lord disciplines those he loves, and he punishes everyone he accepts as a son." This verse tells us why we should not faint under divine chastisements. It is a general rule that all these things are to be referred to the sovereignty, wisdom, and goodness of God. "This," says the apostle, "is God's way; thus it seems good to him to deal with his children; thus he may do because of his sovereign dominion over everything. May he not do what he will with his own? He does this in infinite wisdom, for their good, and to show his love and care for them."

"The Lord disciplines those he loves." Love precedes discipline. It is like this with any father. He has the love of a father first of all, before he disciplines his son. The love meant here is the love of adoption; that is, the love of benevolence, by which God makes people his children.

Everyone. This is not to be taken universally, as everyone is not disciplined; but it is restricted to the people God accepts.

7. Endure hardship as discipline; God is treating you as sons. For what son is not disciplined by his father? This is no new argument in this verse but an inference and special application from verse 6 and an exhortation. This patient endurance of chastisements is of great value in God's sight, as well as being of special value to the souls of those who believe.

For what son is not disciplined by his father? This presumes two things: first, that every son will more or less stand in need of discipline; second, that every wise and tender father will in such cases discipline his son. So the argument is taken from the illustration of the duty that inseparably belongs to the relationship between a father and a son. From this it is clear that God's discipline of believers is his dealing with them as his sons.

8. If you are not disciplined (and everyone undergoes discipline), then you are illegitimate children and not true sons. The principle that the apostle lays down about discipline is so clear, in nature and in grace, that to the inference he made about the evidence of sonship from it, he adds here another, which also serves his purpose: namely, that those who have no discipline are not sons, are not God's children.

Illegitimate children and not true sons. Their state is expressed both positively and negatively to emphasize the assertion. Besides, if he had only said, you are **illegitimate children,** it would not have been so clear that they were not sons, for **illegitimate children** are also sons. But they are not such sons as have any right to the paternal inheritance. They may have gifts and riches bestowed on them by their fathers, but they do not have any right of inheritance by virtue of their sonship. Such people, says the apostle here, are those who are not disciplined.

9-10. Moreover, we have all had human fathers who disciplined us and we respected them for it. How much more should we submit to the

Father of our spirits and live! Our fathers disciplined us for a little while as they thought best; but God disciplines us for our good, that we may share in his holiness. These verses further emphasize the rightness of the exhortation to endure divine discipline patiently. This is a new argument and not just an application of the previous one. The argument is taken from a mixture of principles and experience. It is based on two principles: first, from the light of nature, namely, that children should obey their parents and submit to them in everything. The second is from the light of grace, namely, that there is the same real relationship between God and believers as there is between natural parents and children, though of a different nature. His whole argument is based on these undoubted principles.

The Father of our spirits. The person who disciplines us is the Father of our spirits. He is a father, but of a different nature from them. There is a contrast between human fathers, mentioned earlier in the verse, and the Father of our spirits. While the apostle divides our nature into flesh and spirit, it is clear that "spirit" refers to the rational soul. For although the flesh is also created by God, yet natural generation is used to produce it. But the soul is directly created and infused, as it has no other father than God himself (see Numbers 14:22; Jeremiah 38:16; Zechariah 12:1). This is the basic reason for our patient submission to God in our afflictions, namely, that our very souls are his, the immediate produce of his divine power and under his rule alone. May he not do what he will with his own? Will the broken piece of pottery contend with its maker?

That we may share in his holiness. God's special purpose in divine discipline is that we may share in his holiness. God's holiness is either that which he has in himself or that which he approves of and requires in us. The first is the infinite purity of his divine nature, which can never be communicated to us. However, we may take part in it in a special way, through our interest in God as our God as well as by the effects it produces in us. These are his image and likeness; "put on the new self, created to be like God in true righteousness and holiness" (Ephesians 4:24). We are said to "participate in the divine nature" (2 Peter 1:4).

Submit. As children, we should submit, literally "be subject," to the Father of our spirits. This can be compared with our earthly parents who disciplined us, and whom we respected. This is what Peter refers to in the following way: "Humble yourselves, therefore, under God's almighty hand, that he may lift you up in due time" (1 Peter 5:6).

11. No discipline seems pleasant at the time but painful. Later on, however, it produces a harvest of righteousness and peace for those who have been trained by it.

This verse ends the apostle's argument about sufferings and afflictions and how they should be borne. He states that the good derived from them is overwhelmingly better than their evil. He uses the same argument in 2 Corinthians 4:17, "For our light and momentary troubles are achieving for us an eternal glory that far outweighs them all."

It produces a harvest of righteousness. Not "it will do so," as the Vulgate reads; but "it does so"; namely, in the planned season. It is not a dead, useless thing. God prunes his vine so that it may bear fruit (John 15:2). All of God's dealings here are likened to a farmer with his corn (Isaiah 28:23-29). This harvest produces two kinds of fruit. First, the removal of sin, by putting it to death: "By this, then, will Jacob's guilt be atoned for, and this will be the full fruitage of the removal of his sin" (Isaiah 27:9). The second part of the harvest is increased righteousness and holiness.

Righteousness. The harvest produced is the **fruit of righteousness,** not righteousness itself. Neither our actions nor our suffering is the reason for our righteousness, but they promote it in us and increase its fruit. So the apostle prays for the Corinthians, that God would "increase" in them "the harvest" of "righteousness" (2 Corinthians 9:10). For the Philippians he prays that they may be "filled with the fruit of righteousness that comes through Jesus Christ—to the glory and praise of God" (Philippians 1:11). So **righteousness** here means our sanctification, or the inner principle of holiness and obedience. And the **harvest** of this is to increase in all graces.

And peace. This **harvest of righteousness,** which discipline brings, is "peaceable." "The fruit of righteousness will bring peace" (Isaiah 32:17). "Peacemakers who sow in peace raise a harvest of righteousness" (James 3:18).

Verses 12-17

12-13. Therefore, strengthen your feeble arms and weak knees! "Make level paths for your feet," so that the lame may not be disabled, but rather healed. These verses start the second part of this chapter, which applies the teaching about sufferings and discipline previously insisted on.

Therefore shows that the following exhortation comes from the previous discourse. "Seeing things in this case are as we have declared, this is your duty from now on." Writing in the New Testament follows this pattern as much as this letter does. It states doctrinal truths, backs them up with divine testimonies and reasons, and then applies them.

Strengthen your feeble arms and weak knees! Part of this exhortation is taken from Isaiah 35:3, "Strengthen the feeble hands, steady the knees that give way." The exhortation is directed toward parts of the body that are involved in gymnastics, namely, the hands, the knees, and the feet, through which the body exerts all its strength to win the prize. We must observe, first, the defect they possess; second, the remedy for this defect; and, third, what both of them mean spiritually.

Feeble hands. The defect is in the hands. They are **feeble,** literally "hands that have been wearied." They are so weak that they hang down. Such people become tired of what they are doing and give up.

Weak knees! This is a picture of fear and despondency. "Hearts melt, knees give way" (Nahum 2:10). The knees are weak "my knees give way from fasting" (Psalm 109:24). Both the descriptions of the hands and the knees depict a heartless, slothful person, or one who is so faint in running the race that he is ready to abandon all hope of success and give up.

Strengthen. The same ailment is afflicting different parts of the body, so the apostle prescribes the same remedy for them both. "Raise them to the correct posture; set them right again; apply them to their duty." So it was with the woman "who could not straighten up at all," as she was bowed down, whom Jesus cured, and "she straightened up" (Luke 13:11, 13). In the only place that this word is used in the New Testament, Acts 15:16, it says "I will rebuild," or "set up," David's fallen tent. A restoration to their former state is signified in this word. In our Christian race we must use all our spiritual strength.

13. "Make level paths for your feet." Literally "make straight tracks for the feet." This is a path that leaves a track that may be followed. Obeying God is called "walking before him," and these paths are the "paths of the righteous."

Lame. The apostle continues with his metaphor about running. Those who obey **make level paths** for their feet, but those who are defective here are called **lame.** A **lame** person makes only slow progress and is ready to stop altogether. So, lameness is an ailment different from external hindrances and is not just fainting and weariness, about which the apostle had previously spoken, and which happens to those who are not lame. Lameness points to an inner sickness that needs to be **healed.** We note that many diseases, weaknesses, and disabilities occur among God's flock. God promised that he himself would tend such people with care: "For this is what the Sovereign Lord says: I myself will search for my sheep and look after them. As a shepherd looks after his scattered flock when he is with them, I will look after my sheep" (Ezekiel 34:11-12).

In view of the state of the Hebrews at this time who had received the teaching of the Gospel, which is seen both in this letter and in the Acts of the Apostles, I think that **the lame** were those who retained the Jewish ceremonies and worship alongside the teaching of the Gospel. This is what made them weak and hindered their spiritual progress.

14. Make every effort to live in peace with all men and to be holy; without holiness no one will see the Lord. After his exhortation to the

Hebrews to persevere patiently in their sufferings, the apostle moves on to set out some practical duties. They are necessary at all times, but were particularly relevant for all who wished to remain constant in their profession of the Gospel. For no light, no knowledge of the truth, no courage, will preserve anyone in his profession, especially in times of trial, unless he pays particular attention to holiness and obedience. The apostle starts with a precept that embraces all the other precepts.

The instruction here has two parts: first, our duty toward other people; second, our duty toward God, which guides us in our duty toward other people.

Peace. The essence of our duty toward all other people, in all circumstances and relationships, is to seek peace with them. However, the apostle does place a limit on this when he writes, "If it is possible, as far as it depends on you, live at peace with everyone" (Romans 12:18). Peace with other people is not to be carried out at any price.

Holiness. This **holiness** should not be restricted to chastity but is universal holiness.

15. See to it that no one misses the grace of God and that no bitter root grows up to cause trouble and defile many. From saying what duties they must carry out, the apostle warns against various evils that would ruin their faith if they were overcome by them. His warnings are not directed to particular individuals but to the whole church.

The grace of God. By **the grace of God,** God's gracious favor and acceptance in Christ, as it is proposed by the Gospel, is meant. This consists of all spiritual mercies and privileges in adoption, justification, sanctification, and consolation. These things flow from the love, grace, and goodness of God in Christ, and so are called **the grace of God.**

No bitter root. The apostle has words of Moses in mind: "make sure there is no root among you that produces such bitter poison" (Deuteronomy 29:18). Poisonous sins are mentioned in Amos: "you have turned justice into poison and the fruit of righteousness into bitterness" (Amos 6:12). It is clear from Moses that this "root" is a person who is inclined toward apostasy and departing from God: "make sure there is no man or woman, clan or tribe among you today whose heart turns away from the LORD our God to go and worship the gods of those nations" (Deuteronomy 28:17). This **bitter root** refers to people in the church whose hearts are turning away from the Gospel as they turn either to Judaism or to a sensual life.

And defile many. This is the effect of the **bitter root** growing up. So people who have been made clean by baptism and the profession of the truth can be contaminated again with abominable errors or filthy lusts (see 2 Peter 2:18-22).

16-17. See that no one is sexually immoral, or is godless like Esau, who

for a single meal sold his inheritance rights as the oldest son. Afterwards, as you know, when he wanted to inherit this blessing, he was rejected. He could bring about no change of mind, though he sought the blessing with tears. The apostle specifies evils that corrupt Christian societies and may lead to total apostasy. He brings together sexual immorality and godlessness for three reasons. First, because they are, as it were, the heads of two sorts of sins that men may be guilty of, namely, sins of the flesh and sins of the mind (Ephesians 2:3). Second, they usually go together. Those who are habitually sexually immoral always grow profane; and profane people, of all others, are likely to take sexual immorality lightly. Third, they are the special sins that are rarely sincerely repented of and forsaken.

See that no one is sexually immoral. The first evil mentioned is sexual immorality. The warning is given to the church.

Although sexual immorality is here and elsewhere denounced, here the apostle does not mean every person who may through temptation be overtaken by this sin, but those who live in this sin and make a habit of being sexually immoral. Such are placed at the head of those who will never inherit the kingdom of God (1 Corinthians 6:9). Such are to be excluded from the church as a token of their exclusion from heaven. It is therefore no wonder that the apostle says that it is most difficult for them to recover from such a state.

Godless like Esau. The second evil is godlessness. There are very few people in Scripture about whom more evidence is given of being a reprobate. This should warn everyone not to trust in the outward privileges of the church. Esau was Isaac's eldest son; he was circumcised according to the law and took part in all the worship of God in that holy family. Yet he became an outcast from the covenant of grace.

He could bring about no change of mind. That is, despite Esau's tears, Isaac did not and could not change his mind in conferring the blessing on Jacob. This sad event was brought about by Esau's godlessness. No one knows where deliberate sin may lead. Esau gave little thought that when he sold his inheritance he had completely forfeited God's eternal blessing.

Verses 18-29

18-19. You have not come to a mountain that can be touched and that is burning with fire; to darkness, gloom and storm; to a trumpet blast or to such a voice speaking words that those who heard it begged that no further word be spoken to them. The whole purpose of the apostle's letter is to persuade the Hebrews to persevere in the profession of the Gospel. For at this time they appear to be greatly shaken. So the apostle warns them against apostasy in four ways. First, he warns against an evil heart of unbelief, or the sin "that so easily entangles" (verse 1). Second, he warns against the necessity of Mosaic worship and the old church-state. Third, he warns that persecutions will come for those who follow the Gospel. Fourth, he warns against prevalent lusts and sins, such as godlessness and sexual immorality.

The main argument that he insists on in general is the superiority of the Gospel-state over the old covenant. This he demonstrates in the person and office of its Author. It must be noted that the great honor and privilege of the Jewish church-state was their coming to Mount Sinai, when the law was given. They were to be taken into God's covenant, to be his special people above all the world. There they were formed into a national church and had all the privileges of divine worship committed to them (see Romans 9:4). This is the glory which they still rely on to this day, as they reject the Gospel in their unbelief.

The apostle observes that there was no evidence, in all that was done, of God being reconciled to them; there was no pardon in case they sinned; there was no promise of grace to help them carry out what they were ordered to do; this was the "ministry that brought death" (2 Corinthians 3:7). God was here seen in all the outward demonstrations of infinite holiness, justice, severity, and terrible majesty on the one hand, and on the other, men in their lowest condition of sin, misery, guilt, and death. If there was nothing to come between God and men, all this glorious preparation was nothing but a spectacle, set up for the pronouncing of judgment and the sentence of eternal condemnation against sinners. On this depends the force of the apostle's argument in verses 18-21.

The Israelites at Mount Sinai were sinners under the sentence of the law. Many individuals may have been justified through faith in the promise, but as they stood and heard and received the law, they represented sinners under sentence who had not yet received the Gospel. This is what the apostle intends to show.

One thing must be said about the Gospel-state that follows. All spiritual things of grace and glory, in heaven and earth, are summed up in Christ, as Ephesians 1:10 declares. Our coming to him by faith gives us an interest in them all, so that it may be said that we come to them all. It is not necessary to exercise faith in every one of them, as through our coming to Christ we come to them all, as if every one of them had been the special object of our faith in our initiation into the Gospel.

The apostle records that the people came to seven things. First, to a **mountain that can be touched;** second, to a **fire** that burned; third, to **darkness;** fourth, to **gloom;** fifth, to a **storm;** sixth, to a **trumpet blast;** seventh, a terrible **voice.** They asked that **no further word be spoken to them.**

You have not come to a mountain that can be touched. This was

Mount Sinai, in the wilderness of Horeb, which was in the deserts of Arabia (see Galatians 4:25). The apostle mentions this at the beginning because on the mountain all the laws and directions of the people's approach to God were given (Exodus 19).

Begged that no further word be spoken to them. They were terrified, so they said, "we will die if we hear the voice of the LORD our God any longer" (Deuteronomy 5:25). This voice, the word, this speech, coming straight from God, out of the **fire** and **darkness,** was what heightened their fear. The giving of the law was so full of terror that the people could not bear it but realized that they would die if God carried on speaking to them. The sinner is overwhelmed when he has a sense of the voice of God himself in the law. When he finds God himself speaking in and to his conscience, he can no longer bear it.

20-21. Because they could not bear what was commanded: "If even an animal touches the mountain, it must be stoned." The sight was so terrifying that Moses said, "I am trembling with fear." The command about the animal is not specific, as stated here, but was part of the general prohibition, "whoever touches the mountain shall surely be put to death" (Exodus 19:12). This refers only to people, but in the statement about the kind of death to be inflicted it is added, "He shall surely be stoned or shot with arrows; not a hand is to be laid on him. Whether man or animal, he shall not be permitted to live" (Exodus 19:13). No living creature was allowed to come to the mount. I think this excludes wild animals and reptiles and only includes the cattle that were under the control of men.

The consternation that fell on Moses is expressed in these words, **"I am trembling with fear."** Moses said this. We are told this by the Holy Spirit. But the words themselves are not recorded in the story. They were doubtless spoken then and there, where, upon this dreadful representation of God, it is said that he spoke, but not one word of what he said is recorded. "The sound of the trumpet grew louder and louder. Then Moses spoke and the voice of God answered him" (Exodus 19:19). Yet nothing is added about what Moses said or what God replied. Doubtless he spoke these words, **"I am trembling with fear."** Everyone was at an utter loss and in distress as the law was given again. No relief was derived from this. But "Christ is the end of the law so that there may be righteousness for everyone who believes" (Romans 10:4).

22-24. But you have come to Mount Zion, to the heavenly Jerusalem, the city of the living God. You have come to thousands upon thousands of angels in joyful assembly, to the church of the firstborn, whose names are written in heaven. You have come to God, the judge of all men, to the spirits of righteous men made perfect, to Jesus the mediator of a new covenant, and to the sprinkled blood that speaks a better word than the blood of Abel. This is the second part of the comparison that completes the basis of the apostle's exhortation. In the first part the apostle outlined the state of the people and the church under the law, from its giving and the nature of its commands. In his second part, he declared the state they were called to through the Gospel, to show its incomparable superiority to the old covenant, and how much more beneficial the new covenant was to them.

We have here a blessed, glorious description of the catholic (universal) church and its nature as revealed under the Gospel. We have here the substance of all the privileges that we receive through the Gospel. It is the access ascribed to believers here, and that alone, which will secure their eternal salvation.

Whereas the catholic church is divided into two parts, namely the church militant and the church triumphant, they are both included in this description. For **Mount Zion, to the heavenly Jerusalem, the city of the living God,** refers principally to the church militant, while the rest of the description refers to the church triumphant.

The Roman Catholics have another part of the church, neither on the earth nor in heaven, but under the earth, as they say—in purgatory. But those who come to Christ through the Gospel have nothing to do with this.

The foundation of this universal communion, or communion of the universal church, comprising all that is holy and dedicated to God in heaven and earth, is summed up in and through Jesus Christ: "to bring all things in heaven and on earth together under one head, even Christ" (Ephesians 1:10). This is the only basis for their mutual communion among themselves. Whereas, therefore, we have here an association in the communion of men and angels and the souls of those who have departed, in a middle state between them both, we ought to consider always their recapitulation in Christ as the reason for this. All things were gathered into one by him. "For God was pleased . . . through him to reconcile to himself all things, whether things on earth or things in heaven" (Colossians 1:19-20). God himself is here seen as the supreme sovereign head of this universal church, all of which he reconciles to himself.

But you have come to Mount Zion. Zion was a mount in Jerusalem that had two peaks. The temple was built on the first, Mount Moriah, and so became the center of all the solemn worship of God. On the other mount, the palace and homes of the kings of the house of David were built. Both of these mounts typified Christ; one of his priestly office, the other of his kingly office.

The apostle is not thinking about the physical nature of **Mount Zion** here, but only how it compares with Mount Sinai, where the law was given. "Now Hagar stands for Mount Sinai in Arabia and corresponds to the present city of Jerusalem, because she is in slavery with her children. But the Jerusalem that is above is free, and she is our mother" (Galatians 4:25-26). **Mount Zion** and "the Jerusalem that is above" are the same church.

You have come to thousands upon thousands of angels in joyful assembly. That is, an innumerable company of angels. Having said that they have come to **the city of the living God,** he now shows them who is living there besides themselves. So, through Jesus Christ, we have a blessed access to these angels. Because of our fall from God and the entry of sin into the world, these angels had nothing to do with us except to carry out God's judgment on us. God made use of these angels in the giving of the law, to fill people with dread. But now they are, in Christ, one mystical body with the church, and we serve God together.

To the church of the firstborn. This is another example of the glory of this state that believers have come to. Literally, "an assembly and a church of firstborn ones." Unlike the assemblies that governed cities like Athens, this assembly did not deal with state business but with all the spiritual needs of the society.

Firstborn. There is a double allusion in this word. First, there is reference to the rights of the firstborn in general. Here the apostle seems to refer to Esau, who, being ungodly, sold his birthright. Those who are genuinely interested in the Gospel-church have a right to the whole inheritance. By their adoption they are entitled to all that God has provided, that Christ has purchased, including his whole inheritance of grace and glory. Second, there is a reference here to the firstborn being counted in the wilderness (Numbers 3:40-42). "Your names are written in heaven" (Luke 10:20); "in the book of life" (Philippians 4:3; Revelation 3:5; 17:8); "the Lamb's book of life" (Revelation 21:27). This book of life is the roll of God's elect in the eternal, immutable designation of those who are called.

This, therefore, is **the church of the firstborn, whose names are written in heaven,** namely, God's elect, called, and through gratuitous adoption interested in all the privileges of the firstborn; that is, made fellow-heirs with Christ and heirs of God, or of the whole heavenly inheritance.

You have come to God, the judge of all men. This access to God through Jesus Christ is often mentioned in the Scripture as a great privilege. They have access to God as **the judge of all men.** This may not seem to be a privilege, for everyone has to appear before God's judgment seat. But it is one thing to be brought before a judge to be tried and sentenced as a criminal, and another thing to have a favorable access to him whenever you wish. This is the access that is intended here.

To the spirits of righteous men made perfect. This shows that there are **spirits of ... men** in a separate state and condition, capable of communion with God and the church. These **spirits** are the souls of people who have departed. **Spirits** are that essential part of our nature that subsists in a separate state from the body.

Made perfect. Everyone who leaves this world is just or unjust, justified or not justified. But the spirits of all those who here are just, or justified, and who have left this world, are **made perfect.** They are all **made perfect,** according to the apostle, and so are not in need of our prayers to make them perfect. Being **made perfect** means that they have finished their race, are totally delivered from all sin, and enjoy the reward of God's presence.

To the sprinkled blood that speaks a better word than the blood of Abel. There is no comparison between Christ's sacrifice and the sacrifices before the law. The blood of Abel's sacrifice spoke about the same things that Christ's blood speaks about, though in a dark, obscure way. It did not have the same power as Christ's blood, but it spoke about the same thing.

25-27. See to it that you do not refuse him who speaks. If they did not escape when they refused him who warned them on earth, how much less will we, if we turn away from him who warns us from heaven? At that time his voice shook the earth, but now he has promised, "Once more I will shake not only the earth but also the heavens." The words "once more" indicate the removing of what can be shaken—that is, created things—so that what cannot be shaken may remain.

See to it that you do not refuse him who speaks. The is a command to believe and obey God. Anything less than this is refusing him who speaks. It is not enough to give him a hearing, as we say, unless we also obey him. Hence the word is preached to many, but it does not benefit them, because it is not combined with faith.

If they did not escape when they refused him who warned them on earth, how much less will we, if we turn away from him who warns us from heaven? This is clearly taught by Jesus himself: "I have spoken to you of earthly things and you do not believe; how then will you believe if I speak of heavenly things? No one has ever gone into heaven except the one who came from heaven—the Son of Man" (John 3:12-13). Jesus further added, "The one who comes from above is above all; the one who is from the earth belongs to the earth, and speaks as one from the earth. The one who comes from heaven is above all" (John 3:31). These verses have the same theme as the verses in Hebrews 12:25, namely, the revelation of heavenly things or the mysteries of the will of God through Jesus Christ.

If they did not escape. The apostle infers that their sin was judged, so they would not have been able to escape.

"Once more I will shake not only the earth but also the heavens." When the prophet Haggai wrote, "This is what the LORD Almighty says: 'In a little while I will once more shake the heavens and the earth, the sea and the dry land'" (Haggai 2:6), he goes on to explains these words by saying, "I will shake all nations" (Haggai 2:7). The prophet Haggai and the apostle are referring to spiritual things. In the kingdom that remains after the shaking, the believers receive spiritual things.

28-29. Therefore, since we are receiving a kingdom that cannot be shaken, let us be thankful, and so worship God acceptably with reverence and awe, for our God is a consuming fire.

The apostle here sums up both the doctrinal and the hortatory parts of the letter. For what through all his arguments he had shown concerning the preference and superiority of the Gospel of the church over the law, he gives as the reason why they should obey God and persevere in their Christian faith.

Kingdom. The apostle is referring to a **kingdom,** a heavenly, spiritual state, under the rule of Jesus Christ, whom God has anointed and set up as his king on his holy hill of Zion (see Psalm 2:6-7). The Gospel and Christ's rule were represented from the beginning by the name and idea of a kingdom, and rightly so (see Isaiah 9:7).

Since we are receiving a kingdom. Believers receive this **kingdom.** Their interest in this kingdom is spoken of as **receiving** it, because they possess it through a gift, grant, or donation from God their Father. "Do not be afraid, little flock, for your Father has been pleased to give you the kingdom" (Luke 12:32).

So worship God acceptably. That is, so that we may be accepted or find acceptance with him. As it relates to worshiping God, this is sometimes applied to the people who lead the worship and sometimes to the worship itself. With both, it signifies what is well pleasing to God, what he accepts (Romans 12:1-2; 2 Corinthians 5:9; Ephesians 5:10; Philippians 4:18; Colossians 3:20; Hebrews 11:5-6).

With reverence and fear. Directions about how this duty should be carried are now given. It is to be done **with reverence and fear.** These are not used together or apart with respect to the service of God anywhere else in the New Testament. The meaning of the words here is best seen in what they are opposed to—the contrast with a lack of a due sense of the majesty and glory of God, and a lack of a due sense of our own vileness.

29. For our God is a consuming fire. This is the reason that makes the previous duty necessary. "Therefore we should serve God with reverence and fear, because he is a consuming fire." The words are taken from Deuteronomy 4:24, where they are used by Moses to deter the people from worshiping idols or graven images. This is a sin God will not put up with. In this metaphor God is called a **consuming fire,** because fire burns every combustible thing it comes into contact with. In the same way God will consume and destroy sinners who are guilty of the sin that is here forbidden. Such sinners, namely, hypocrites and false-worshipers, realize that God is like this when they are convicted (Isaiah 33:14).

Hebrews
Chapter 13

Verses 1-8

1. Keep on loving each other as brothers. The duty commanded is **loving . . . as brothers,** and the way to do this is to **keep on** doing it. Love is the fountain and foundation of all mutual duties, moral and ecclesiastical. **Loving . . . as brothers** is the basis of the love that is commanded here. "Everyone who loves the father loves his child as well" (1 John 5:1). It is by adoption that we are all taken into and made brothers in the same family: "you have one Father, and he is in heaven" (Matthew 23:8-9). This loving as brothers is a special grace of the Spirit. "The fruit of the Spirit is love" (Galatians 5:22), and is most often linked with faith in Christ Jesus (Philemon 5; 1 John 3:23). Nobody has this gift in himself, as it a gift that comes from above. Brotherly love was commanded by Christ himself. He calls it his commandment in a special way (John 15:12), and thus it is "a new commandment" (John 13:34; 1 John 2:7-8; 2 John 5). Christ's purpose in this is that it should bring special glory to God and be a witness to the world that we are his disciples: "By this all men will know that you are my disciples, if you love one another" (John 13:35).

2. Do not forget to entertain strangers, for by so doing some people have entertained angels without knowing it.

Strangers, even among pagans, were thought of as people who were almost sacred, under God's special protection. So says Emmaus to Ulysses: "O stranger! It is not lawful for me, though one should come more miserable than you are, to dishonor or disregard a stranger; for strangers and poor belong to the care of God" (Homer, *Odyssey* 14:56). The Scripture frequently commands and encourages this duty (see Deuteronomy 10:19; Isaiah 58:7; Matthew 25:35; Luke 14:13; Romans 12:13; James 1:27; 1 Peter 4:9).

3. Remember those in prison as if you were their fellow prisoners, and those who are mistreated as if you yourselves were suffering. This is the second way to show brotherly love. The first concerned strangers; this concerns sufferers. People who are **in prison** must be remembered. It seems that those who are free are apt to forget Christ's prisoners, so it is necessary to remind them to **remember those in prison.** This involves caring for prisoners (Philippians 4:10); it involves being compassionate toward prisoners, **as if you were their fellow prisoners** (10:34). This also involves visiting prisoners (Matthew 25:36, 43).

4. Marriage should be honored by all, and the marriage bed kept pure, for God will judge the adulterer and all the sexually immoral.

And the marriage bed kept pure. Literally, "undefiled." This is in contrast to adulterers who defile the honorable state of marriage. The apostle gives instructions about keeping marriage within proper bounds (1 Corinthians 7:2-5; 1 Thessalonians 4:3-7).

5-6. Keep your lives free from the love of money and be content with what you have, because God has said, "Never will I leave you; never will I forsake you." So we say with confidence, "The Lord is my helper; I will not be afraid. What can man do to me?"

Free from the love of money. How we live is of great importance in our Christian lives. A guideline the apostle gives here is to **keep your lives free from the love of money,** literally, "without love of money," or, without covetousness (see Luke 16:14; 1 Timothy 3:3; 2 Timothy 3:2). Covetousness is an inordinate desire to enjoy more money than we have, or than God is pleased to give us: "People who want to get rich fall into temptation and a trap and into many foolish and harmful desires that plunge men into destruction. For the love of money is a root of all kinds of evil. Some people, eager for money, have wandered from the faith and pierced themselves with many griefs" (1 Timothy 6:9-10).

"Never will I leave you; never will I forsake you." Literally, "by no means . . . nor . . . by no means." The force of the negative here is emphasized by three negative particles. The aim is to remove all objections that fear and unbelief give rise to. "Let people do what they will, let any circumstances arise, I will not at any time, on any occasion, for any reason, leave you, nor forsake you." Positive blessings are contained in these negative expressions. **Never will I leave you** assures us of God's presence: "whatever your state or condition I will never withdraw my presence from you"; **never will I forsake you** assures us of God's help, as the apostle emphasizes in the next verse: "I will never allow you to be helpless in any trouble; my help will continue with you."

6. So we say with confidence, "The Lord is my helper; I will not be afraid. What can man do to me?" Each of us may say as David did in a similar situation, "The Lord is with me; I will not be afraid. What can man do to me?" (Psalm 118:6). In the same way the psalmist says, "When I am afraid, I will trust in you. In God, whose word I praise, in God I trust; I will not be afraid. What can mortal man do to me? . . . In God I trust; I will not be afraid. What can man do to me?" (Psalm 56:3-4; 11).

"What can man do to me?" There is a double contrast here. First, a contrast between God and man: "The Lord is on my side; I will not fear what man can do." Second, there is a contrast between what God will do—"he will help"—and what men can do—"What can men to do me?"

7. Remember your leaders, who spoke the word of God to you. Consider the outcome of their way of life and imitate their faith.

Remember your leaders. The apostle means all who had spoken or preached the Word of God to them, whether apostles, evangelists, or pastors.

Imitate their faith. "Think of their work in preaching the Word of God, and follow or imitate them in their faith." To **imitate** is to follow someone else's example. The word is often translated as "follow" by the apostle. "For you yourselves know how you ought to follow our example. . . . We did this, not because we do not have the right to such help, but in order to make ourselves a model for you to follow" (2 Thessalonians 3:7, 9; see also 1 Corinthians 11:1; Ephesians 5:1; 1 Thessalonians 2:14; Hebrews 4:12). We are to **imitate their faith.** We are not to follow mere men, not even the best of men, as our model and example in all things is Christ alone. But we can learn to emulate Christian graces where we see them displayed in Christian leaders. So the apostle says that he himself is an example to believers (1 Corinthians 4:16; Philippians 3:16; 1 Thessalonians 1:6), but adds a limiting factor, that they should only follow him in as much as he followed Christ: "Follow my example, as I follow the example of Christ" (1 Corinthians 11:1).

8. Jesus Christ is the same yesterday and today and forever.

The same. Christ does not change. In his work he is the same from first to last. While various changes were made in the institutions of divine worship, and there were many parts of divine revelation, yet in and through them all Jesus Christ was still the same. So we do not need to fix a specific moment to **yesterday,** or to **today,** or to **forever.** Through this proverbial speech the apostle is talking about all seasons, to denote the eternity and immutability of Christ in them all. The same purpose is behind the words, "grace and peace to you from him who is, and who was, and who is to come" (Revelation 1:4).

The correct consideration of Jesus Christ, especially in his eternity, immutability, and complete power, as he is always the same, is the great encouragement of believers in their whole profession of the faith and in all the difficulties they may meet on account of this. A constant clinging to the truth about the person and work of Christ will stop us from listening to various strange teachings that damage our souls.

Verses 9-14

These verses seem abstruse, and the apostle's thinking is not easy to follow. But expositors usually overlook this general thinking and only concentrate on the exposition of individual verses. To find out the mind of the Holy Spirit as a whole in these verses, we must consider the purpose of the apostle here and how he deduces one thing from another. Once this is done we can turn to expounding each verse.

1. There was at this time not only an obstinate adherence to Mosaic ceremonies among many of the Jews who professed the Gospel, but also an endeavor to reinforce their necessity and to impose their observation on others. The apostle is against these things throughout his letter. When he mentions Christ and his unchanging nature in the church, the apostle adds an exhortation not to continue to observe these rites from the old covenant, as was taught by some from Judea. "Some men came down from Judea to Antioch and were teaching the brothers: 'Unless you are circumcised, according to the custom taught by Moses, you cannot be saved'" (Acts 15:1).

2. The apostle gives this reason for his warning: such belief and behavior is inconsistent with the Gospel, the nature of Christian religion, and its great principle that "Jesus Christ is the same yesterday and today and forever" (13:8). From this he moves on to various acknowledged principles that he takes for granted or explains.

First, he supposes that the spring of all their observances about meals, eating or not eating, and consequently of the other rites of the same nature was from the altar. With reference to this, clean and unclean things were determined. What was allowed to be offered on the altar was clean, and what was not allowed to be offered on the altar was unclean. And there were various laws as to which sacrifices might be eaten by the priests and which ones might not be eaten.

Second, the foundation of religion lies in an altar, for that is where atonement for sin was made. And through it all our worship is offered to God, which cannot be accepted in any other way. So the apostle affirms that we also have an altar, but not one that makes a distinction between meats, verse 10.

Third, whatever the benefits of our altar, the way to partake in them is not through the administration of the services of the old tabernacle.

3. The reason given by the apostle for this comes from the nature of our altar and its sacrifice. In its very type it was declared that there was no right of eating or any distinction between meats. For in the solemn sacrifices of expiation and atonement, the blood from them was taken into the holy place, and the bodies of the animal sacrifices were burned entirely

outside the camp; so the priests themselves had no right to eat anything from them (verses 11-12).

4. In answer to this, the Lord Christ, who is himself both our altar and our sacrifice, as he offered himself, carried his own blood, in the efficacy of it for atonement, into the holy place of heaven, and suffered in his body "outside the city gate" (verse 12), or in the place answering to that outside the camp where the bodies of the animals that were sacrificed were burned. So this leaves no place for eating or any distinction between meats.

5. Here a new state of religion, answering to the nature of this altar and sacrifice, is introduced, in which those observances that depended on the nature and use of the altar in the tabernacle were utterly inconsistent. So, whoever adhered to them renounced our altar and the religion founded on our altar. Nobody can have an interest in two altars at the same time, as they are so different and involve such different religious observations.

6. He adds, in the last place, what we learn from the nature and use of our altar and sacrifice, in contrast with the meats that belonged to the old typical altar. Here the apostle mentions the patient bearing of the cross, or suffering for Christ (verse 13); self-denial, concerning any interest in temporal enjoyments (verse 14); the continual worship of God in and through spiritual sacrifices made acceptable in Christ, our altar, priest, and sacrifice (verse 15); and usefulness among men in all good deeds of piety and charity (verse 16). These are the only sacrifices that we are not called to make.

9. Do not be carried away by all kinds of strange teachings. It is good for our hearts to be strengthened by grace, not by ceremonial foods, which are of no value to those who eat them.

Do not be carried away by all kinds of strange teachings. It is clear that these **strange teachings** were evident in the churches of the Hebrews. This is clear in the special instance given about **ceremonial foods.**

Not by ceremonial foods. Literally, "not by foods." The heart cannot be strengthened by **ceremonial foods.** For the apostle immediately says they **are of no value to those who eat them.** This does not mean that there are two ways to become spiritually strong, one by grace, the other through **ceremonial foods.** Rather, grace is the only way, though some people have stupidly supposed that it might happen through **ceremonial foods.** The apostle often makes the distinction between the value of grace and the lack of value in **ceremonial foods.** "For the kingdom of God is not a matter of eating and drinking, but of righteousness, peace and joy in the Holy Spirit" (Romans 14:17). "But food does not bring us near to God; we are no worse if we do not eat, and no better if we do" (1 Corinthians 8:8; see also Colossians 2:16; Hebrews 9:10).

10. We have an altar from which those who minister at the tabernacle have no right to eat. The sole ground of all distinction of meats and other ceremonies among the Jews was the altar in the tabernacle, with its nature, use, and services. The apostle lets them know that, now that this altar has been removed, we have a different kind of altar, which gives different services from the previous ones, as described in verses 13-15. This is what the apostle is saying here.

We have. That is, "we, who believe in Christ according to the Gospel and worship God in spirit and truth also have an altar. We have everything in substance that they previously only had in name and shadow."

There have been disagreements about what this altar is that the Christian church has and uses, which caused superstitions in latter ages. Some say this altar means a physical altar made of stone, on which an unbloody sacrifice of the flesh and blood of Christ is offered by priests every day; plainly of the same kind, nature, and use as that in the tabernacle. Others think that the table that the church uses to celebrate the Lord's Supper is here metaphorically called an altar, because of the communication of Christ's sacrifice that is made at it. But these things are wholly foreign to the purpose of the apostle. The altar that we now have is Christ alone and his sacrifice. For he was both priest, altar, and sacrifice, all in himself, and still continues to be so for the church. The sacrifice that we offer through this altar is "a sacrifice of praise" (verse 15), which is "the fruit of lips that confess his name" (verse 15). This takes us away from any thoughts about any physical altar.

Which those who minister at the tabernacle have no right to eat. The people who are excluded from having the right to eat are those who **minister at the tabernacle.** The apostle uses the present tense for those who are ministering and continue to **minister.** He ignores the fact that the temple had replaced the tabernacle, as no changes were made in the worship itself.

To eat. Eating was the only way to take part in the meats from the altar, where everyone received their portion to eat. Hence the apostle uses the word **eat** here to indicate any kind of participation. He does not mean that we have an altar where some may eat of the sacrificed meats that they had no right to, but rather, that they had no right to benefit from our altar in any way at all. They had no right or title to this by virtue of any divine institution. The apostle does not absolutely exclude these people from ever attaining an interest in the altar. He does say this is true in two ways. First, they had no right because of their office and links with the tabernacle; second, while they kept that privilege and used these meats to gain peace with God, they could not have any interest in our altar.

11-12. The high priest carries the blood of animals into the Most Holy Place as a sin offering, but the bodies are burned outside the camp. And so Jesus also suffered outside the city gate to make the people holy through his own blood.

Jesus also suffered outside the city gate. That is, outside the city of Jerusalem, which corresponded to the camp in the wilderness, after the tabernacle had been established there. Four things are seen here.

First, he left the city and church-state of the Jews, about which he denounced their destruction as he went out of the gate: "Jesus turned and said to them, 'Daughters of Jerusalem, do not weep for me; weep for yourselves and for your children. For the time will come when you will say, "Blessed are the barren women, the wombs that never bore and the breasts that never nursed!" Then "they will say to the mountains, 'Fall on us!' and to the hills 'Cover us!'"'" (Luke 23:28-30).

Second, he put an end to all sacrificing in the city and temple, as far as that would be accepted by God. All was now ending.

Third, he declared that his sacrifice and the benefits from his sacrifice were not included in the Jewish church, but were extended to the whole world. "He is the atoning sacrifice for our sins, and not only for ours but also for the sins of the whole world" (1 John 2:2; see also John 11:52).

Fourth, he declared that his death and suffering were not only a sacrifice but a punishment for sin, namely, the sins of the people who were to be sanctified by his blood. For he went out of the city as a criminal and died the death that by divine decree was a sign of being cursed. "Christ redeemed us from the curse of the law by becoming a curse for us, for it is written: 'Cursed is everyone who is hung on a tree'" (Galatians 3:18).

The Lord Jesus, out of an unimaginable love to his people, would spare nothing, avoid nothing, deny nothing, that was necessary for their sanctification, their reconciliation, and dedication to God. He did it "with his own blood." "To him who loves us and has freed us from our sins by his blood" (Revelation 1:5; see also Acts 20:28; Galatians 2:20; Ephesians 5:25-27).

13-14. Let us, then, go to him outside the camp, bearing the disgrace he bore. For here we do not have an enduring city, but we are looking for the city that is to come.

Go to him outside the camp. The **camp** in the wilderness was the area in which the people pitched their tents as they were camped around the tabernacle all the time. The bodies of the animals that had been used for the sin offerings were carried to the camp and burned. This corresponds to the city of Jerusalem, as is clear here. In verse 12 it says that Jesus also "suffered outside the city gate"; in this verse it says that he is **outside the camp.** Clearly the apostle means the same thing by "city gate" and "camp." Now the camp and the city were the center of all the political and religious meetings for the church of the Jews. To be "in the camp" is to have a right to all the privileges and advantages of the citizenship of Israel and the whole divine service of the tabernacle. For if anyone lost that right for any reason, even if it was just for a short time, they were removed from the camp. "As long as he has the infection he remains unclean. He must live alone; he must live outside the camp" (Leviticus 13:46; see also Leviticus 24:23; Numbers 5:2; 12:15).

The main point the apostle makes here is that a moral and religious purpose is served by going from this camp. These Hebrews valued nothing so highly as their moral and religious life and their citizenship in Israel. They could not understand how all the glorious privileges given of old to that church and people should stop so that they had to forsake them. So most of them continued in their unbelief about the Gospel; many would have combined its teaching with their old ceremonies. But the apostle shows them that by Christ's suffering outside the gate or camp, they were called to something quite different.

All the privileges and advantages, whatever they were, were to be renounced. Anything that was inconsistent with having Christ and participating in him must be forsaken. The apostle states this at length: "If anyone else thinks he has reasons to put confidence in the flesh, I have more: circumcised on the eighth day, of the people of Israel, of the tribe of Benjamin, a Hebrew of Hebrews; in regard to the law, a Pharisee; as for zeal, persecuting the church; as for legalistic righteousness, faultless. But whatever was to my profit I now consider loss for the sake of Christ. What is more, I consider everything a loss compared to the surpassing greatness of knowing Christ Jesus my Lord, for whose sake I have lost all things. I consider them rubbish, that I may gain Christ and be found in him, not having a righteousness of my own that comes from the law, but that which is through faith in Christ—the righteousness that comes from God and is by faith. I want to know Christ and the power of his resurrection and the fellowship of sharing in his sufferings, becoming like him in his death" (Philippians 3:4-10).

To him. They were to go **to him.** Christ went outside the city gate and suffered. We must go after him, and **to him.** This means we have to relinquish all the privileges of the camp and the city for his sake. We have to leave them behind and go to him. We must cling by faith to his sacrifice and through this to sanctification, in place of all the sacrifices of the law. We must own him under all that reproach and contempt that were heaped on him during his suffering outside the gate. We must not be ashamed of the cross of Christ. We must go **to him** in his office of king, priest, and prophet of the church.

14. For here we do not have an enduring city, but we are looking for the city that is to come.

We do not have an enduring city. Whatever facilities they might have here in this world for a time, they still do not have a city that endures forever, nor one in which they could live in forever. Probably, the apostle is showing here the difference between the Christian church and the church under the old testament. For the church under the old testament, after they had wandered in the wilderness and elsewhere for a long time, was brought to rest in Jerusalem. But he says, **We do not have an enduring city, but we are looking for the city that is to come.**

The city that is to come is the heavenly state of rest and glory.

Verses 15-17

The apostle summarizes our Christian duties under three headings. 1. Spiritual, with respect to God (of which he gives us an example in verse 15). 2. Moral, with respect to all kinds of people (an example of which is given in verse 16). 3. Ecclesiastical, in the church-state into which we are called through the profession of the Gospel (the main duty required here is stated in verse 17).

15. Through Jesus, therefore, let us continually offer to God a sacrifice of praise—the fruit of lips that confess his name.

Sacrifice of praise. The nature of Gospel obedience consists in being grateful for Christ and having grace through him. This may be summed up as our **sacrifice of praise.** The apostle describes it as presenting our bodies, that is, our whole beings: "Therefore, I urge you, brothers, in view of God's mercy, to offer your bodies as living sacrifices, holy and pleasing to God—this is your spiritual act of worship" (Romans 12:1). But in the description in Hebrews 13:15 the apostle limits his description to the duties of worship and praising God with our lips.

Continually. The **sacrifice of praise** that is commanded is to be offered **continually.** We are to pray always, without ceasing (see Luke 18:1; 1 Thessalonians 5:17). Two things are included here. First, there should be freedom from appointed times, seasons, and places. The sacrifices under the law had their times and places prescribed to them, apart from which they were not accepted. But as far as we are concerned every place and every time is equally approved. Second, diligence and perseverance are included. We should be careful to do this, that is, **continually,** as occasions, opportunities, and appointed seasons require.

The fruit of lips that confess his name. The apostle explains how we are to offer this sacrifice to God. Through **the fruit of lips that confess his name.** It is generally agreed that this comes from Hosea 14:2, "Say to him: 'Forgive all our sins and receive us graciously, that we may offer the fruit of our lips.'" The psalmist speaks in a similar way: "What right have you to recite my law or take my covenant on your lips?" (Psalm 50:16).

Because the praise of God mainly consists of acknowledging his glorious deeds, to **confess his name**—that is, so to profess and acknowledge those things in him—is the same as to praise him. The apostle uses the phrase **confess his name** here because he means the praise which consists of solemn acknowledgment of the wisdom, love, grace, and goodness of God, in the redemption of the church in Jesus Christ. This is to **confess his name.**

16. And do not forget to do good and to share with others, for with such sacrifices God is pleased.

To do good. This concerns the whole of our lives. "To those who by persistence in doing good seek glory, honor and immortality, he will give eternal life" (Romans 2:7). We are told not to become weary in doing this: "Let us not become weary in doing good, for at the proper time we will reap a harvest if we do not give up" (Galatians 6:9; see also 2 Thessalonians 3:13). We are also encouraged to do this, "For it is God's will that by doing good you should silence the ignorant talk of foolish men" (1 Peter 2:15; see also 1 Peter 3:17; 4:19).

Three things are included in **do good.** First, it includes a gracious propensity and readiness to do good to everyone. "The noble man makes noble plans" (Isaiah 32:8). Second, it includes carrying out this inclination in every way and everything, spiritual and temporal, through which we may be useful and helpful to humankind. Third, it embraces all occasions and opportunities to show pity, compassion, and loving-kindness on the earth. It requires that our lives, according to our abilities, should be spent in doing good to others, according to our abilities. This corresponds to the list of duties in the second half of the Ten Commandments.

17. Obey your leaders and submit to their authority. They keep watch over you as men who must give an account. Obey them so that their work will be a joy, not a burden, for that would be no advantage to you.

They keep watch over you. This word is unique to this place, and it denotes a watchfulness with the greatest care and diligence, even if this involves trouble or danger. Jacob kept and watched the flocks of Laban at night. But these **leaders,** literally, "keep watch over your souls." This summarizes the whole duty of the pastoral office. It is as if he said, "The work of these leaders is solely to take care of your souls: to keep them from evil, sin, and backsliding; to instruct them and feed them; to encourage their obedience and faith, and so lead them safely to eternal rest."

As men who must give an account. That is, of their office, work, duty, and how they carry it out. This "giving of an account" refers to the last day of universal account. But attention needs to be paid to their present duties. First, they **must give an account** of their work. They are not owners, but stewards; they are not sovereigns, but servants. They must give an account of their work and of the flock committed to their charge to the "great Shepherd of the sheep" (verse 20) and to "the Chief Shepherd" (1 Peter 5:4). Second, they must behave **as men** who are entrusted with this responsibility and are accountable in this way. Such people act with care and diligence. Third, every day they **must give an account** to Jesus Christ for the work they have been entrusted with. If those in their care thrive, if they flourish, if they go on to maturity, they **give an account** of this, and thank Christ for the work of his Spirit and grace among them. If those in their care are diseased, slothful, and have fallen into sinful ways, they still have to **give an account** to Jesus Christ. They spread this before him, mourning with grief and sorrow. Indeed the following words—**joy** and **not a burden**—seem to show the different ways of giving this account. This account may need to be given with joy or it may need to be given with sorrow.

Verses 18-25

There are three parts to these closing verses. First, the apostle's request that the Hebrews pray for him (verses 18-19); second, his solemn prayer of blessing (verses 20-21); and, third, a report about Timothy's condition, and the usual greeting (verses 22-25).

18-19. Pray for us. We are sure that we have a clear conscience and desire to live honorably in every way. I particularly urge you to pray so that I may be restored to you soon.

Pray for us. This is his request for prayer. He speaks in the plural, **us,** but, as usual, it is himself alone that he means. He acknowledges that the prayers of the humblest saints may be useful for the greatest apostle. Hence it was usual for the apostle to request the prayers of the churches to whom he wrote (2 Corinthians 1:11; Ephesians 6:19; Colossians 4:3; 2 Thessalonians 3:1). For mutual prayer for each other is a main part of the communion of saints, in which they help each other, at all times, places, and circumstances.

19. I particularly urge you to pray so that I may be restored to you soon. Some things may be observed here. First, he had been with them previously. Second, he desires to be **restored** to them; that is, to come to them again, so that they might have the benefit of his ministry and he the comfort of their faith and obedience. Third, he is earnest in this desire and therefore the more urgent in requesting their prayers that his desire might be accomplished.

20-21. May the God of peace, who through the blood of the eternal covenant brought back from the dead our Lord Jesus, that great Shepherd of the sheep, equip you with everything good for doing his will, and may he work in us what is pleasing to him, through Jesus Christ, to whom be glory forever and ever. Amen. Having requested their prayers for him, he adds to this his prayer for them, and so gives a solemn end to the whole letter. It is a glorious prayer, including the whole mystery of divine grace, both its origin and the way it was brought through Jesus Christ. And he prays that the fruit of all he had instructed them about may be grow in them, for the substance of the whole doctrinal part of the letter is included here. The nature of the prayer itself shows that it came from a spirit full of faith and love.

The God of peace. The title given to God, or the name by which he calls on him, is, **the God of peace.** Our apostle often refers to God in this way (Romans 15:33; 16:20; Philippians 4:9; 1 Thessalonians 5:23).

That great Shepherd of the sheep. They belong to God. This **great Shepherd** was promised of old (see Isaiah 40:11; Ezekiel 34:23; 37:24). What is meant here includes the whole office of Christ as king, priest, and prophet of the church. For as shepherd he feeds, that is, rules and instructs us. As the shepherd who laid down his life for the sheep (John 10:11), this refers to his priestly office and the atonement he made for his church by his blood. All the elect are committed to him by God, like sheep to a shepherd, to be redeemed, preserved, saved, through virtue of his office. This relationship between Christ and the church is often mentioned in the Scripture, with the security and consolation that depend on it. We are taught here that he died as part of his work, as the **great Shepherd of the sheep,** which shows the excellency of his love and the certainty of the salvation of the elect.

He is not said to be a shepherd in general, but the **Shepherd of the sheep.** He did not lay down his life as a shepherd for the whole flock of mankind, but for the elect who were given and committed to him by the Father, as he declares in John 10:11, 14-16.

21. Equip you with everything good for doing his will. The first thing he prays is that they will be equipped, that is, made fit and able. It is as if he said, "This is a thing that you in yourselves are not prepared for; no matter what light, power, freedom may be in you, this will not make you suitable for this." What he prays is that they will be enabled to work as God requires them to.

And this is to be **for doing his will,** that is, for every good deed. The whole of our obedience toward God and duty toward man consists in good deeds (see Ephesians 2:10). Hence he prays that they may do the will of God, which is the sole rule of our obedience.

So it is clear what grace the apostle is praying for here. In general, he is asking that God's grace, through the mediation of Christ, may bring about their sanctification. We are enabled to do God's will through God's constant work of grace in our souls. In this way they are prepared to carry out their Christian duties. While many, at least of the Hebrews, might have indeed already received this grace in their initial conversion to God, as all believers do, the apostle prays that they may daily increase in it. For all this strengthening and growing in grace consists in the increase of this spiritual habit in us.

22. Brothers, I urge you to bear with my word of exhortation, for I have written you only a short letter.

My word of exhortation. This is the truth and teaching of the Gospel applied for the building up of believers, whether by way of exhortation or consolation, as each includes the other.

I have written you only a short letter. Out of his life and concern for them he had written or sent this letter to them, so they should **bear with** him in it. He had given them no more trouble than was necessary, in that he had **written . . . only a short letter.** But how can this said to be **a short letter** since it is of considerable length? Considering the importance of the subject matter, the whole purpose and mystery of the covenant and institutions of the law, and the office of Christ, and the danger of their eternal ruin, all that the apostle had written might be thought of as **a short letter.** He had given them a compressed summary, literally, "few words" about the teaching of the law and the Gospel, which they ought to take in good part.

23. I want you to know that our brother Timothy has been released. If he arrives soon, I will come with him to see you. He writes to them about the good news of Timothy's release.

24. Greet all your leaders and all God's people. Those from Italy send you their greetings. To **greet** another person is to convey one's kindness and affection to them. This the apostle desires, for the preservation and continuation of complete love between them.

25. Grace be with you all. This was the normal way he ended all his letters. This he wrote with his own hand, and it would have been a way to know that he had written the whole letter (see 2 Thessalonians 3:17-18). He sometimes varies the expression, but this is the substance of all his endings, **grace be with you all.** And by **grace** he means the whole goodwill of God through Jesus Christ, and all the blessings that flow from this.